Marketing for Keeps

Building Your Business by Retaining Your Customers

Carla B. Furlong

JOHN WILEY & SONS, INC.

New York • Chichester • Brisbane • Toronto • Singapore

In recognition of the importance of preserving what has been written, it is a policy of John Wiley & Sons, Inc. to have books of enduring value published in the United States printed on acid-free paper, and we exert our best efforts to that end.

Library of Congress Cataloging-in-Publication Data

Furlong, Carla B.
   Marketing for keeps : building your business by retaining your customers / Carla B. Furlong.
     p.   cm.
   Includes bibliographical references and index.
   ISBN 0-471-54017-X
   1. Consumer satisfaction. 2. Customer service. 3. Consumer satisfaction—United States—Case studies. 4. Consumer satisfaction—Canada—Case studies. I. Title.
   HF5415.5.F87 1993
   658.8—dc20   92-40872

Printed in the United States of America
10 9 8 7 6 5 4 3 2 1

To all the special "little people" in my life: Adrian, Bronwyn, Desmond, Connor, Kamir, Myfanwy, and Calum. May you grow up to a truly brave new world.

Preface

When all is said and done, a lot more is said than done.

Lou Holtz[1]

You'd have to have been living under a rock these past few years not to have heard of the quest for quality in both the public and private sectors. A laudable goal certainly but for most, not realizable: too fuzzy, too intangible, a lot more talk than action. A Conference Board of Canada study, for example, found that seven out of ten companies fail in their attempts at quality.[2]

Contrast that with customer retention, the subject of this book. A strategy focused, not on making customers or putting smiles on their faces, but on keeping customers and getting more of their business. "Since [customer] defection rates are measurable," note authors Frederick Reichheld of Boston consultants Bain & Co. and Earl Sasser, Jr. at Harvard Business School, "they are manageable."[3]

This book revolves around the presentation of an implementation model for customer retention. Each chapter represents a step in this model that reflects the "Best in Class" from over 35 retention champions across North America. A tangible application of the model is presented at the end of each chapter using a real-life company.

Making customer retention *really* happen takes more than models and strategies; it takes people. Brave words, tough assignment; one the traditional organization is incapable of carrying out. Revised approaches to decision making, structure, and compensation are needed to implement the retention process. A few of the concepts we'll look at include action orientation; individual accountability throughout the organization; a focus on error and recovery, not perfection; starting from the inside customer out; and a willingness to live with a little risk and a lot of flexibility. Not rocket science but common-sense ideas whose time has come again.

Acknowledgments

I'm the only one who gets her name on this book but there's been a raft of folks who really deserve some billing. I'm not about to let them be on the dust jacket (only room there for one big ego!) but I would like to say thanks to the many people who put me on the right research track:

Chip Bell, Performance Research Associates, Inc.
Stephen Brown, Arizona State University

and

Kristin Anderson, Performance Research Associates
Earl Bahler, J. Walter Thompson
Jim Barnes, Memorial University
Paul Bates, Marathon Brokerage
Ken Bernhardt, Georgia State University
David Bond, Hongkong Bank of Canada
Lillian Book, The Rogers Group
Doris Bradstreet, Merit Kitchens
Stanley Brown, Price Waterhouse
Catherine Callaghan, *Small Business*
Clay Carr, U.S. Department of Defense
Karen Castleane, Ernst & Young
Jim Eagles, Ernst & Young
Dick Earthy, Surrey Credit Union
Roy Fithern, Royal Bank of Canada
Phil Forman, J. Walter Thompson
Keith Haydon, Heydon Marketing Services
Jim Hilborn, Hilborn Information
Cal Hodock, Comart
Aleta Holub, First National Bank of Chicago
Bob Inglis, Technalysis
Bonnie Irving, *B.C. Business*
Carol Jennings, Bain & Co.
Timothy Keane, Retail Target Marketing System

Marlene Klassen, Great-West Life
Eileen Layman, Ernst & Young
Shelley Lazarus, Ogilvy Direct
John LeCave, National Commerce Bancorporation
Laura Liswood, Liswood Marketing Group
Bob MacKay, Russell & DuMoulin
Melissa Manson, The Tom Peters Group
Linda McAleer, The Melior Group
Don Mizaur, Laventhol & Horwarth
Bill Neil, SDR, Inc.
Maryann Rasmussen, American Express
Jim Rogers, The Rogers Group
Joel Rosen, Price Waterhouse
Gretchen Rowe, Arizona State University
Len Schlesinger, Harvard Business School
Diane Schmalnese, Opinion Research
Jim Shanahan, MBNA America
Jack Snader, Systema Corporation
Don Tuline, Richmond Savings Credit Union
Randy Vandermark, British Columbia Institute of Technology
Darleen Viggiano, The Tom Peters Group
Jim Walker, Royal Bank of Canada
Wayne Walker, Investors
Stacy Wanaga, Bain & Co.
Edwin Weinstein, Brendan Wood, Tutsch and Partners
Peter Wigram, Institute of Canadian Bankers
Betty Wishard, Wishard & Associates
Dave Zielinksi, *The Service Edge*

Thanks also to Roberta Domae, who worked her way through more than 90 hours of tapes with grace and speed. To the staff of the B.C. Central Credit Union Library and Resource Centre, in particular Shirley Shipley and Georgia Whiten who helped me track down many a wayward footnote citation. And, finally, to my friends and family who were always there to buck me up and keep me slugging away.

I couldn't have done it without all of you. Many thanks everyone.

Contents

you're operating on executive intuition at best; at worst, on innuendo and rumor, when you should be "managing by fact," as Edward McEachern, pathologist at West Paces Ferry Hospital, puts it. Yet in a survey of executives by a Michigan management firm, Sandy Corp., only 42 percent performed any customer surveys.[3] Even fewer used comment cards or hotlines. So how are they tapped into the customer pipeline—by telepathy?

CHAPTER 4   Focusing on Your Best Customers:

The stories in this chapter reaffirm the relevance of the old adage, 'You can't be all things to all people'. "Because any company's capability is necessarily limited, it cannot span the entire (customer) dimension," insists Harvard Business School professor Benson Shapiro and colleagues.[4] That's the subject of this fourth chapter.

CHAPTER 5   Empowered Employees: Your Greatest

A company's best ideas can come from its most humble constituents. Only makes sense that those closest to the customer may know a thing or two about customer needs and wants. That runs counter to popular management doctrine that those at the top have all the answers. This chapter refutes this notion and suggests a new role for managers, that of liberator of human ingenuity.

CHAPTER 6   Internal Customers: Building Success

Research by management professor Benjamin Schneider confirms that employee satisfaction with the way they're treated is directly related to customer satisfaction. Consultant Frederick Reichheld of Bain and Co. agrees, "Customer retention and employee retention feed one another."[5] The undisputable conclusion: customer retention, like charity, begins at home.

CHAPTER 1

Customer Retention: The Key to Growth and Profit

You've got to hold on to the people who took you to the dance.

Mike Miller, president
Miller Business Systems

A focus on keeping customers has kept MBNA America, a large U.S. credit card company, in the black in recent years. It hasn't always been so. In fact, in 1982, president Charles Crawley was fed up with the ever-increasing rate of customer defections. He called together the full MBNA workforce and announced his commitment to keep each and every customer from that time forward. That set some wheels in motion; feedback from outgoing customers was gathered, analyzed, and acted upon. Eight years later, MBNA's defection rate stood at just 5 percent, half the industry average, a difference that translated into a sixteenfold increase in profits.[1]

A small Canadian company came across a similar pot of gold when it ventured into the realm of retention marketing. In 1990, Bow Valley Credit Union, a financial institution with two branches nestled near the Canadian Rockies in and around Banff, Alberta, worked up an all-in-one small business account it called "Strictly Business." The first mailout of a direct response piece went to existing business accounts, about 20 percent of the credit union's membership. "The results just blew my mind," insists general manager Larry Bohn. Commercial account business increased 50 percent over a short three-month span, with significant spin-offs beyond small business. "The entire credit union's assets grew 10 percent."

The moral of these stories: paying attention to existing customers pays off. Or, as management professor Michael LeBoeuf at the University of New Orleans says, "The big bucks aren't in making customers. They're in keeping customers."[2] Granted, getting more from those you've already got is not really a revolutionary idea. Most sellers do give the notion a passing nod but few exploit it profitably. Today's organizations depend instead on massive marketing machines geared to customer acquisition with little thought given to retaining these people once they're on board. In a 1987 survey by The Forum Group, a U.S. management consulting firm, employees of U.S. and Canadian companies said that "attracting customers" was considered a priority at their workplace twice as often as "keeping customers."[3] This can be a costly mistake.

Retention—On the Minus Side

According to American Management Association statistics, you'll have to lay out five times as many greenbacks to coax new recruits into the customer fold as to keep those already inside.[4] That can eat a sizeable hole in any budget. In the financial services industry, for example, estimates from the Council for Financial Competition, Washington, D.C., suggest a potential loss of more than 17 percent profit each year.[5] Figure 1.1 expands this to business in general.[6] Then there's the "churn factor" that can further erode the bottom line. "Churn" is defined as the number of customers who leave

The Cost of Lost Customers.[6]

Customers Lost Per Day	Revenue Loss	
	If Customers Spend $10 Weekly	If Customers Spend $100 Weekly
1	$ 189,800	$ 1,898,000
5	$ 949,000	$ 9,490,000
10	$1,898,000	$18,980,000

FIGURE 1.1 Revenue from lost customers can eat a sizeable hole in any organizational budget as illustrated by these figures. Bottom line: paying attention to existing customers pays off.

over a year's time divided by the number of new customers. If you lose half as many customers as you gain each year, for example, your churn is at 50 percent. High churn is an unfortunate but routine reality for many organizations; some cable systems, such as HBO, regularly see a customer churn well over 100 percent.[7]

Retention—On the Plus Side

There's a positive side to keeping close tabs on current customers. Reducing the customer exodus by as little as 5 percent a year plumps profits up to 85 percent. Figure 1.2 provides some specifics here.[8] In the insurance business, says Life Insurance Marketing and Research Association vice president, Albert Sheridan, long-term policyholders are 50 percent more likely to keep their accounts in the black than first-time buyers. "And agents who keep in touch with their best customers enjoy greater repeat business and are less likely to get shot down on their cross-selling pitches."[9] Other industries can benefit as well. In his book *Managing to Keep the Customer*, Robert Desatnick credits the U.S-based research firm, Technical Assistance Research Programs, with the following price tags on customer loyalty:[10]

- An automobile retailer—$140,000 revenue over a customer lifetime.
- A supermarket—$4,000 in revenue per year per customer.
- An appliance manufacturer—$2,800 revenue per customer lifetime.

The older the customer relationship, the better: data from Boston-based consulting firm Bain & Co. shows that a 10 percent profit from a one-year-old relationship with a customer can grow to over 60 percent if the customer tenure exceeds seven years.[11] Fortune seems to favor the mature.

Customers who've stuck by you over the years are more apt to recommend your establishment to their friends and family. For example, a top U.S. home builder credits more than 60 percent of its sales to referrals from existing clients.[12] And current customers are more likely to greet your cross-selling offers with enthusiasm than are prospects who don't know you from Adam or Eve. In fact, Council on Financial Competition research points to a twofold

The Plus Side of Customer Retention.

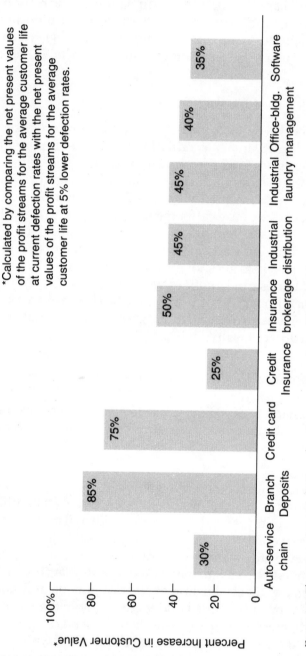

Reducing Defections 5% Boosts Profits 25% to 85%

*Calculated by comparing the net present values of the profit streams for the average customer life at current defection rates with the net present values of the profit streams for the average customer life at 5% lower defection rates.

Percent Increase in Customer Value*

	Auto-service chain	Branch Deposits	Credit card	Credit Insurance	Insurance brokerage	Industrial distribution	Industrial laundry	Office-bldg. management	Software
Value	30%	85%	75%	25%	50%	45%	45%	40%	35%

FIGURE 1.2 There's a plus side to keeping close tabs on current customers. Reducing the customer exodus by as little as 5 percent a year plumps profits up to 85 percent across a variety of industries. Desatnick, Robert L. *Managing to Keep the Customer: How to Achieve and Maintain Superior Customer Service Throughout the Organization,* p. 4. Copyright 1987 by Jossey-Bass.

advantage for direct mail and telemarketing campaigns aimed at current customers versus outsiders.[13]

As a final bonus, a focus on keeping customers loyal can keep your organization well out in front of the competitive pack, even ahead of those with unit costs below your own. In the credit card industry, for example, cutting customer defections by just 20 percent means the same to the bottom line as a 10 percent cut in costs.[14]

Retention—Why Now?

Today's world is one where customers have a lot of options. As author and consultant Laura Liswood says, "There are too many retail stores, too many banks and too many airlines all going to the same place."[15] And the competition's just beginning to heat up. As trade barriers tumble, the competitive threat will be increasingly global, and white-hot according to Paul O'Neill, chairman of Aluminum Co. of America.[16] Such a variety of vendors makes for a very picky customer. Al Endres, at the Juran Institute, believes customers in the 1990s have an increasing rate of expectation, and a decreasing tolerance level.[17]

All this boils down to one hard reality: most potential customers today are already attached and companies without enough are sure to come looking to lure yours away. When that happens, all your "tried and true acquisition tricks," as Liswood calls the traditional marketing ploys, will fall flat.[18]

Retention—Customer Service with a New Face?

Retaining existing customers—isn't that just what we've all been struggling to do the last few years using the precepts of customer service and quality? Not quite; granted, customer retention and customer satisfaction are interrelated; dissatisfied customers rarely hang around for the sequel. Still, if you fancy staying around yourself, you have to do something more than just create a customer "with a big smile on his face," as Warren Blanding at the Customer Service Institute quips. You have to separate customers from their money. "Satisfaction isn't what you make your money off of," contends Blanding, "You make your money off people buying things from you."[19]

Besides, the quest for quality as a business strategy hasn't been all that successful. Research done in 1991 by the Conference Board of Canada reveals that a whopping 70 percent of organizations trying to execute total quality strategies are failing.[20] Beyond the hype and the training workshops, there's often little to show for the effort and the expense. "The majority of quality efforts fizzle out early, or give some improvements but never fulfill their initial promise," says Boston Consulting Group vice president Thomas Hout.[21] Adds Dean Silverman, executive vice president of Temple, Barker & Sloane Inc., a management consulting firm in Lexington, Massachusetts, "For many . . ., quality programs have turned out to be just another drag on the bottom line, costing the buck without producing the bang."[22]

Service—good, bad, or indifferent—also doesn't often distinguish between prospect and customer; retention strategy does. Where your customers come from is beyond the scope of retention and almost irrelevant in a marketplace where customers are all but spoken for already. Just two strategies hold any realistic promise for future profits: "hanging on tight" to existing customer stockpiles or pilfering from the competition. Retention zeroes in on the former. And that's a business strategy that's tangible and actionable, something that the fuzzy goals of quality and service just can't be. "Many business leaders have been frustrated by their inability to follow through on . . . service quality," note authors Frederick Reichheld of Bain & Co. and Earl Sasser, Jr. at Harvard Business School. "Since [customer] defection rates are measureable, they are manageable."[23]

Retention—Why This Book on the Subject?

Marketing for Keeps: Building Your Business by Retaining Your Customers is specifically aimed at improving relations and business with your present customer base, offering practical aids to growing, as well as keeping current customers. Emphasis on the practical: too many other publications are long on why's and short on how's. The employee development director at a large U.S. chemical company encapsulates the frustrations of many when he says of a recent journalistic offering, "We got lots of people to read the book, but we don't know what to do with the ideas."[24] With real-life illustrations from a cross-section of organizations, sectors, and regions, executive interviews, and a "Making it Happen" section ending each chapter, *Marketing for Keeps: Building Your Business by Retaining Your Customers* concentrates more on getting there than on being there.

The focus on existing customers isn't the only thing that sets this book apart from other publications. Many business books tend to be poor testaments to the doctrines they preach. The writing style and layout make reading heavy going. There's little attempt to enliven visually through graphics or to make it easy for the reader to extract information quickly. *Marketing for Keeps: Building Your Business by Retaining Your Customers* is different.

The critical path to customer retention laid out in these pages highlights a series of steps; each chapter represents a strategic link in this chain. From strategies follow tactics, and these are developed for each step, chapter by chapter. I've tried to practice what I preach, and have presented these tactical concepts in small, digestible chunks. Each tactic is illustrated with bitesized anecdotes from real-life, making for rapid reading and quick comprehension.

This book revolves around the presentation of an implementation model for customer retention. I scoured the North American countryside for retention champions, amalgamating all I learned into a practical framework. No one organization has been the inspiration for or can provide the illustration of this model because no one organization has done everything best. Rather, the model reflects the "best in class" from over 35 organizations. Both retail and business-to-business strategy is represented from both sides of the Canada–U.S. border—from the massive Xerox Corporation out of Rochester, New York, to the minute Manning Jamison, a 46-member accounting firm located in Vancouver, British Columbia; from airlines at America West to wallpaper with B.B. Bargoon's. Even a few government agencies, an association, and a couple of hospitals are thrown in for good measure.

A cautionary note before we continue: in the real world, the best-laid plans go "oft astray." Be wary, then, of those bearing recipes for success. Such off-the-shelf programs may yield some good results in the short term but can set you up for disaster over the long haul; you need to think framework and flexibility instead. That's because we're talking about a culture change here, a metamorphosis of your organization from one focused on itself to one focused on its current customers.

Each chapter in this text presents one of twelve steps or "transformation points" along this evolutionary path (see Figure 1.3).

The first section of each chapter outlines the principle of the step in question. The final section, entitled "The Practice—Making it Happen," maps out recommendations based on the model for one particular company, a small West Coast professional services firm. Seeing how the model might come to life for this organization can go a long way to demonstrating how it could work for you, but it may not cover all the bases so be prepared to fine-tune.

The Planning Guide in Theory

The "Model for Customer Retention" is made up of three parts and twelve steps. Part I, "Mobilizing the People and the Organization for Customer Retention," is really a short warmup where we mobilize our people and our organization for the task at hand— customer retention. Part II, "Building Organizational Commitment to Customer Retention," is about building commitment to the retention cause by chalking up some small victories quickly. Reorienting your organizational culture around customer reten- tion is no small task; there'll be plenty of naysayers and skeptics blocking the transition. And they won't be convinced by words; they'll need to see results, such as the 90 percent reduction in patient diet errors for one nursing ward at a 586-bed hospital in B.C., Canada, achieved in a mere three months using this model.

Finally, in Part III, "Organizational Integration," with a solid arsenal of victories under our belts and our opponents in disarray, we're ready to tackle the task of integrating the retention focus throughout the organization, reworking traditional lines of author- ity, communication, and compensation. That'll ensure that reten- tion doesn't become just another passing fad but is firmly en- trenched in a new corporate culture.

Before we examine the twelve steps of the model, I'd like to clarify a few points.

1. *This Model Is a Management Model*—Customer retention isn't just for the marketing types in your organization. On the contrary, everyone up and down the hierarchy should jump quickly on the retention bandwagon, which is fast proving to be *the* business strategy for the nineties. To quote a colleague: "It is important to recognize that the traditional organization is incapable of retaining customers. New approaches to management, decision-making, organization and learning must [first] take place."[25]

The "Customers For Keeps" Model—the 12 Steps.

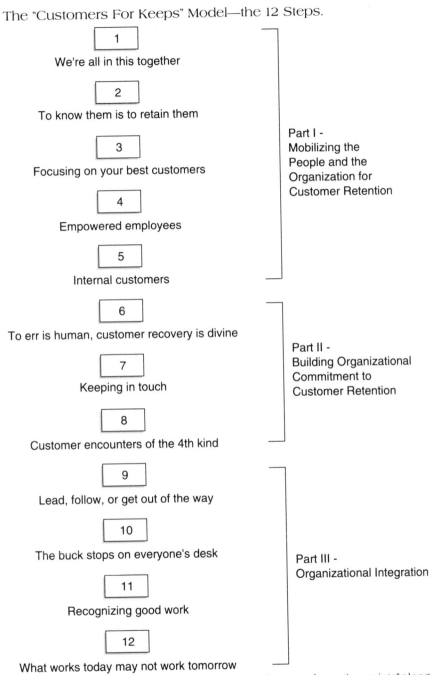

1

We're all in this together

2

To know them is to retain them

Part I -
Mobilizing the
People and the
Organization for
Customer Retention

3

Focusing on your best customers

4

Empowered employees

5

Internal customers

6

To err is human, customer recovery is divine

Part II -
Building Organizational
Commitment to
Customer Retention

7

Keeping in touch

8

Customer encounters of the 4th kind

9

Lead, follow, or get out of the way

10

The buck stops on everyone's desk

Part III -
Organizational Integration

11

Recognizing good work

12

What works today may not work tomorrow

FIGURE 1.3 Each chapter in this text presents one of 12 "transformation points" along the evolutionary path from an organization focused on itself to one focused on its current customers.

2. *This Model Is Cyclic*—The model laid out in this book is not a static snapshot of a customer retention strategy but rather a dynamic cycle, reflecting the way the world really works, like it or not. In his book *The Fifth Discipline*, Peter Senge has said so eloquently, "Reality is made up of circles but we see straight lines." Our customer retention model reflects this belief.[26] To use the model, you start by targeting your best customer group, work your way through the twelve steps of the model using this group as a point of focus, then start all over again with your next best customer group, and so on.

3. *This Model Is about Action and Accountability* (see Figure 1.4)—As mentioned above, action is really the name of the game in retention and in this model. That's because action is so often what's been missing with other approaches to the problem of keeping customers around. I like the way Robert Schaffer and Harvey Thomson, principals of the management consulting firm, Robert H. Schaffer & Associates of Stamford, Connecticut and Toronto, Ontario, put it; "The performance improvement efforts of many companies have as much impact on operational and financial

People—Powered Retention—A Model

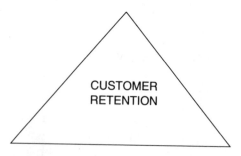

ACTION
"Nothing will ever be attempted
if all possible objections must be
first overcome" (Samuel Johnson)

CUSTOMER
RETENTION

ADAPTABILITY
"Don't be afraid to take a big step... you
can't cross a chasm in... small jumps"
(David Lloyd George).

ACCOUNTABILITY
"There is no outside... you and the
cause of your problems are part of
a single system" (Peter Senge,
The Fifth Discipline).

FIGURE 1.4 The three key principles behind the Model for Customer Retention—
individual accountability, an action orientation and organizational adaptability.

results as a ceremonial rain dance has on the weather."[27] They suggest you bypass what they call "lengthy preparation rituals" and get down to making measurable gains quickly.[28] I couldn't agree more; that's what this model is all about.

The "Model for Customer Retention" is also about accountability, something I believe has gotten lost in the shuffle of late. Sooner or later, rhetoric has to be recast into action, and that action's only accomplished by people, whether at the top, in the middle, or on the bottom, but always and only *people*. In the words of an executive at the Bureau of Labour Information, a Canadian government agency that collects, analyzes, and disseminates information on collective bargaining to the industrial relations industry, "Our only significant assets ride up and down the elevators."[29] That leads us right into the last key point about this model, that retention must start from inside the organization and progress outward to our existing customers.

4. *This Model (and Retention) Must Progress from the Inside Out*— All the strategic savvy in the world won't cut much ice if your people aren't on your side. "Customer relations mirror employee relations," claims author Robert Desatnick. "Eighty percent of the opportunity for productivity and profitability lies in effective management of the work force."[30] In other words: if you want to retain good customers, you'd better get your mind around the idea of retaining good employees first.

The Model in Practice

To give you a more tangible illustration of the customer retention model, each chapter ends with a look at how model principles might work in practice. This is accomplished using a *real* company to "model the model," which we'll call "Retention Inc." (The names of the staff have also been fictionalized.)

Retention Inc. is a midsize West Coast company that has specialized in financial advice and products for more than four decades. A two-office setup serving the local market, the firm now generates $3.5 million in revenues each year. Its client base, currently at more than 500, is concentrated in the areas of owner-managed private corporations, and nonprofit and health care organizations although the firm does cater to individual customers. Many of these have been with the company for years. Bob, one of the firm's original employees, believes this is because Retention Inc. hasn't grown away from its dedication to personally serving its existing clients. That mission makes the company a prime candidate for retention management.

The organization chart at Retention Inc. is simple: each of the company's nine partners works with a team of three to six staff members. That keeps the atmosphere informal but professional, believes Mike, one of the nine, "All partners operate with an 'open door' policy and on a first-name basis." At a weekly meeting, the partners work through major decisions including any concerning customer service and retention. These aren't seen as distinguishable at this company so there's no separate monies set aside for retention per se.

The Twelve Steps

Part I—Mobilizing the People and the Organization for Customer Retention

Step 1—We're All in This Together (Chapter 2).   A pox on internal competition and the image of the solitary hero standing against all comers. If we're to stand any chance of keeping our customers, we need to stand together. That's the essence of this first step. As Apple Computer's John Sculley counsels, worship no more the lone cowboy on horseback. Make the team and its results the stars.[31] And get personalities out of retention problem solving while you're at it. Nip the "it's not my fault, it's your fault" reaction in the bud and depersonalize the situation by focusing on repairing the process, not on reprimanding the people. Faulty processes eat up most of an organization's energy anyway, leaving customers neglected and ripe for abandoning ship. For example, Misercordia General, an Edmonton, Alberta hospital, estimates that only 16 cents of every dollar goes to patient care; the rest is sucked into an administrative black hole.[32]

Step 2—To Know Them Is to Retain Them (Chapter 3).   Sure, we all buy into the idea that, if you want to know what your customers really want, you need to ask them. Or do we? A survey of 686 executives by Sandy Corp., a management and staff training firm in Troy, Michigan, suggests not. Although 68 percent of top brass in that study felt confident that less than 10 percent of their customers were "dissatisfied," only 42 percent of their companies performed any customer surveys.[33] So how were they tapped into the customer pipeline—by telepathy? Even with conventional customer research, a lot of reading between the lines may be needed if you're to know what's really on customers' minds.

Step 3—Focusing on Your Best Customers (Chapter 4). You've probably come across the 80/20 rule before, the notion that 80 percent of your business comes from just 20 percent of your customers. This is not just a myth. Take the financial services industry, for example. Statistics from The Liswood Group in Seattle prove that 10 percent of a bank's customers account for 90 percent of monies on deposit.[34] Let's go from the macro to the micro, and look at one specific financial institution headquartered in Vancouver, B.C. A minuscule 1 percent of this trust company's clients hold over 30 percent of that firm's assets. So what's my point? It's this: focus on your best, first.

Step 4—Empowered Employees (Chapter 5). This step is all about unleashing the power of human ingenuity to make customer retention really happen. It's about management acting as a catalyst to retention efforts throughout the organization; if necessary, stepping out of the way to let others get on with the job. "Russia proved you can't do it all centrally," comments Digital Equipment's president Kenneth Olsen. It's also about management accepting the lion's share of the responsibility for defecting customers. "Failure is usually the price a company pays for poor management policies," claims Donald Potter of the research firm of Windermere Associates.[35]

Step 5—Internal Customers (Chapter 6). Results from an executive survey conducted by Kaset International, a Florida-based consulting company, put the human element way out front in a list of key obstacles to effective customer relations.[36] That's because too many employees don't see themselves connected to the external user in any way, shape, or form. The fact is, some of them don't see themselves connected to anyone else internally, either. As author Peter Senge puts it, "What was once a convenient division of labor [has] mutated into . . . 'stovepipes' that all but cut off communication between functions."[37] And without this cross-functional cooperation, that is, getting your internal links to line up with external customer needs, all customer retention efforts are doomed to failure.

Part II—Building Organizational Commitment to Customer Retention

Step 6—To Err Is Human (Chapter 7). In a recent book, author Linda Lash cites studies from a U.S. research firm, Technical Research Assistance Programs, that suggest a customer with a problem that's been resolved may prove more loyal than a customer satisfied by ordinary good service.[38] Besides, an organizational focus on error and recovery sits better with the average worker who reacts poorly to programs geared to perfection, according to American Quality Foundation statistics.[39] It also comes closer to the customer's needs than some absolute standard of service. As IBM Canada executive Don Myles puts it, "If I were using the traditional North American mentality, I'd say our service level is 97 percent. That means if I send out a million invoices to 200 customers, I'm statistically sending out wrong invoices to every customer almost every month." This is not conducive to good customer retention.

Step 7—Keeping in Touch (Chapter 8). Corporate absence does not make the customer's heart grow fonder. On the contrary, it's "out of sight, out of mind." If you want customers to stay around, you need to keep in touch. Richard Wettergreen, vice president of Corporate Communications at Foremost Insurance Group, contends that "Any customer contact is an influence over retention." Simple but effective ways of making contact with your current customers are outlined in this step.

Step 8—Customer Encounters of the 4th Kind (Chapter 9). If customers have one product with your institution, there's a 15 percent likelihood they'll stay loyal to you for five years. With two products, that likelihood rises to 45 percent; with three, it's up to 90 percent.[40] Service consultant Laura Liswood calls this the "glue" of cross-selling, just one of the customer bonding techniques discussed in this step of the "Model for Customer Retention."

Part III—Organizational Integration

Step 9—Lead, Follow, or Get Out of the Way (Chapter 10). Here we integrate our action-oriented retention model into the management infrastructure. Managers lead by doing, by getting off their duffs and getting involved. Forget the arms-length attitude from the executive chair; get down and dirty with both employees and customers alike. Members of the Xerox executive team rotate the role of customer service officer one day every month. If it's "Customer Care Day" and a client's on the line, the manager on duty drops everything and takes the call.

Step 10—The Buck Stops on Everyone's Desk (Chapter 11). The effective use of power implies a sense of responsibility and an understanding of its limitations. Neither comes easily to managers or employees accustomed to the yoke of structure. "If you've been in a protective cocoon for years," explains Don Myles at IBM Canada, "it's like, 'You can't really mean that.' " We will take a pragmatic look at how to make everyone accountable for customer retention.

Step 11—Recognizing Good Work (Chapter 12). Consultant, author, and academic Michael LeBoeuf tells us that we get more of the behavior we reward.[41] Yet in a national poll taken by the Public Affairs Foundation, only 22 percent of workers saw any connection between how hard they worked and how much they were paid.[42] So if it's customer retention you're after, pay for that, like Foremost Insurance Group does. Rebecca Spratlin, vice president of the company's AARP Business Division, explains, "All sales reps have a specific percentage of [customer] renewals that they have to obtain to maximize their bonus payouts," giving everyone at Foremost a vested interest in whether or not the customer sticks around once a policy's booked. The latest in motivational research, though, reveals that it takes more than money to motivate employees, so we won't neglect nonmonetary aspects of charging up the troops.

Step 12—What Works Today May Not Work Tomorrow (Chapter 13). Marketing for keeps with existing customers means accepting that trial-and-error is usually the only way to fly, one of the key ideas expressed in this final step in our retention model. Don't panic over a false start; it's natural and it won't spell disaster. No canned 90-day wonder will work so accept that your retention programs will need time to mature and a considerable amount of fine-tuning. All this requires a high level of organizational flexibility—pretty scary for some, but the only way to go nonetheless. "You can't buy these . . . systems off the shelf," insists David Garvin, a Harvard business school professor. "The most successful efforts tailor ideas to the organization."[43]

PART I

Mobilizing the People and the Organization for Customer Retention

CHAPTER 2

We're All in This Together: Using Cooperation to Keep Your Customers

> *[The] lone cowboy on horseback is not the figure we worship anymore at Apple. Now more teams are heroes.*
>
> John Sculley
> Apple Computers[1]

When physicians are asked what would make them brag about working with 294-bed West Paces Medical Center in Atlanta, Georgia, they answer that if their available time in that hospital could be maximized, that would be a nice start. One prominent source of time loss for surgeons is the wait for the operating room. In 1989, the Operating Room (OR) staff of the $140-million institution reasoned that if they could reduce the length of time it takes to turn over an operating theatre that would keep doctors from having to stand around wasting time. What they didn't realize was that much of this delay resulted from processes outside OR and beyond the control of OR staff.

The OR department's staff team began its resolution of this process by studying the causes for OR time lags. A key one emerged: patients awaiting surgery averaged 23 minutes in a holding area largely because only 17 percent had been preadmitted for required lab or X-ray workups. This was not a people problem so much as a process problem and one that was fixable.

The team made three important changes based on its analysis. "No one really owned the process of trying to get patients preadmitted so (the team) assigned that job to the woman who schedules patients for surgery," says hospital president Chip Caldwell of their first recommendation. Now, anywhere from two to three days before their surgery date, patients are called to come into the hospital to have any preoperative tests done. A group of OR nurses has been given responsibility for ensuring this preparatory session is efficiently handled and all reports come back to them. Further, surgeons are enjoined to impress upon their patients the importance of the preadmission step. This three-pronged approach took a significant slice out of surgical holding time, the original 23 minutes dwindling to 16.

The West Paces story illustrates three critical points about maintaining customer retention that are true in most organizations: (1) that a group of individuals working together can solve problems they couldn't solve on their own; (2) that everyone's responsible but no one's at fault; and (3) that more than 9 times out of 10, it's the process that's at fault, not the people. Ninety percent of calls coming through the customer hotline at Delta Hotels & Resorts, as just one example, concern things that need fixing, notes president Simon Cooper. "They're not employee related." Yet, when problems arise, most of us are pretty quick to point the finger at some other group or individual. If the marketing people didn't always have their heads in the clouds, if the computer department could communicate in English, if the salespeople took shorter lunch breaks, if the mailroom folks weren't so slow . . . the list is endless. The purpose of this first step in our retention model is to bury this archaic, destructive ritual of we-versus-they bashing, once and for all, with the following recommended steps.

1. Remember, We've Got to Stand Together if We're to Stand a Chance of Keeping the Customer. . . In too many organizations today, too many people spend too much time covering their butts and their territories and too little time working together for the customer. How many times have you encountered folks spouting off about team effort only to find the team's an exclusive club dedicated to preserving itself rather than the customer. Most of this teamwork rhetoric is sound and fury signifying little, and accomplishing less, according to Harvard management professor Chris Argyris. "A team may function well with routine issues. But when [it] confronts complex issues that may be threatening, the "teamness" seems to go to pot."[2]

Isn't it time to pitch the politics and just get on with the job? After all, as author Anne Petite puts it, any organization is simply a "community of customers dependent on each other."[3]

But what if no one can agree on exactly what the job is? According to Steve Graziano, vice president of Market Information at Fidelity Investments Institutional Group, everybody's priorities are different. For example, the people on the operations side of his company are hell-bent on getting the statement out on time to customers; the marketers, on the other hand, want to see all the client problems resolved with despatch.

Come on, we all know what the job is: it's what the customer says it is. Concentrating on the external customer can eliminate what Aleta Holub at First Chicago National Bank calls "the noise factor." When political infighting and bureaucratic empire building begin to gnaw away at productivity, a customer refocus can get things back on track, because "there aren't too many people who will dispute that the customer is important."

2. . . . So Keep Staff Focused on the Outcome for the Customer . . . In the words of consultant and author Anthony Putman, "Everyone in the organization, top to bottom, has to recognize that this is a community of people dedicated to a single overriding purpose, to make an important, positive difference in the life of the customer." That's the only reason anyone draws a salary, he insists; maximizing value for shareholders or making profits should come in a distant second or third.

There's something Putman calls the "technical trap," that can really get in the way of a focus on the customer. "Each technical area [in an organization] has its own logic; the logic of computing is quite different from the logic of advertising [for example]." In order to be good at any discipline, you need to achieve some mastery of its technical logic. The problem is too many people get wound up in this stuff; it tends to take on a life of its own and everyone forgets about the customer. You've got to rigorously put that customer focus in the foreground, keeping any technical logics in check. If the computer system needs fixing, you take your attention off the customer temporarily and get involved in the logic of computing. But only until the problem's solved; then, it's back to the customer focus again.

Working well with other people in an organization for the client's welfare doesn't just mean being the kind of person who's really nice to have around, according to Jody Bonneau at First Chicago National Bank. "I mean, how useful is that?" She's trying to build teamwork in her department based on giving and receiving feedback on what really cuts it from the customer's point of view, whether internal or external. People are naturally frustrated by criticism that their work isn't up to snuff. "I work hard," they say, but no one's going to reward you for putting in 14 hours a day. "[Customers] don't care how hard you work; they [just] want the outcome they're after and they're only going to reward you [for that]." Stress customer outcomes, not employee inputs.

Customer-focused feedback on staff work isn't particularly easy to execute. "Most of us are not used to getting honest feedback," believes Bonneau, so before we can accept it we need to be trained in how to receive it. She and colleague Patricia (Trish) Barr, a vice president with the bank's Cash Management Sales Department, conduct training courses on this subject. "I walk through mock-ups of task evaluations with my staff," explains Bonneau. "I say, 'Okay, I just dropped this on your desk, how do you feel?' Then we work our way through the stages of shock, anger, rejection, and finally acceptance of the criticism." She also reminds staff that it's only the people who care about you who venture any censure. "It's the people who aren't telling you who are not on your side."

The ideal situation for any company, says Digital's Earl Haight, indirect sales manager, U.S. Direct Marketing, is that everybody's either helping pick up an order from a customer or is helping support that order. "If you're not in one of those two situations [at Digital], we're looking to put you in one."

Luckily, keeping everyone tuned into customer needs isn't as tough as it sounds. As Xerox's manager of Service Marketing, David Spindel, says, "I've never met an employee yet who doesn't want to satisfy the customer."

3. . . . *Even if Some Staff Feel the Customer's Not Their Job.* As mentioned above, some people in your organization may not believe they have any connection to the end customer. That's what happened when BellSouth Mobility, part of BellSouth Cellular Corp., the $1.7-billion cellular phone subsidiary of BellSouth Corporation, presented a customer satisfaction guarantee to its 2,500 employees in the summer of 1989. In order to make good on

such a service pledge, customer contact employees at BellSouth had to rely on the good graces of their colleagues throughout the company, something not always forthcoming. "They don't seem to have the same sense of urgency about this as we do" was a common complaint from the front line. This was a major stumbling block. Customer service people were running into not a lack of customer concern but a simple ignorance as to how each person's job impacted the customer.

As a result, BellSouth designed a series of one-day workshops to enlighten staff on how each job within the company results in a direct impact on a customer, be it an internal or an external one. Each session involved a mix of 20 to 30 employees from all functions and levels, although supervisors were separated from nonsupervisory staff.

This operational intermingling proved a boon to discussion. This was one of the first opportunities that employees had to get together in a cross-functional setting. There was a lot of knowledge gained in those workshops (apart from that about the external customer); participants were saying, "I had no idea what I did affected you so directly."

The workshops followed a fairly specific agenda and included a good measure of participation. First off, an off-the-shelf training package with a few BellSouth modifications introduced attendees to the concept of everyone being responsible for customer retention. "The workshops encouraged people to talk about what they saw as problems in dealing with customers and what brought on these problems," explains Early Davis, BellSouth Mobility's director of Customer Operations, Region 2. Next up was a viewing of a training video that featured a mock trial about "Who Killed Service?" Workshop participants were invited to step into the roles of judge and jury and investigate the "crime of poor service." "This exercise treated everyone in the company as a suspect." says Davis.

During the second half-day, management presented the concept of the guarantee with backup stats on why they were convinced BellSouth could make this strategy work. To further drive home the importance of the strategy, employees were asked to contribute personal stories about their own experiences, good and bad, with other organizations that offered guarantees. Then it was open season on guarantees. "Facilitators asked employees if they shared the company's confidence," says Davis, "and got a lot of interaction on that."

"The training sessions created a tremendous surge in employee pride," claims Davis. "Employees earned the personal satisfaction of knowing they actually have an effect on what happens in the company."

4. *Don't Pit One Internal Group Against Another. . .* It's always been rather fashionable to describe the world of business as being one of dog-eat-dog where only the strong survive. This kind of fanciful notion of competitive drive is held up as the ideal way to separate the wheat from the chaff, but it can have disastrous effects if it's directed inward, say many competitive experts, including Alfie Kohn in his 1986 book, *No Contest: The Case Against Competition.* Excellence and victory are conceptually distinct, he contends. Competitive situations, in which several people or groups are seeking the same end but not all can achieve it, tend to be less efficient and result in poorer quality products.[4]

When winning becomes an end in itself, ideal performance standards like "customers for keeps" lose meaning. Why bother upping the ante on customer retention if your nearest rival's still choking on your dust? "Doing better than others, but doing the least to stay ahead becomes the goal," claims Rosabeth Moss Kanter, Harvard business school professor, consultant, and author of *When Giants Learn to Dance.*[4]

Simon Cooper, president of Delta Hotels & Resorts, a 25-location hospitality chain headquartered in Toronto, Ontario, believes one of the most insidious of all in-house rivalries is that which pits staff on the firing line against the back-office folks. "One can create the myth that one group is important and the other isn't." His $300-million company has been careful to avoid any sort of guest recognition program, for example, that asks for direct evaluation of any one individual from the hotel's 6,500 employees. "These tend to highlight the front-of-the-house employees because those are the only ones who come in contact with the guest. Yet the waitress or waiter is only as good as the food that the chef behind the range has put on the plate."

5. *. . . Especially When it Comes to Money. . .* At Roots Canada, a speciality retail chain with annual sales of $15 million, product incentives called "spiffs" are divided equally among all staff on the floor. This is particularly true on Saturdays when business is brisk and someone has to take over the cash register for the whole day. That person misses out on the chance to do any cross-selling to

customers and thereby earn a few extra dollars in spiffs. "We don't want competitiveness between our employees," explains Rima Greenberg a manager with the Canadian company, "because it frightens off some of the teamwork."

Gary Cartwright, an administrative plant manager, says the company he worked for before joining the $500+ million Milwaukee commercial printing and publishing firm Quad/Graphics was one where his success depended on making sure someone else or some other department failed. At Quad/Graphics, there's a lack of territorial imperative among the different company departments. "Here, we succeed better as groups than individually. The more money that's in the pool, the more we're all going to get."

If the pot's divvied up strictly on individual performance levels, says Cartwright's colleague Ron Nash, then for you to get more, someone else has to get less. "So you're always going to try to keep secrets to yourself," inevitably at the expense of the customer. That's why no one at Quad/Graphics, and that's more than 6,000 people over eight locations, is on commission. Instead, managers share equally in a bonus fund. "There is no seniority here; everybody gets the same cut," explains Carl Bennett, vice president of Administration. "That's why we work very hard to help one another make a sale," continues Cartwright. "We all put more money in our pockets at the end of the year."

6. . . . *Stress Cooperation Instead.* At the Defense Logistics Agency Personnel Support office, the $13-million support arm of the Defense Logistics Agency (a part of the U.S. Department of Defense), branches weren't so much competing with as ignoring one another. They weren't cooperating either, and that was costing everyone potential customer trade. Before the customer contact function was amalgamated into one unit in 1990, each of the four Columbus, Ohio, branches did its own thing. "Everybody was serving his or her own interests," recalls program manager Bernard Lukco. That meant any project that potentially crossed branch lines didn't get picked up, and, even within units, the laissez-faire attitude resulted in a good many inefficiences. Lukco elaborates, "The development branch people would go and get a contract that involved not only development but also delivery, the classroom instruction. But the people doing development didn't have as much competency to do delivery [as the delivery group in the department did]."

At first, the various groups in the 150-person activity flinched at the loss of independence. But as new contracts, spin-offs from other agency customers, popped up on their doorsteps, says Mary Albright, associate director, they began to appreciate that the sum of the parts can indeed be greater than the whole. "There's a growing recognition that business that's good for the [agency], whether its my part or somebody else's, is ultimately good for me."

Agency customers, typically other groups within the Department of Defense, also gained from this new spirit of cooperation. Albright explains, "We are able to identify those kinds of projects that one field activity wants us to do that may be common to several activities so we can spread the cost around or sell it as an agency-wide project, and that's more efficiently funded." For example, the California office of the Defense Industrial Plant Equipment Center put in a request to instruct technicians working on specialized tank, ship, and airplane equipment. One major drawback: the training package had a sticker price of $150,000, a considerable bite out of any single unit's budget. After we did some checking around, says Albright, we found the Pennsylvania and Tennessee operations believed this kind of training would suit their people as well. "We were able to arrange for funding at headquarters so nobody has to singly bear the cost."

7. Focus Organizational Energy Not on Bad People But on Bad Processes. . . Paul Redelheim, director of Quality Improvement for Mental Health at Hospital Corporation of America (HCA), a $4.68-billion health-care consortium of 79 institutions and 60,000 employees headquartered in Nashville, Tennessee, has a great anecdote that hits the nail right on the head on this point. Once upon a time, not long ago, there was a psychiatric hospital administrator whose food services department made a poor showing on a patient satisfaction survey. Her first response was a typical one, to think about beating up the food services director. Redelheim swerved her off this course by taking her step-by-step through the food delivery process. "As we walked through the flowchart, it became really clear that the patient's evaluation was not of the performance of Food Services but of the performance of a whole series of integrated processes that have to work together to get the food from the kitchen to the patient."

It's a production that includes a cast of many, says Redelheim, and dietary people aren't the only ones performing: a nurse has to open the unit door, a housekeeper may need to wash a table for the food tray, a physician may have to redraft therapy schedules so appointments don't conflict with meal times, and so on. All of a sudden, the administrator began to realize that there was a lot more to all this than simply search and destroy the lowest performer. "The assumption had been, find that person and motivate them with pain. Without any consciousness whatsoever that the processes within which that person works have more to do with that score than the effort of the person doing the work."

Most organizations aren't even looking for bad processes, much less fixing them. They're really not thinking at all about processes, like filling a client order or opening an account, but are focused on functions, like Marketing or Accounting. But when it comes to customer retention, the functional setup just won't work, period.

8. . . .And Bad Policies. Bad policies can be just as much a barrier to customer retention as bad processes. A perfect example of this is the Madison, Wisconsin Fleet Street story.[5] In 1983, an audit commissioned by then mayor Joseph Sensenbrenner revealed big problems at the city's garage. In particular there were long delays in repairs for the city's 765-unit fleet of squad cars, dump trucks, refuse packers, and road scrapers. The report said nothing of solutions, though. Recalls Sensenbrenner, "The audit gave a depressingly vivid . . . picture of the problem . . . but it offered no clear explanation of why things were so bad."

Sensenbrenner's first instinct ran along the same lines as the aforementioned HCA administrator. "I felt inclined to call in the shop boss [and] read him the riot act." Instead, he convinced the Fleet Street garage crew and union reps to form a team. "We gathered data from individual mechanics and from the repair process itself." They discovered they weren't the problem; the inventory was. "We found that . . . delays resulted from the garage not having the right parts in stock." The general consensus was that it was the Parts people who were to blame, but when those folks had their say, they pointed to the mishmash of makes and models that formed the 765-unit fleet. "We discovered . . . 440 different types, makes, models, and years of equipment." "Why the bewildering variety?" the Parts manager was asked. "City policy," he answered, "it's always been, 'Go for the lowest sticker price, end of criteria.' " On to the Parts purchaser. "I'd be happy to narrow the field for parts suppliers," he said, "but Central Purchasing won't let me." Next stop, Central Purchasing. "We're with you on this," they said here, "but if we tried to change that policy, our paperwork would come back 'No can do' from the Comptroller." Enter the Comptroller. "Sounds good to me," he agreed, "but it won't get by the City Attorney." Last stop, the City Attorney's office. "Why of course you can do that," he said. "In fact, I assumed you were doing it all along!"

There is a happy ending to all this. The Madison purchasing policy for city vehicles was changed. The results? Twenty-one of 24 steps in the repair process bit the dust bringing a nine-day average turnaround time down to just three. Sensenbrenner sees two morals to this story: (1) The problem didn't get solved until everyone worked together; and (2) It was the system that was flawed, not the workers. "The source of the downtime problems was upstream in the relationship of the City to its suppliers—not downstream where the worker couldn't find a missing part."

9. Get Your Facts Straight on What's Really Wrong.   Another HCA psychiatric hospital anecdote shows how easy it is to misread a customer situation. On the surface, the two hospitals appeared to have a similar problem—Dietary taking it on the chin in a patient satisfaction survey. However, in the second case, a more in-depth look at survey results revealed the main source of the griping about food originated with patients in the Eating Disorders Unit (EDU). "These people have a psychological hatred of food," explains Redelheim, so naturally they'd see little to praise at mealtime. "Once we broke out the EDU patients from the other psychiatric units, the scores were fine."

10. Rate the Group's Output, Not the Individual's Input.   Mediocre customer ratings rarely reflect an individual's performance in isolation. As marketing vice president Jody Bonneau at First National Bank of Chicago explains to me, "[Customers are] not evaluating Carla Furlong. They're evaluating the [organization's] responsiveness to customer inquiries [for example] or our lockbox services." The 1985 fixup at the bank's letter-of-credit department illustrates this precisely.

Customer complaints of being bounced around the credit unit prompted the setup of a quality team to get to the root of the problem. The culprit, it turned out, was not the credit staff but the department's assembly-line infrastructure. A customer's request went on a four-day journey through dozens of steps and nine employees before a letter of credit was finally issued. Letting each customer deal with just one employee, the same one for each new order, was the answer. Today, it requires less than a day to process a letter of credit and, in 1990, First Chicago issued 1,450 such letters, double the 1985 figure, using 49 percent fewer personnel.

First Chicago's process-not-people focus applies internally as well. In-house project sponsors are asked to grade a task performed by another department, say Marketing, not to pass judgment on the people involved. That wasn't always the bank's modus operandi, admits Bonneau. "We actually went the other way [first but] came back to doing it by function." This was for three solid reasons: first, according to quality guru Ed Deming over 85 percent of service quality problems result from bad processes, not bad people, proof that you should be hard on the problem, easy on the people;[6] second, to keep a positive tone in the customer service process ("it shouldn't be threatening," insists Bonneau); and finally, because the bank doesn't want to be all talk and no action when it comes to the concept of teamwork.

11. Depersonalize the Atmosphere.   Concentrating on issues rather than individuals helps eliminate the typical finger-pointing defense to a problem. That's certainly the way it worked for customer service pilot teams at a 586-bed hospital in Burnaby, B.C., according to Betty Frenette, the Canadian institution's director of Admitting. "Once they realized we were focusing on the process and not the people, it became very easy to work together. The most defensive people in the beginning turned out to be real champions at the end."

Team participants in the hospital's Customer Care Program could be candid in their comments without fear of fisticuffs or sulky withdrawals from their compatriots, adds colleague Clara Pi, director of Dietetics. "It provided them with an opportunity to be honest with each other and point out problems; [for example] 'I don't like the way you do things' or 'Do you realize the consequences of what you're doing?' " A hospital team member's comment brings this home very clearly. "There's a fear factor at the beginning, like someone's putting you under the microscope. You get through that when you realize these people are all on your side."

You might need the credibility of research to move staff off their defensive positions. For example, at Norrell Services, an Atlanta-based staffing service company, a time-and-motion study done by a branch design team showed the cause of most branch foul-ups to be design problems, not people problems. Twelve of the firm's 200+ branches were involved, every process monitored with a stopwatch plus two people shadowed for a solid week. "We got a picture of what a branch is like from Monday morning to Friday afternoon," explains the design team head Georgia Connors, vice president of Customer Service for the $378-million company. The results really took the pressure off everyone and got them excited, according to Stan Anderson, vice president and general manager of Norrell's Eastern Division. "We confirmed that 80 to 90 percent of all problems are in delivery and the system; only 10 to 20 percent are the people."

12. *Don't Just Focus on Bad Processes; Watch Out for Missing Ones as Well.* For want of a little process, things that affect customer retention can fall through the cracks. The $17.5-billion Xerox Corporation had a client who'd tried unsuccessfully for three years to cancel a nonexistent service contract on his Xerox electronic typewriter. If it hadn't been for a new customer-contact program called "Customer Loyalty," a callback system to customers whose service contracts are up for renewal,[7] he might well have been still trying. "It wasn't until we created a process whereby a telemarketing rep was put into position to talk to that customer that we were able to solve the customer's problem," claims David Spindel, service marketing manager at Xerox Corporation's U.S. Marketing Group.

The computer flagged this customer as someone wanting to cancel a service contract, but when a Xerox telemarketer phoned and asked why, the customer denied ever having such a contract. "The customer said, 'We don't have a service contract [and] I don't understand why you keep sending me this letter saying, "If you don't notify us, we're going to renew your service contract." Everytime you send that letter, I send a letter back saying, 'I don't want to renew.' "

Of course, the contract invoice had remained unpaid over the three years as well—it wasn't a large enough amount to warrant any collections effort, according to Spindel. "Oops, we've goofed," admitted the rep, and, with one keyboard stroke, cancelled the contract, clearing the account of any outstanding debits at the same time. "It was the lack of process that caused this problem in the first place," insists Spindel.

"When we use the word 'process' at Xerox," continues Spindel, "we define it as a series of consecutive steps, one adding value to the next, each with an output and a customer, internal or external." Some might see this approach to customer retention as a bit confining, "more tedious, less imaginative because it's hard-core blocking and tackling step 1, step 2 . . .," says Paul Cahn, vice president of Consumer Marketing. The Xerox Corporation rejects such criticism.

"Process is what maneuvers your people into customer contact," contends Spindel. "[It] is a series of steps that says when this happens you do that and it culminates with somebody talking to the customer and, at that point, the individual does exercise creativity to solve the customer's problem." Besides, if you don't know why your organization isn't able to deliver on customer retention, how can you even begin to change things around, wonders Cahn. "In the absence of a documented process, it's very difficult to improve [things]. We believe the focus on process will get the desired results."

13. Do a Little Process Training. It isn't second nature for most people to look objectively at a problem. What comes more naturally is a defensive stance, "It's not my fault," or an offensive tactic, "Someone else is to blame." Some process training can help give workers at all levels a shared language. Without that commonality, it's hard to keep personalities out of problem-solving, claims Lou Marth, product manager of Xerox's New Build Operations. "Problems were identified by saying something like, 'I'm having trouble with so-and-so over in Production' and so-and-so in Production would reply, 'I'm not the problem, it's Joe Blow in Design,' and so forth. Now we have specific step-by-step methods that identify and state the problem explicitly and provide [the] means of solving it." Figure 2.1 outlines the standardized technique that all Xerox personnel now use in problem solving.

A particularly good way to help employees analyze why a given problem exists is to have them map out the process using a technique called "flowcharting." It's a visual way to walk through the process and see where the "pinchpoints" are, that is, where things break down. Figure 2.2 outlines an example of a flowchart for the medication dispensing process at Brigham and Women's Hospital in Boston, Massachusetts.[8]

West Paces Medical Center has perfected a system that's given

Xerox's Problem-Solving Process

1. Identify and select a problem.
2. Analyze the problem.
3. Generate potential solutions.
4. Select and plan a solution.
5. Implement the solution.
6. Evaluate the solution.

FIGURE 2.1 A common problem-solving technique helps Xerox workers look objectively at any organizational problem.

its employees a headstart on making team meetings work. Gathering people into group sessions is a cornerstone of the customer retention process, yet few employees (or managers for that matter) have much of a clue on how to run an effective meeting. That's where the "center-step meeting process" comes to the rescue.

Medication Process Flowchart—Brigham and Women's Hospital, Boston.

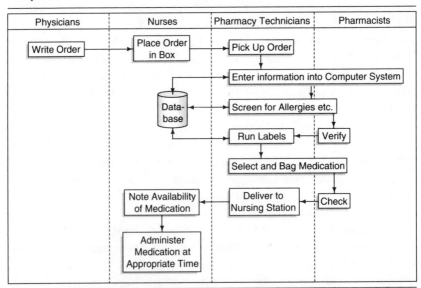

FIGURE 2.2 It isn't second nature for most people to look objectively at any problem. A little process training can help such as the technique called "flowcharting", a visual way to walk through any organizational process and see where things are breaking down. This figure illustrates an example of a flowchart for the medication dispensing process at a Boston hospital.

A clear objective that relates to the customer issue at hand with three or four agenda items is set for each meeting, which is restricted to one hour in length. Each team has a facilitator, leader, timekeeper, and recorder; the last three change with each session. The leader has responsibility for the meeting's content and the team process over time, explains Edward McEachern, a pathologist at West Paces. "[Then] there's the recorder whose job is to record and a timekeeper who says, 'We have eight minutes left, what's the team's pleasure?' [Finally, there's] the facilitator [who] is the custodian of the *process* of the meeting, not the content."

Trained to assist team leaders and chosen on the basis of their people skills, West Paces' facilitators float across several departments, adds Sandra Walcsak, assistant vice president, but they keep well in the background at team meetings. "The facilitator will assist [only] if the team is getting off on a tangent."

At the outset of any work session, the team reviews the agenda, assigns the roles of leader, timekeeper, and recorder, and then works through the agenda until the hour's up. It's a powerful tool, claims McEachern, and he illustrates with a story about a meeting he facilitated with a group of physicians. "I hadn't been invited in on the process before this session," he says, "so the group had none of the above structure. They just wandered all over the place for two hours but, in the end, they got the point. These doctors are really sold on this meeting process [now]; they wouldn't willingly go back to anything that's substandard."

14. *Close that Loop.*   No process is worth anything if there's no way to ensure that what gets solved stays solved or if what appears solved really isn't. Xerox put in an automated postinstallation service in July 1989. "We had always asked our customer relations groups to follow through with every new equipment purchase," says business planning manager, Peter Waasdorp. But there was a good deal of variation across the different units. "We wanted the districts to be able to customize the process." The problem was that some used phone calls and some used mail surveys, and many were running below 95 percent satisfaction. "We should be at 100 percent," he claims; "after all, these people have only just made the decision to join the Xerox customer roster."

The postinstallation system at Xerox is now centralized and consistent—"every customer who receives a new product or service from Xerox gets a postinstallation survey (by mail within 60 days) that goes to the person designated by the customer as the [one] accountable at the customer site." It's just one more way, according to Waasdorp, for area management to close that loop.

The Practice—Making It Happen, Part I—Step 1

What?

A series of workshops aimed at clearing the air and getting past the "We've been here before" and "This too shall pass" attitudes.

Why?

To convince your people that this is a unique twist on a familiar theme.

How?

1A. "We're all in this together Workshop 1.1" with Retention Inc.'s 23 partners, managers, and professional staff to clear the air and introduce "Model for Customer Retention" concepts.
    a. Highly participative group discussion exercises, for example:
        i. "If you were a customer of Retention Inc., what things would make you consider taking your business to a competitor?"
        ii. "What makes it difficult for you to do what it takes to keep your customers at Retention Inc?"
        iii. "What are the positive and negative forces at work that prevent Retention Inc. from keeping its customers?" Use the Total Quality Management (TQM) technique of "force-field analysis."[9] (See Figure 2.3.)
        iv. "If you were the president of Retention Inc. for a day, what one change would you make to improve customer retention?"
    b. Model concepts stressed:
        i. *"Diagonal-slice" accountability,* i.e., people up and

What's in the Way of Making Retention Happen—Force-Field
Analysis: Example - "Should the Office Be Moved?"

Driving Forces				Restraining Forces
Limited space	→		←	Close to service providers
Lack of parking	→		←	Many restaurants nearby
Lack of public transportation	→		←	Newly installed network system
Poor climate control	→		←	Employees have moved to be close to office
Limited access for service vehicles	→		←	Great view of city
Hiring 20 percent more employees	→		←	Close to airport
High rent	→		←	Expandable space

FIGURE 2.3 This figure illustrates an example of a visual technique known as "Force-Field Analysis" which is used to understand the nature of the forces that are opposing positive change, for example, customer retention.

down and across the organization taking responsibility for customer retention. **"A catalyst from
the top, energy from the bottom, and solutions
from the middle."—Hal Hoare, Simon Fraser
University, Vancouver, B.C.**

   ii. *Retention errors, not ideals*—a focus on fixing tangible customer retention problems, not on attaining
perfection.

  iii. *Getting personalities out of problem solving*—introduction to the concepts of "Objectivity" and "Partnership," and to specific tools for depersonalizing
retention problems, e.g., focusing on the big picture and customer, and flow charting.[10] (See Figure 2.4.) Also a discussion of the importance of
looking at *how* people work together as well as on
what tasks or issues they work on. For example, at
B.C. Hydro, a Canadian utility, "empowered
work teams" measure their performance on four
"climate goals"—integrity, innovation, commitment, and teamwork.

  iv. *Retention fact, not fiction*—a focus on managing
customer retention issues based on solid customer
research (this step anticipates Step 3 of the model;
see Chapter 4). **"It's not what you don't know that
can hurt you; it's what you know that ain't so."—
Will Rogers.**

c. Discussion and selection of an individual responsible
for coordinating the company's retention program.

An Example of a Flowchart.

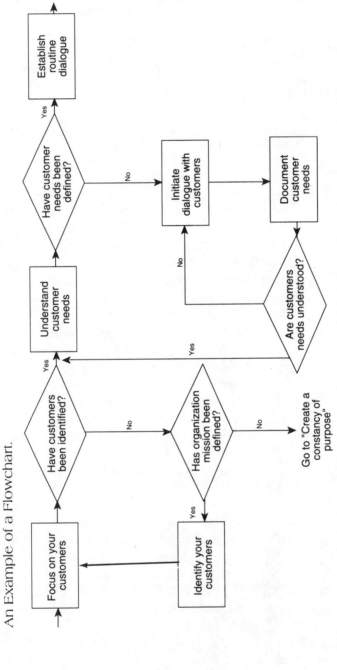

FIGURE 2.4 By focusing on the process rather than the people involved, teams are able to get beyond personalities and onto customer retention. This figure provides part of a detailed flowchart on the customer retention process.

d. Presentation of the "We're all in this together survey" for all Retention Inc. staff; questions specific and actionable, for example:

    i. "If a team of Retention Inc. personnel could be put together to tackle specific issues that would enhance your ability to keep your customers, which issues would you like to see addressed first?"

    ii. "Think for a moment about the customers you serve *within* Retention Inc. If a team of Retention Inc. managers and staff could be put together to tackle specific issues that you believe would enhance the satisfaction rating of your *internal* customers, which issues would you like to see addressed first?"

    iii. "If a team of Retention Inc. managers and staff could be put together to tackle specific issues that would enhance your work satisfaction rating, which issues would you like to see addressed first?"

e. Presentation of a simple framework for managers to: (i) introduce model and survey to their direct reports in 30-minute manager/employee minimeetings, and (ii) elicit recommendations from staff for peer-elected reps from all job categories, levels, functions, and departments within Retention Inc. These peer-elected reps will attend the "We're all in this together Workshop 1.2" for general staff (Step 1B below).

1B. "We're all in this together Workshop 1.2" with peer-elected manager/employee reps as determined from Step 1Ae:

a. Exercises and concepts similar to those introduced in Workshop 1.1.

b. New exercises:

    i. Summary and discussion of results of "We're all in this together survey."

    ii. Creation of the "Retention Advisory Group," a group of 8 to 12 members that will act as an "advisory board" to the individual/unit designated as Retention Coordinator. This "board" will assist in the gathering and screening of retention issues for employee/manager problem-solving teams, as well as in the internal marketing of the retention program. For example: "How are we going to keep everyone informed?"

1C. Communication of results of Workshops 1.1 and 1.2 to all Retention Inc. staff through internal marketing vehicles recommended by the Retention Advisory Group formed in Step 1B (exercise b. ii).

When?

Month 1.

CHAPTER 3

To Know Them Is to Retain Them: Researching Customer Wants and Needs

Do not do unto others as you would have them do unto you; their tastes may not be the same.

George Bernard Shaw[1]

There's a story that's told around the coffee pot at First Chicago National Bank about senior executive Larry Russell and the birth of the bank's customer quality measurement office in 1983. Russell was on the job only a few days when there was a major foul-up with one of his product groups. He was called on the carpet by chairman Barry Sullivan who said, "This is not your fault but it's most certainly your responsibility to make sure it doesn't happen again."

Russell went back to his team and asked, "What happened guys?" Around the conference table that day was a wide disparity of opinion on this. Russell listened for awhile and then said, "There's no one's opinion in this room that matters." Dead silence. "Because there are no customers here. Go out and ask your customers what's important to them," he told the chastened group. "If we concentrate on that we're not going to find ourselves in this kind of trouble again."

These are definitely words to live by for any would-be customer retention organization. Unless you get it from the horse's (customer's) mouth, you can't be sure your information is valid. Without that, you're operating on executive intuition at best; at worst, on innuendo and rumor, when you really should be "managing by fact" as Edward McEachern, physician and quality improvement consultant at West Paces Medical Center, puts it. Even when customers seem unable to make sound judgment calls, it's risky to sidestep them. Conventional psychiatric wisdom has it, for example, that mental health patients can't assess their own mental well being. A 1990 study by Hospital Corporation of America (HCA), a $4.68-billion health-care corporation with 79 facilities across the United States, blew that notion clean out of the water, says Eugene Nelson, HCA's director of Quality Care Research. Psychiatrists in the study rated their patients' mental health status; their patients also rated themselves. "The correlation was almost perfect, better than .9 on a 0 to 1.0 scale."

Knowing what your customers really want from you can save a lot of wear and tear on your bottom line. That's what this chapter's all about.

1. Don't Get Too Attached to Your Own Opinion . . . Avoid the temptation to rely on your own instincts or what passes for gospel among your colleagues. If you're not typical of your existing customer base, then what you think doesn't really count. And that could mean you're pouring resources into areas that don't really matter a fig to your customers. "Left to our own devices, we pay more and more attention to things of less and less importance to the customer," insists Ron Zemke, author of *Service America*.[2] Fidelity Investments Institutional Group was determined to get statements to its pension plan sponsors in record time. That's what they thought customers wanted. "The industry norm is 30 days," says Steve Graziano, vice president, Market Information, "but that didn't satisfy those in charge. 'We'll push for 25,' they said, and when that line was crossed, it was, 'Go for 20.' So we made everybody run faster. Then we're down to 18, and it's, 'Should we push for 10?' " Fortunately for those, by now, frantic back-office Fidelity staffers, a customer satisfaction survey intervened.

"Eighteen to twenty days is more than acceptable," customers said in this research, "In fact, we'd be just as happy if the thing showed up within 25 to 30 days." "So, we'll stick with where we are at 20," says Graziano, "and not make our people jump through any more hoops."

What customers did want, though, was more responsiveness: that's "insuring the right person answers the phone at the time I have a problem." The happiest among the surveyed customers were those whose problems with the investment firm had been resolved within 24 hours. It was more like three days, though, for the more unfortunate, and most disgruntled, respondents. That was due to procedural protocol for telephone pickup at the company. In the past, when a customer's Fidelity contact was unavailable, the call was bumped to an open pool, where, often as not, no one knew him or her from Adam or Eve. Following on the survey results, that's changed. A backup person is now on tap, with a full client profile at the touch of a button, thanks to some improved technology. We've put our resources where we'll get the best bang for our buck with customers, contends Graziano.

2. . . . Or to Your Vantage Point. Sometimes, what's good for the company, at least in the short term, isn't so hot for the customer. See the world from your customer's viewpoint, not your own or the corporation's. This was a lesson Xerox learned on the heels of a 1986 task force report based on hundreds of interviews with its customers. It was apparent that the company's views of what constituted quality differed markedly from how the customers saw things, admits Peter Waasdorp, business planning manager for Xerox's U.S. Marketing Group.

Customers wanted accurate billing, for example. Xerox, on the other hand, was intent on whittling down its "days of sales," a measure of how quickly customers paid up. "Get your act together on billing errors and we'd be happy to cough up the cash," was the customer attitude. "What we found was customers were very dissatisfied with our five percent error rate." That lead to a major company effort to focus on invoice quality and the ease of correcting bills, an effort that's paid off. "We're approaching one percent," contends Waasdorp, "and continuing to focus on driving that number even lower."

3. Being Higher Up Doesn't Make You More in Touch. Being higher up the chain of command doesn't necessarily make you any better at reading your customers. It can make you more arrogantly sure you've got the customer pulse though, claims David Thomson, former senior vice president of Marketing at Delta Hotels & Resorts, a 15-unit hospitality chain based in Toronto. He recalls an incident where his own president, Simon Cooper, misjudged guest preferences and was forced to "eat crow" as a result.

The multibillion-dollar hotel chain regularly surveys customers through a program called "Partners in Performance" (PIPS). At one PIPS session, a breakfast focus group in 1990, guests were asked to comment on trays of room amenities, such as soap and shampoo. "We showed them a number of different types of bottles and asked which of these would they prefer for what reasons." Cooper initially saw little reason to bother clients with such stuff as he felt he knew just what they wanted. "He'd be willing to listen, though, if we wanted to take it to the customers first," recalls Thomson, who openly laughs at the result. "The look the president liked the most was what the guests liked the least."

Cooper wasn't Delta's only executive to fall prey to the I-know-what's-good-for-them trap. Some years back, an experiment to entice the female executive market at a West Coast Delta location bombed completely, admits Pam Paquette, regional director of Marketing. Some enterprising folks at the hotel believed they were already well acquainted with the needs of the female traveler. That being the case, there was no need at all to ask these women about an idea for a new kind of room, designed just for them. I bet you can guess what comes next.

These "leading ladies rooms" had a very special decor, all soft and fluffy, and totally wrong, according to subsequent research. "Women said, 'Don't single us out. Give us equal treatment, not pink powder puff rooms.' " So much for management intuition.

4. *Go to the Source.* Much of the success of any customer retention endeavor depends on the quality of your research intelligence. And if you want that information you've got to go to the source. That's where market research, and the following tips, come in.

4a. *Don't Balk at the Cost of Research.* Don't eschew research because you believe it costs too much. Admittedly, the price tag can get pretty hefty. The most basic of customer audits can run you close to $10,000 and a full-scale investigation by a consultant can reach the $100,000 mark in no time. Even a group session with your customers averages $3,000. You can keep expenses in line, though, by sticking to research on what's valuable and actionable rather than on what's just interesting. Or train some employees to do telephone surveys, like Bank of Boston did for its research blitz on upscale clients in 1986. Over 1,000 of the bank's people were only too happy to earn a few extra dollars moonlighting as evening researchers.[3]

Exploit the resources available through local university and college business programs. Many commerce or MBA curricula can accommodate projects submitted by local companies. University of British Columbia (B.C.) students, as an example, dug up some good starting-point data on small businesses for the B.C. Central Credit Union in Vancouver, Canada.[4]

4b. Apply Multiple Research Techniques and Don't Reinvent the Wheel. There are many paths to customer understanding. You can tap into research other people have done, called "secondary research," or you can create your own. The latter, or "primary research," can take two forms, "qualitative" or "quantitative." Qualitative research such as employee or customer group interviews is used as a first shot at understanding your customers; quantitative research such as mail or telephone surveys gives you a statistical dimension to the issues raised in qualitative research.

Take advantage of all available research avenues. Figure 3.1 gives you a good starting point on determining which options are best for your organization.[5] First define your research objectives: what are you trying to learn and what action are you going to take? Don't reinvent the wheel; scour your local libraries, governments, and associations for what others have done before. They say genius is not in having a good idea, but in knowing how to use someone else's.

Research Technique Effectiveness (based on a survey of American Management Association membership and that of the Society for Consumer Affairs Professionals, 1987)

Technique	Percent Rating Most Effective	Effectiveness Rating (out of 5)	Cost (average annual)
800 numbers	36	4.08	$384,000
Focus groups	25	3.89	91,000
Mail/phone surveys	36	3.75	145,000
Comment cards	13	3.33	103,000
Point-of-purchase surveys	11	3.59	83,000

FIGURE 3.1 There are many paths to customer understanding and retention. Take advantage of all available research avenues including studies done by others, called "secondary research". This figure compares various available research options.

4c. Start from the Inside Out.   Start your research from the inside out and from the least expensive to the most costly. Look to your company's computer files and employees first before venturing into the outside customer world. Dig into client transactional records, for example, and root out why they take some of their business elsewhere because you can be sure they do. "Many companies have much of what they need (in-house) but have never organized it in a formal way," claims Ian Gordon, a partner in the Toronto office of Ernst & Young Management Consultants and author of the 1989 book *Beat the Competition!* "Internal sources may provide as much as 80 percent of what you need."[6]

4d. Get Staff to Play Detective.   Save a few dollars by getting your own people to do some customer retention research and get their commitment to the results at the same time. It took face-to-face meetings with dissatisfied customers, for example, to convince union workers at U.S. Steel's Gary Works mill in Gary, Indiana, that business as usual would soon mean no business, and no jobs.

In 1987, Gary Works, which accounts for 60 percent of U.S. Steel's shipments, was courting disaster. Key customers like General Motors and Ford Motor were heading for the door, the plant was losing more than $100 million a year, and employee morale was all but nonexistent. That's when new plant manager John Goodwin pulled hourly worker Bill Barath off his job as galvanizer and into the customer's shop, specifically Ford's Chicago Heights plant. Barath got an eyeful—the anticorrosion skin he'd so carefully coated at Gary on steel bound for Ford never made it intact through the customer's production line. The problem was traced to a faulty machine at the Gary mill that was suppose to trim zinc buildup off the steel edges. Barath went back with that intelligence and under Goodwin's hands-off management, the problem was fixed.

Word spread and other U.S. Steel customers wanted their own Barath equivalent. Now, the Gary Works customer team includes five union workers who call on automotive customers and three more who visit nonautomotive clients. With the exception of a regular Monday meeting with Goodwin and other managers, team members spend their working week on site with customers. "A lot of times, we can just call a manager at the plant from the road, tell him what the problem is, and it gets fixed right away," says pioneer team member, Jeff Grunden. "Other times it's more complicated, but everybody you need is there in that Monday meeting." It's been a successful experiment. As an illustration of just how much, General Motors, which had all but struck U.S. Steel off its bid lists, increased Gary Works purchases fivefold since 1987.[7]

4e. Use Employee and Customer Group Interviews.   An excellent way to gain valuable insight into customer opinions and concerns is through small group interviews, called "focus groups." Customers are invited to these group sessions to speak freely and at length about their views on your organization and its products and services. "It's nothing more than a discussion that's channelled and controlled by a moderator," explains Doug White, head of British Columbia-based White/Barton Research Associates.[8]

Focus groups can be used to sample customer opinion in a variety of situations. Anne Provost, a vice president with Heffring Research Group Ltd. in Calgary, Alberta, recalls the case of a Vancouver food processor that used focus groups to fine-tune television ads announcing a new product. The spots focused on the technology behind the product, but customers sent the advertiser back to the drawing board when they said the ads were boring. "The [original campaign] was effective for the people who ran the company," says Provost, "but it wasn't for the consumer."[9]

One of the classic uses of focus groups is to decide what types of questions to ask in a follow-up survey for a larger number of participants. A word of caution here. Focus groups offer organizations a chance to capture a range of opinion on a given question or issue. They don't say how many people think the same way. That's the province of the survey.

Focus groups don't work in every situation either. One-on-one interviews, for example, are a better bet if potential respondents are too scattered, like pulp and paper foremen, or if the subject matter's on the sensitive side, such as personal finances or competitive secrets.

You get your best results from focus group sessions if you spring for two groups per topic and an outside researcher who'll be able to act as objective moderator for the actual interviews. "Quite often the client is just too close to the product or service to be objective," warns White. Good moderators get everyone relaxed, he continues, and keep their own opinions under wraps.[10]

Clients do have a place at focus groups, watching the action through a two-way mirror. Managers from an electrical-panel maker that wanted to redesign its product, for example, watched electricians take competitors' panels apart in no time. But when it came to the Toronto firm's product, participants were bogged down by having to use three different screwdrivers. "The difficulty just hadn't occurred" to the client, says Toronto market researcher Bob Inglis and president of Technalysis Inc., "until they saw these guys struggling."[10] But be prepared to keep a stiff upper limit if you view these sessions. As Casey MacKenzie, executive vice president at First Nationwide Bank, says, "It can be agony . . . listening to ordinary people complain about your business."[11] Figure 3.2 provides some guidelines for focus group viewing.

But don't just hone in on existing customers. Save yourself some future grief by getting input on what's working and what isn't from your own customer service people, branch managers, and sales staff. James Shanahan, now sector vice president of Marketing for MasterCard International, notes how employee input can add significantly to the design of any new service. When his former employer, a large full-service U.S. bank, introduced a financial planning service, the company opted to keep the customer fact-finding questionnaire simple—too simple, as it turned out. Through debriefing sessions, employees passed on customers' comments: money is serious business and the questionnaire should reflect that tone.[12]

4f. Observe Customer Behavior. Get a feel for actual customer habits by taking up an observation post in the lobby of your

Guidelines for Focus Group Viewing

1. Don't expect focus group participants to care as much about your product, service, or organization as you do. It represents only a small part of their lives.
2. Don't expect your focus group participants to be people like you or to be people unlike you.
3. Don't expect focus group participants to be consistent and don't label them as hypocrites when they aren't.

FIGURE 3.2 An excellent way to gain valuable insight into customer opinions and concerns is through small group interviews, called "focus groups". You get your best results from these sessions if you spring for an outside researcher who'll be able to act as objective moderator. You can watch these proceedings through a two-way mirror or on a videotape. Keep these guidelines in mind, though, when viewing.

organization. A western U.S. financial institution, for example, observed that traffic flow to one of its ATMs was practically nonexistent. When accosted in the bank, customers said they couldn't find the thing; it turns out that it was obscured by a post in the foyer.

4g. Back Up Soft Research with Hard Numbers. Don't limit your research to soft techniques like focus groups. Follow through with surveys—by mail, telephone, or in person—to quantify your results and add a statistical edge to your data.

4h. Design Research Questions in the Customer's Own Words . . . Even when you're trying to design questions that will help you get on your customer's wavelength you're still apt to miss the boat on occasion, as United Services Automobile Association (USAA) researchers discovered. Every year, the nation's fifth largest insurer of privately owned automobiles and fourth largest of homes randomly surveys by mail 2 percent of its two million customers and policyholders in what research executive director Frederick (Tim) Timmerman, Jr., calls "living samples." A lot of time and effort had gone into the survey design, yet a pretest of one for the life insurance division in late 1990 showed there was still more work to do. "We were asking questions [customers] didn't understand; we were culture-locked." Based on that focus group, the survey's been completely revised.

- *. . . Make them simple . . .* The initial efforts from HCA measurement design teams offered too many choices for a simple, self-administered survey. "We wanted the questionnaire to be something a person could complete in half an hour," says HCA's Eugene Nelson. But over a 36-month period in 1986–89, these teams labored over an immense database to build a family of quality monitors for each of five key hospital customers—patients (medical, surgical, and psychiatric; inpatient and outpatient), physicians, employees, the community, and payors (major employers). The employee measurement system, for example, grew from six focus groups and 82 one-hour sessions with personnel across all hospital ranks. "We call it wallowing in the reality," says Nelson.

  A set of quality dimensions for each customer group began to take form, and within each dimension, a list of key quality characteristics emerged. To illustrate: a major dimension of what makes physicians brag about a hospital is the quality of nursing; two key characteristics of that dimension are the use of temporary nurses and the stability of nursing staff. All this effort generated just too much information to squeeze into a simple customer survey. As an example, when the employee system team mapped out the characteristics of the supervisory system, a major dimension of what it takes to wow hospital staff, the list of characteristics was 40 items long. So the task of whittling down began, aided by a second round of focus groups to get some rank ordering by customers. Over time, the HCA teams crafted five easy-to-do questionnaires.

• *. . . And make them actionable.* Survey questions that generate answers that nobody can do anything about may be technically sound but, in practice, useless. That's why, in 1990, Bridgestone/ Firestone opted for a customer satisfaction sampling technique with statistical flaws and a survey that covered a very limited range of topics. An aborted test of a more full-blown option proved the wisdom of this simpler course. Survey results from a 1987 pilot in Columbus and Memphis showed up as a whole lot of gobbledygook to store managers. Retail tire marketing manager, Rick Bangs, elaborates: "If I was a manager and I got my report, I couldn't make head or tails of it. When I did understand it, it wasn't at an actionable level."

"We knew from the pilot what our problem was," says Bangs. "We weren't fixing cars right the first time. Bottom line is we can't afford to spend millions on measuring a problem we know we've got. We decided [instead] to focus our attentions and expenditures on fixing that problem."

The $1-billion tire and service retailer also wanted any measurement and follow-up action to take place at the store level. And that means that *simple* and *actionable* needed to be the operative words. The result: a six-question card is placed on the customer's rearview mirror by the sales associate, the technician assigned to the car signs off when the work's completed and, when the survey results are mailed back, they go directly to the store manager. Bangs accepts the inevitable distribution bias this approach may foster. After all, "customer retention only happens at the store level."

4i. Do Customer Exit Research. This may seem the epitome of closing the barn door after the livestock's on the loose but research here can be very useful in heading off a major customer exodus. Every other month, "closed account" customers at Harleysville National Bank and Trust Company receive a survey in the mail. The $260-million Pennsylvania institution uses survey results to spot trends in specific markets; for example, is a major problem brewing in one particular branch?[13]

4j. Get a Reading From Multiple Users. Watch that you don't confine your research to the obvious operational customer contacts. That focus works nicely for individuals and smaller businesses where operational people usually double as the decision maker. In larger customer organizations, however, the two functions rarely coalesce in one person.

To accommodate just such a broad spectrum of decision influencers, IBM Canada totally revamped its customer measurement system in 1991. "We were surveying [only] the MIS directors and a lot more users have influence over what decisions are being made; more budgets are shifting out," says Lee Kea, formerly director of Strategy and Business Management. Quite simply, the company was surveying the wrong people. The annual survey was reformatted as a quarterly and aimed more deeply into the customer hierarchy. "We now have twelve times as many people surveyed inside the MIS group and we've gone to a whole new [user] population."

4k. Research the Competition. Don't lose sight of the other guys. Everything customers perceive about your organization is tied to their perceptions about who they see as your rivals. They're going to constantly compare you against the competition so you'd better get a good handle on the basis for that comparison.

Get on competitor mailing lists for such things as client newsletters, pay the competition a visit to critique their services and ask your customers who does what better. An Ontario, Canada, machine-parts manufacturer, for example, found it was losing customers to a rival business. When talks with the competitor's suppliers, customers, and ex-employees identified precision machinery as its competitive edge, the manufacturer was able to upgrade his own equipment and recapture lost market share.[14]

If you think you can forgo the cloak-and-dagger of competitive intelligence, think again. Someone is probably out there right now analyzing your firm and taking a shot at your customers, so it makes sense to know as much about them as they do about you.

Quips Ernst & Young's Gordon, "I don't want to sound paranoid. But the fact is even paranoids have enemies"—and competitors.[15]

5. Be Creative in Getting Customers to Talk. Customers won't always say what they really mean. Most of the time they won't volunteer any information at all; they'll just quietly pull up stakes and disappear from your balance sheet. Research confirms that 91 percent of unhappy customers won't lodge a complaint with the offending business, but they won't return either.[16]

The following story illustrates how difficult it can be to coax information from reluctant customers. In 1985, an external contractor was hired by a U.S. Department of Defense unit to work with in-house technical experts. Their assignment was to develop a series of training modules on the safe operation of agency motor vehicles. Five years later, there was nothing to show for their efforts. Within three months of a new team of customer contact specialists being assigned to the account, however, the first module rolled off the presses, followed by seventeen more over the next two years. "We turned the project around completely," claims Mary Albright, associate director of the Civilian Personnel Service Support Office, Defense Logistics Agency (DLA). "We accomplished in two years what we had barely begun in the previous five."

Why the poor showing for this project initially? It took just one visit by the new customer team to ferret out the reason. The contractor was sold on the idea of in-depth training but that wasn't what the customer wanted. "Operating a nuclear-powered airship might need that kind of detail," laughs program manager, Bernard Lukco. "But we were looking at a palette jack. You weren't going to fly it, just push it across the floor." Albright chimes in, also with a chuckle, "What he wanted was something like, 'When you operate a forklift, don't run into walls.' What we were doing was more like, 'When you operate a forklift, you get on, left foot first, you put this foot on this pedal and you turn this knob counterclockwise.' "

So why hadn't the client just spit out his objections to this amount of detail; why let things drag on with the contractor as they did? The reasons were twofold. First, having to deal with such an array of experts had tied the customer's tongue. "[He] seemed reluctant to complain to the technical people," explains Lukco. "He felt these people ought to know what they were doing." Second, even when he did venture a comment, he couldn't properly articulate his concerns. "The customer didn't know how to explain exactly what it was he was looking for; all he knew was what he saw wasn't what he wanted."

DLA's new customer liaison team now provides a nice link for agency patrons. These people often are more at home with the liaison staff than with the functional group and they now have an objective contact person for any problem-solving. "They have somebody who is not involved in the project but has a link with management who would help solve [any] problem," concludes Lukco.

You might have to get pretty creative to persuade customers to talk. Getting them together with their peers can sometimes stimulate conversation and give you good insight into how you can serve them. One such example is the ServiceMaster customer seminar featuring keynote speaker and management guru Peter Drucker. "We asked CEOs from the health-care industry to join us," explains Chuck Stair, president and COO of ServiceMaster Management Services, which provides supportive management services to healthcare, education, and industrial facilities. At the seminar, Drucker discussed industry challenges, such as employee turnover, and encouraged lots of input from the floor. It was an opportunity for the $1.61-billion corporation to see what customers believed to be the key issues facing them over the next few months and years. "This was another way to listen to [our] customers as they interacted with a respected source of leadership [Drucker]."

6. *Read Between the Lines.* Your customers don't necessarily think the way you do, so they won't come up with data that addresses your corporate concerns right away. They'll talk about what's meaningful to them and that may not jive with industry jargon. Clint Vardeman tells his Rural/Metro emergency crews not to expect customers to extol the virtues of their technical proficiency. "I've yet to see a customer comment card that says, 'These guys were wonderful, they attached my tourniquet just so and I observed their sterile technique and it was perfect.' "

Some reading between the lines may be in order. Customers may say one thing in a focus group, for example, but do something quite different when it comes to putting hard money on the line. One client of Boston-based consulting firm Bain & Co., for example, found minimal correlation between its elaborate satisfaction results and actual customer defections.[17]

It's often a matter of misplaced priorities; customers may consider the same things important that your organization does but they don't attach the same weight to them. Fidelity Investments' top choice for customer satisfaction, for example, got little more than a passing nod from customers in the company's 1990 study of customer expectations. The survey tracked the effect of 72 attributes on satisfaction, both from a positive and a negative perspective. "The goal," explains John Post, marketing manager for Retail Services, "was to figure out which ones were critical to improving the overall level of satisfaction but also which ones would prove to have the greatest negative impact. We were not looking at what drew them to Fidelity; we were looking at what would keep them."

Customers bypassed performance, which the company believed most important, in favor of courtesy and friendliness, accuracy and timing, and being treated like a person. In response, Fidelity designed a new training series for all its phone reps called "Extraordinary Customer Relations." "It's been a real hit with customers. Out of 100 calls in the past, a 'Gee, you're terrific' sentiment from a customer was a rare commodity," admits Post. Not so today; "Now, I definitely hear that."

If you don't straighten out what's really crucial for customers, you might soon find you haven't any. I like the way Mark Hanan and Peter Karp say it in their 1989 book *Customer Satisfaction:* "A supplier that satisfies the 80 percent of things that do not count as "musts" and fails to satisfy the 20 percent of the things that make or break a [customer] relationship is in the wrong business."[18]

7. Don't Just Research to Make Them Happy, Research to Make Them Stay. Fifty percent of customers surveyed by a major U.S. retailer said they were fairly satisfied. With a little prodding, though, they admitted they wouldn't be back.[19] This is the reality of customer retention—your job isn't just to ward off dissatisfaction in your customer base, it's to make sure they don't take their business elsewhere. So, in your research, get beyond what turns them on or ticks them off and on to what keeps them coming back for more.

These are not always one and the same thing, claims James Miller at Xerox's U.S. Marketing Group in Rochester. When it comes to guarantees, for example, customers aren't so much taken by the promise of money back as by the sense of control. That's why Xerox allows equipment exchanges at the customer's discretion under the conditions of its "Total Satisfaction Guarantee." "The way you get customers to stay is to delight them [not merely satisfy them] and that's not always what they initially tell you," Miller contends.

His colleagues, David Spindel, manager of Services Marketing, and Paul Cahn, vice president of Consumer Marketing, have also found similar inconsistencies with customer research. Using what they call "leads and clues questions," they are able to build a sense of what factors contribute to customer satisfaction—things like billing accuracy or fixing the customer's machine on the first call. Yet, when these are correlated with what keeps customers frequenting Xerox outlets, often there's no match. Spindel provides the following example.

"The question customers most frequently check [on surveys] that they're most dissatisfied with is frequency of paper jams. Yet, we found a relatively low correlation between customer dissatisfaction with paper jams and overall customer satisfaction with Xerox." Spindel believes it's because customers expect paper jams. Adds Cahn, "The frequency with which customers say, 'We're dissatisfied with something' and the actual importance of that when you rank it in terms of customer retention sometimes gives you two very different kinds of answers."

This research conundrum isn't restricted to the high-tech industry; it pops up elsewhere. U.S. research shows that although the top complaint for financial services customers is long lineups, they don't switch suppliers for that reason. It's only when something goes wrong with their account and they're forced to do battle with the organization—that's what ultimately forces them out the exit door for good.

8. Don't Neglect Research on Customer Expectations. Customers form expectations about what your organization can do for them and compare these against their perceptions of what you actually deliver. Too large a gap between these two and they'll start looking elsewhere for satisfaction. Just how much of a shortfall customers will tolerate is the stuff of important retention research. Texas A&M and Duke University professors A. Parasuraman, Leonard Berry, and Valarie Zeithaml recommend you start by establishing the customer's "zone of tolerance," that is, the difference between what's desired and what's perceived as adequate. Figure 3.3 illustrates this concept visually.[20]

The Zone of Tolerance

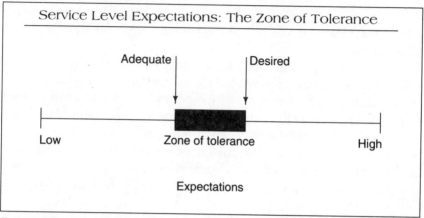

FIGURE 3.3 Customers form expectations about what your organization can do for them and compare these against their perceptions of what you actually deliver. Too large a gap between these two and they'll start looking elsewhere for satisfaction. This "zone of tolerance" is illustrated in this figure. The "desired" service level is the service your customer hopes to achieve by doing business with you, a blend of what he or she believes "can be" and "should be". The "adequate" service level is that which the customer finds acceptable. It is in part based on the customer's assessment of what the service "will be".

9. Develop a Customer Profile. Everything you ever wanted to know about your customer packed into one convenient package—that's the essence of the "customer information file" (CIF), an automated client profiling system that integrates all transactional and demographic data available on a particular customer into one record. This is a very useful research tool for would-be customer retainers.

CIF is not new. It's been around for more than a decade. In its simplest form, CIF is a name and address file that also identifies the customer's different accounts at that institution. The most sophisticated CIFs use complex database architectures to provide a detailed snapshot of the customer and document his or her complete relationship with the organization. At Brooklyn Union Gas Co., for example, where a new CIF was installed in 1990, 500 hand-held computers link field personnel to the main-office computer, allowing up-to-the-minute information about customer account status and service requests.[21]

Recent CIF subsystems, particularly relationship database technology, allow you to slice and dice your customer data in more ways than a Cuisinart—the total number of banking customers within a two-mile radius of a specific ATM, for example. You can also add third-party data, such as census information, to the basic file, and perform what-if calculations.

The real payoff with a CIF comes from its application to cross-selling and relationship pricing. Between 1987 and 1989, George Mrkonic, Jr., CEO of Eyelab, boosted sales by collecting data on eyeglass purchasers and offering regular promotions to get them back into the stores for new glasses. Now, as head of Kmart's speciality-stores division, he's built up huge customer lists of do-it-yourselfers, bargain hunters, and sports lovers.[22]

A last reminder on CIFs: the system is only as good as the data it contains: the old axiom "garbage in, garbage out" applies. So keep your CIF data current and accurate.

10. Remember, Customer Research Is Part of Customer Relations. Asking customers what they want does more than just generate good information, claims Bob Jamison of accounting firm Manning Jamison (MJ), a 50-employee company based in Vancouver, Canada. Clients are also impressed that their input matters. In one case, a $30,000-a-year MJ client who had considered tendering his company's audit not only stayed put but was the source of three good referrals in less than a year. Why the change of heart? Jamison believes attendance at the company's group interview with customers in 1990 did the trick. "He said, 'Any company that would go to such lengths to listen to its customers was a company I wanted to work with.' "

11. Let Everyone In on What You've Learned. Hoarding research results serves no useful purpose. Consider providing copies to anyone in your organization who'd benefit from the information. The list should include branch managers, customer service reps, and administrative staff heads. A good example of this philosophy is Lexus, the $100-million luxury division of Toyota Motor Sales, which passes on to dealers every snippet of customer information it collects via satellite connections across its North American market. For example, service histories of all Lexus cars are compiled in one central location allowing the company to broadcast details every other week on what service problems have cropped up and tips on fixing them.

The California-based firm also conducts a broad spectrum of customer satisfaction surveys, the results of which are provided to one and all. Included in the data exchange are customer letters—good, bad, and ugly—plus outside satisfaction research on the company, such as the Customer and Dealer Satisfaction Indices done annually by J. D. Power & Associates Inc. And that information sharing is not limited to the people at the main office or on the sales desk; it's shipped right back to the factories in Japan where the cars are built. That way, says Raymond Lindland, national customer satisfaction and training manager, "the people who design the car know exactly how the customer feels about the vehicle."

There are two key monitors that form the cornerstone of the Lexus satisfaction research strategy—a "New Vehicle Sales & Delivery Survey" that is mailed to the customer within 45 days of purchase or lease, and the "Service Satisfaction Survey," mailed at the time of the car's second free maintenance checkup or whenever additional service work is done. The returned surveys are compiled and feedback is generated monthly to the dealers via the satellite. A percentage index of satisfaction is derived from the survey material, both sales and service, and this also finds its way to the front line.

The Lexus survey questions and format were built up from versions designed a few years ago by the customer relations staff at Toyota. The outside research firm of J.D. Power & Associates also had a hand in development. The choice of questions is important, explains Lindland. This is not a vague popularity contest; the information derived needs to be actionable at the grass-roots level. An answer to a question like, "How did the people at the dealership treat you during the sale?" can help training staff gauge the effectiveness of their programs. "We also ask questions like, 'Did you see anything wrong with the car?' " continues Lindland. "We use that information for improving our product."

Survey results are also keyed by individual sales consultant. "Our customers will cite specific individuals," says Marjorie Crosby, customer satisfaction operations manager. "We want to see that gets back to the dealership." The dealers are encouraged to use this information to provide positive feedback, as well as coaching opportunities if all's not as it should be.

All this quizzing at Lexus has paid off. In 1992, the company ranked first for the third year in a row in the industry's annual owners' satisfaction survey.

12. *Don't Get Mired in Measurement.* Customer retention facts and figures can be pretty intoxicating at times; they give us such a

wonderful feeling of accuracy. There's no question, of course, that good research keeps us better in touch with what customers really want, and it's oh so tempting to keep up the good work and keep on researching until the last bit of error's been squeezed out. That's never going to happen, however, and there comes a time when you've just got to bite the bullet and make that decision, according to Xerox's James Miller. "You can analyze the heck out of it but, at some point, it's going to be a leap of faith." Or as one businessman observed, "Statistics are no substitute for judgment."

13. Do Something with Your Research. It's one thing to measure customer retention, says HCA's Eugene Nelson, and quite another to use those measurements constructively. The problem isn't in terms of customer measurement per se. It's in "making that measurement applied, useful, and used." For many organizations, research reports merely collect dust on bookshelves. In a 1991 survey of the hospitality industry, marketing professor Chekitan Dev and his colleague Bernard Ellis found that only about 45 percent of the data obtained from guests was ever used.[23]

At HCA, however, employees have been able to make good use of their company's family of customer measurements. In just one instance, a team working off the patient measurement system reduced the time required to deliver pain medication on the wards by nearly 50 percent in just 12 months.

Talk about listening and responding to customers comes cheap, claims America West Airline's Mark Coleman, former senior vice president, Sales & Product Development. For his company's key patrons, frequent business travelers, only money and action talk. Getting there on time is critical to how well these customers rate an airline and America West committed over $18 million just to ensure it remains tops in this category. The company maintains three airplanes at its Phoenix base, gassed up and ready to go any time in case of breakdown elsewhere in the fleet. "They're just sitting there," says Coleman, "in case it fogs in at Omaha. That airplane is ready to pick it up here." All flights are scheduled to arrive on time or early 80 percent of the time, versus an industry norm of 50 percent. Coleman explains, "It averages an hour and five minutes to Los Angeles [from Phoenix]. We will actually schedule an hour and fifteen minutes."

The biggest snag to on-time performance is connecting baggage handling, notes Coleman. And that's where the company's $18 million found a home. A laser baggage system in America West's new terminal in Phoenix sorts and escorts luggage to connecting flights. "There's an inbound baggage belt that takes the bag from one airplane [right at the airplane, no carts], then sorts and delivers it to the next flight by reading the laser tag on it."

The airline's also added a special baggage-handling service for the elite of its frequent travelers, members of "The Chairman's Club." Special tags identify members' luggage and a new procedure expedites baggage delivery at the traveler's final destination. "The bags are put on the plane last in a special area; as a result, they're always the first bags to come off."

Such serious response to customer comments has earned America West championship status two years running. "We've been voted national champion for '88 and '89," says Coleman, "and continue to be the most on-time airline in the entire U.S. airline industry." It's an accolade that doesn't come free, though. "You've got to put your money where your mouth is."

14. *Keep All Research Efforts Coordinated.*   Too many organizations pay too little heed to a coordinated research effort. That means that every department or branch is doing its own thing and it doesn't take a genius to figure that's a poor use of resources.

15. *Remember, Sometimes No Amount of Research Is Going to Help.* Often customers don't really know just what they want from you, or what you can do for them, for that matter. You have to adapt, says ServiceMaster's Stair; try new approaches (including trial and error) to bring client needs to the surface. "Some customers will not realize immediately what they're telling you is a need; over a period of listening, though, you'll find it. At other times, you will have to initiate action and have the customer respond, then readjust until you're going down the right road." For an Atlanta health-care facility, determining what would make major employers express delight about having their staff hospitalized was a major headache. "We've been at it over a year and a half," admits West Paces Medical Center administrator Chip Caldwell, "and we still don't have the answer completely." They did find a partial solution, though.

Interviews done over a period of a year with businesses like Hewlett Packard and Prudential Insurance indicated that value, not simply cost, is the critical yardstick a payor uses to judge a medical institution. "The first thing that comes out of their mouths is, 'We want to reduce the cost,' " Caldwell says. "But when you start exploring how that might play out, they end up saying, 'We don't want to reduce the quality, what we really want is value.' " So how do you determine the value of an employee's gall bladder surgery? Not an easy task, even for the hospital itself. "We looked at ourselves as payors and asked, 'When would we express delight about the health care we're paying for?' "

An answer did eventually emerge. Using teams of physicians, the hospital applied quality management techniques to the four most common diagnoses occurring in the workforce—back injuries and lower back pain, mental and chemical dependency, cardiogenic complications, and pregnancy and childbirth. The team assigned to the last issue saved payors over a half-million dollars by reducing the number of caesarean (c-section) deliveries for pregnant employees. Pathologist Edward McEachern picks up the story at this point.

McEachern's c-section team brought together the full gamut of people who understand the delivery process, including nurses, physicians, and administrative staff such as the admitting clerk and the obstetrics educator. It's not the way things would have been arranged in the past. "We would have gotten a bunch of doctors together and said, 'Okay, what do you think?' "

After a two-week stint on data collection, group members had quantified the actual process on a flowchart they called a "clinical process map." Plus they'd uncovered an intriguing fact about why c-sections are done; reason one is medical but reason two is by patient request. "Why is that?" they asked themselves, and then the patients. "It turns out the mother's mother was saying, 'Once a c-section, always a c-section.' " That prompted the inclusion of grandmothers-to-be in a class for expectant mothers who'd already delivered by c-section. This was one of several initiatives that brought the c-section rate at West Paces down from 22.8 percent to 15.1 percent in two years.

The Practice—Making It Happen, Part I—Step 2

What?

To begin the process of researching what makes customers stay, what makes them grow, and what makes them leave by tapping the employee pipeline.

Why?

Research tells us that front-line employees can predict 90 percent of the time that customers will have complaints but 70 percent of them are afraid to speak up.

How?

2A. Set up a series of videotaped focus groups with employees, two per employee group, e.g., two for executive staff, two for clerical/administrative staff, etc. The participants for these groups will be randomly selected by an outside researcher. **Objective:** to elicit top-of-mind awareness on customer retention issues. **Examples:**
   a. "What are the top two complaints you hear from your key customers? from other clients?"
   b. "If you were a customer of Retention Inc., what would make you consider leaving?"
   c. "If you were a customer of Retention Inc., what would make you consider referring the company to your friends or family?"
   d. "If you were a customer of Retention Inc., what would make you consider bringing more of your business to that company?"
   e. "Think of the customers you or Retention Inc. has lost. What do you believe or know about what made them leave?"
   f. "If you were CEO of Retention Inc. for a day, what one policy would you change that would make sure customers don't leave?"
   Homework: homework assigned to staff participating in these focus groups. See Step 3A for details.

2B. To statistically quantify the results from focus groups in Step 2A, circulate a self-administered questionnaire to all Retention Inc. employees.

2C. Elicit employee/manager recommendations for "Retention Monitors," special staff trained by an outside researcher in a half-day workshop to objectively measure the successes of employee/manager problem-solving teams in later steps. Introduce this concept in the focus groups (Step 2A) but use the questionnaire (Step 2B) to elicit actual names. The final name selection here will be made by the Retention Coordinator and the Retention Advisory Group formed in Step 1.

2D. Copies of videotapes and summary report of focus groups made available to all staff through internal marketing vehicles recommended by the Retention Advisory Group formed in Step 1.

When?

Months 2 and 3.

CHAPTER 4

Focusing on Your Best Customers: The 80/20 Rule

> *Because any company's capability is . . . limited, it cannot span the entire (customer) dimension.*
> Benson Shapiro et al., Harvard Business School.[1]

In 1987, San Antonio Savings and Loan Association (SASA), a $3.2-billion financial institution, wanted to do a service upgrade for the top fifth of its customer base. It was common knowledge that these folks were good for the company; what no one guessed was just how good. That detail showed up in an automated report generated by the company's $290,000 customer information file system. This single group of customers accounted for the bulk of the company's deposits, 91 percent of assets to be exact. A little more research, though, revealed they held only 40 percent of their funds with the Texas company, parking the rest of their wealth elsewhere.

Executive vice president and marketing manager Russell Cobler wanted to know why these key customers didn't entrust all their money to his organization. When he and his marketing staff asked what would entice them to up the San Antonio portion, they said, "Give us a special way to conveniently access the funds we now have with you, and we'll consider sending a few more dollars your way." This the savings and loan did through a home-banking facility staffed six days a week. Full-service banking was now just a phone call away.

In theory, the service was available to all San Antonio customers

("We didn't want to run the risk of alienating the balance of our customer base," notes Cobler). In practice, however, promotion of home banking is confined to best customers through a special informational magazine, entitled *SASA Money Advisor*. Coddling of key customers has paid off for the 53-branch organization. In one year alone, these customers contributed new loans of $17.5 million and added deposits over $80 million.[2]

The SASA story, among others in this chapter, reaffirms the relevance of the age-old adage, "You can't be all things to all people." "Because any company's capability is necessarily limited, it cannot span the entire (customer) dimension," insist Harvard Business School professor Benson Shapiro and colleagues. "If it tries to, the poor focus will leave the company vulnerable to competition. The result . . . is reduced profitability."[1] Some suggestions for getting a focus on the best of your customer base is what this chapter's all about.

1. Know Who Your Best Are. This is no trivial exercise. Most company systems aren't geared to ferreting out the more profitable among your customers. They can usually point to who buys the most, but not necessarily who's best for the bottom line. And these often aren't the same.

Take the case of a prominent producer of capital equipment that started up a national account program in the hopes of garnering more business from its largest accounts. The new program was chocked full of goodies: generous volume discounts, heavy sales support with experienced account managers, hands-on input from top executives, and expedited delivery. After a false start, sales from these accounts did rise, justifying even higher levels of support. Unfortunately, company profits didn't follow suit. It was only then that the company discovered these big accounts were generating big losses along with their big volumes.[3]

Profit, of course, is the difference between dollars coming in and dollars going out. Shapiro et al. dub these two flows "net price" and "cost to serve" and have developed a means of classifying customers along the two dimensions, displayed in Figure 4.1.[4] The trick, they believe, is in understanding the actual cost to serve any one customer group. Many managers slip up on this one. They manage more by anecdote than by good cost accounting practices.[5] For one U.S. equipment manufacturer, for example, winning bids meant losing money.[6]

Know Who Your Best Are—The Customer Classification Matrix.

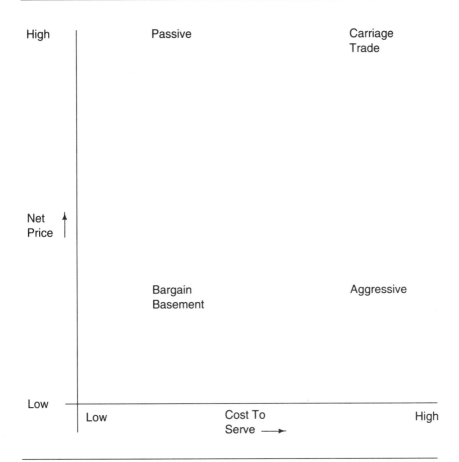

FIGURE 4.1 Because your organization's resources are limited, you need to focus on your best shot among your current customer base. This is no trivial exercise though. Most company systems aren't geared to ferreting out the most profitable among their customers. This figure illustrates a technique for classifying the best of your customer crop. The vertical axis is net price realized from your customers; the horizontal, cost to serve these customers including presale, production, distribution and postsale costs. "Passive" customers are your best bet; they're willing to pay top dollar but cost little to serve. "Carriage trade" customers come next; they're also willing to part with their pesos but they expect a better bang for their buck. "Bargain basement" customers are sensitive to price but inexpensive to serve. And finally, "aggressive" customers who want it all—best service and low prices.

What should be included in the cost to serve a customer? In their 1987 article, Shapiro et al. detail four key factors:[7]

1. *Presale*—Examples: "How many sales calls does it take to close a deal? Do our top people need to be on the job? Is there any need for presale support services like custom design work?"
2. *Production*—Examples: "Does the client want fast delivery or can we schedule this order for off-peak hours?"
3. *Distribution*—Examples: "Do we need to ship at a distance? Does the client want special logistics support such as a field inventory?"
4. *Postsale service*—Examples: "What kind of training packages are we including in the offer? Do we lump repair and maintenance charges with the sales price?"

Even after you've narrowed down your customer costs and plotted a profit dispersion as in Figure 4.1, don't expect the work to be over. A one-shot effort is of little use; customers and competitors change. An American metal manufacturer producing pollution-control components for the auto industry, as one example, found little competition and fat margins in the mid-1970s. Not so in the next decade when others wanted a piece of the action. Customers started drifting away to new competitors but company management didn't notice. Result: a prolonged earnings slump.[8] Shapiro et al. recommend a minimum once-a-year analysis unless your industry's changing rapidly. Then it's preferable to consider a more frequent review.[8]

2. Use Technology to Segment Best Customers.   Technology can be a handy tool for separating the wheat from the customer chaff. Particularly with what's called a "customer information file" (CIF), an automated client profiling system that can provide a detailed snapshot of any customer's complete relationship with your organization (for more details on CIFs, see Chapter 3). A Canadian credit union, Richmond Savings Credit Union, uses just such a system to isolate its most profitable customers from the hangers-on. A $1.5-million microcomputer network and relationship database CIF at Richmond details the type of business each member does with the company, including volume of checks written, withdrawals, and ATM usage.

In 1988, Richmond realized its pricing position was penalizing best customers. "Some members were giving us a lot of business but weren't being adequately rewarded," explains then chief executive officer, Don Tuline. "Other members who took most of their business elsewhere were taking advantage of many of our services without paying for the value they were receiving." A new regime of service charges at the $566-million institution embraced a user-pay philosophy. This was not just to give credit where credit was due for the big users. Nor just to flush out unprofitable clients who weren't pulling their own weight, but rather to persuade these miscreants to mend their ways. An alteration in banking habits for most of the company's marginal customers could put their accounts in the black; the CIF allowed branch staff to advise them on ways to do this.

Best customers weren't neglected either. A phone call to the company's top 3,000 clients offered specific suggestions on reducing the impact of the new charges and introduced a savings vehicle for large depositors, a Treasury Bill (T-Bill) account. The Richmond "pay as you go" approach has paid off. Service charge income grew by $500,000 a year and, out of a customer base of 38,000, only 300 elected to take their business elsewhere. Plus, the new T-Bill account chalked up nearly $100 million in new deposits.[9]

3. *Price for Profit.* Once you know who your best customers are, make sure you pay them to make you profitable, like Richmond Savings Credit Union did with its user-pay philosophy. Forget democracy; pay for *frequency*.

Just recently, I transferred my account from a bank to a credit union (the aforementioned Richmond Savings). I'd been bypassed once too often by my ex-bank's promotional offers. It was always a free teddy bear for new mortgage customers, or some such thing, but nothing for me, in spite of the fact that I'd been faithfully contributing to the bank's coffers for six years. So what's so bad about this kind of goody giveaway? The fact is, for most industries, 80 percent of profit comes from just 20 percent of customers. In the financial services industry, that's 90 percent from 10 percent.[10] One trust company in Canada, for example, discovered 31 percent of its assets were held by a mere 1 percent of its client base.

So where's the rationale for treating new customers the same way as long-term ones? There simply isn't one, and frankly, customers don't expect this kind of democracy. I know if I shelled out a bigger wad of cash for an airline ticket or clocked a few more miles, I'd be able to enjoy linen tablecloths and a plush seat. My nose isn't out of joint, though, when I don't get such niceties in the economy section; I didn't pay for them, so I don't expect them. Neither do your customers. Let's examine how frequent-user programs can work for best customer retention.

3a. They Do Pay Off. Frequent-user programs cost significant bucks to run and, as they now appear to be a dime a dozen, you might ask, "Where's the value in putting one into my organization?" Roger Dow at Marriott Corporation has an answer for that. In 1984, when his company started such a program, the "Honored Guest Award" (HGA), it was greeted with a major yawn from competitors, Hyatt for one. "Who cares?" was the general attitude. "We found out lots of people care," says Dow, and so did the Hyatt executives.

One in particular whose out-of-town relative regularly parked himself at a Hyatt when passing through on business. On one such occasion, there hadn't been the usual call asking for a special deal, so the executive at the Hyatt dialed up his kinsman, and asked, "What's up?" "I'm at the Marriott" was the reply. "They've got this great program that will let me save up for a free jaunt to Hawaii?" "That's when he realized this was pretty serious," says Dow with a smile.

HGA points are actually awarded, not by number of stays, but by how much you spend at Marriott. In the past, a lot of people checked in, ditched their bags, and made a bee line for a restaurant off the premises. "We want to capture more business in the hotel." The program also gives Marriott the flexibility to pump up business at any property where numbers aren't up to capacity. "We can go to our Honored Guests and give special rates at our resorts when we know we're going to have some open rooms."

The HGA program's working very nicely, claims Dow. "The Honored Guest spends more than the nonhonored guest and he/she stays longer [average guest's length of stay, 1.6 days versus an Honored Guest at 1.9]." And with 4.5 million of these bigger spenders, that translates pretty quickly into major dollars.

3b. You Can Get More From Your Best. The HGA program gives Marriott the ability to market to guests specifically based on frequency. Normally, says Dow, promotions are pretty hit and miss. "You run an ad that says, 'Stay at a Marriott two nights and get a weekend free.'" That means a level playing field for all guests, no matter how many times they frequent your establishment. And it does zip for encouraging heavy users to up their ante.

With the new system, targets for rewards can be tied directly to an individual's past activity, making them easily attainable and therefore very motivating. Dow elaborates: "Let's say you stay with us five times over a three-month period, and someone else stays fifteen times over the same period. What we can now say is, 'Dear Carla, over the past three months, you've stayed with us five times. We're having a summer special; if you stay with us seven times in the next three months, we'll do the following for you.' We go to the fifteen-night person and say, 'You've stayed with us 15 times, stay with us 22 and we'll do this.' "

3c. But You'll Need Some Technological Aid. All the specific detail of a frequent-user program requires some pretty substantial record-keeping, a technological reality that adds up to a huge barrier to entry, says Dow, and kept enrollment in the Marriott HGA program to a minimum at the beginning. When the program first started in January 1986, it was all done with little cards. Guests would receive a batch of these, on which each stay's expenditures would be tallied up and keypunched, all by hand. When we rolled out our first mailing to 200,000 guests, we really had no capability to handle their stays, admits Dow. Now, an Honored Guest checks out and, one second later, the computer has updated the points record. "We went from bandaids and paper to a sophisticated computer program."

3d. Stick to Your Knitting . . . Watch that you don't get carried away with auxiliary promotions as part of your frequent-user programs. When BellSouth Mobility inaugurated its frequent caller program in November 1990, it tested the idea of exchanging points earned for nights-on-the-town coupons. That idea fell flat. What customers were really interested in was free airtime usage. "They told us that time and time again," says Annette Loper, strategic market planning manager.

Frequent caller benefits are reserved for the very best of its frequent users, members of BellSouth's upscale "President's Club." The package includes a quarterly point statement accompanied by a personal appreciation from the company's president and a few newsy tidbits. Racking up revenues for the company isn't all it takes to warrant membership in the club, says Loper. "We also look at loyalty, customers who have been with us for a long time no matter what their usage."

The BellSouth frequent caller initiative achieved three objectives for the company—to retain customers, to differentiate itself from the competition, and to help drive airtime usage. Staff and clients found it to their liking as well. "The sales force is very excited [and] we're hearing from customers daily who write in [to say] 'This is great, we love it.' "

3e. . . . And Go with the Familiar. Don't try to get too fancy with your frequent-user efforts; that can lead to customer confusion. America West Airlines started off down the wrong road with its frequent-flyer program by using a dollar-based rather than mileage-based design. "We thought the idea was unique and would be a refreshing change," recalls Mark Beauvais, former managing director for Sales & Marketing Programs. Wrong: people were used to mileage yardsticks; they understood that. So two and a half years into the process, in late 1989, the Arizona-based airline switched midstream. A difficult decision but one that paid off. Within 16 months of the new format, membership had doubled.

At Marriott, the point structure for the HGA program—for every dollar spent you chalk up 10 points—was not arrived at by serendipity. "We made [it that way] so it would come close to what an airline schedule is," explains Dow, "because people are so familiar with [that]."

3f. Consider Recognition As Well As Reward. A Canadian hotel chain, Delta Hotels & Resorts, favors a recognition-heavy scheme to woo frequent users rather than one that stresses reward. Regarding its program, "Delta Privilege," corporate vice president Warren Markwart says it's designed to help the "road warrior" beat some of the inconveniences of travel. When you're clocking 50,000 miles a year, you soon build up a massive store of points. After a few European treks on the house, the bloom is off the rose, and you're less than thrilled at the prospect of yet another frequent-flyer-type initiative.

What will turn your head, though, is the chance to avoid those pesky lineups, the bane of any pilgrim's existence. "When you look at research," notes Markwart, "lineups are always up there in the top three things that bug frequent travelers the most." The check-*in* line's not so bad because most hotels have that all but licked. Then there's the check-*out* line. "Nobody's truly beaten that." That is, until now, with Delta Privilege.

With the aid of a state-of-the-art central reservations system linked to the chain's 17 locations, detailed profiles of all Delta Privilege customers are available at the touch of a button. On member signup, you tick off a list of preferences such as location in the hotel, type of bed, and class of room—standard, moderate, or deluxe. Even down to whether your allergies preclude a feather pillow. Then, when you present yourself and your credit card at the front desk, your room's been preselected and you're zipped through a VIP check-in in no time flat.

3g. Let Employees Know Who's Top Dog. Recognition programs for the pick of your customer crop are worth nothing if employees don't know who these folks are. Plus, when you start to get closer to your key customers through any kind of frequent-user program, they get closer to you, claims Marriott's Dow. "They begin calling you, asking for their point totals," for example. All of which puts a good deal of pressure on your staff. Give them a hand by letting them in on who's top dog among your clients.

At Marriott, frequent guests are distinguished by special cards. If you're a newcomer to the frequency game, your card is red. Stay a bit more often and you're bumped up to gold. If you're one of Marriott's best meeting planners, you rate the next level, which is black. Finally, if you stay 75 nights or more a year, you're at the top of the heap and your rank's platinum.

"The reason we have different card levels is so our people know who's a really big guest," explains Dow. "We can signal the hotel that this person stays a lot." That's essential if you want to ensure 48-hour guaranteed availability, which is what platinum card holders dearly value. It works this way. "The Chicago Marriott is sold out next week. You have a platinum card, you call our reservation center and voila, a room opens up," complete with a basket of sweets and a welcome note from the general manager. It's nice to be recognized.

3h. Throw a Little Training into the Pot As Well. Follow the lead of America West Airlines where 40 percent of a two-week training course for phone operators focuses specifically on the importance of the airline's top frequent flyers. Of the 1.2 million people who qualify for the airline's frequent-flyer program, "Flight Fund," about 30,000 fly more than once a week. This elite group has special status as "Chairman Club" members, making them eligible for a raft of amenities including bonus miles, special vacation packages, and privileges at the "Phoenix Club," America West's top-notch airport lounge. Plus a private 800 number that gives them number one priority so their call jumps to the front of any call-waiting lineup, past the regular call-prompting system and right to a human being. It's here that the training comes in. That human operator is specially trained to respond with red carpet treatment. "We talk to them about who these people are, how often they fly us, the kind of dollars they spend with us, why they are valued," explains Mark Beauvais. "I always talk to these classes myself and make them realize that every time they get one of these phone calls, it's our last possible chance to keep that customer, the one and only time you can do anything significant to retain that business and make a difference to America West."

4. *Consider "Adios" Strategies for the Also-Rans.* If you intend on focusing on your best, it follows that you'll need to neglect your worst. That's called "demarketing" and it can be a pretty tricky thing to manage. A large New York–based bank, for example, botched an attempt to limit teller access to large customers only. The press got wind of the new policy, and soon stories of widows and orphans languishing in ATM lineups dominated the news. That was the end of preferential treatment for the bank's best customers.

In contrast, another financial institution, Wachovia Bank and Trust Company, a full-service institution headquartered in Winston-Salem, North Carolina, faired much better. For nearly 20 years, this $11.7-billion firm has built its reputation on the concept of assigning a personal bank representative to each customer. Research in the late 1960s confirmed the strategic strength of such a policy. Consumers find most financial institutions large and impersonal, explains Robert Reagan, vice president of Financial Institutions. "It is often difficult to find your way through the many departments and services . . . You find yourself getting shoved from one person to another." Wachovia found the personal banker message created a special niche. ". . . It gives people a distinct reason for doing business with us."

In 1989, the 214-office company made a significant adjustment to this successful program. The original concept was to assign every customer a personal banking contact. Having to deal with the least profitable of their client bases, however, left Wachovia's personal bankers, now predominately college graduates, with little quality time for better customers. "The relationships [with the bottom 20 percent] are not profitable enough to justify the calibre of person we have in the personal banker job," explains John Ramsey, senior vice president of Retail Banking. Something had to give.

The decision was made to continue to allow less-profitable customers *access* to the personal banking group; however, they'd no longer be *assigned* a personal banker. Also, for better customers, a memory-jogging message would appear on all bank correspondence, reminding them of the names and telephone numbers of their banking contacts. For the bottom 20 percent, there would be no reminder. Subtle, but effective.[11]

The Practice—Making It Happen, Part I—Step 3

What?

Second stage of customer retention research focused on key customer groups: who they are and what will make them stay with Retention Inc.

Why?

For most organizations, the 80/20 rule applies, that is, just a few customers account for most of the profit.

How?

3A. **Homework** assigned to employees in focus groups (Step 2) and to reps attending Workshop 1.2 as follows: "Do some research to profile Retention Inc.'s best customers. (Use all of the company's available information. Break out Retention Inc.'s profit/sales/revenue by customer and by product.) Find out what percentage of their business Retention Inc. has. Why don't we have all their business, i.e., what's the competition doing with them and why is it working?"

3B. Analysis of company records to determine best customers. This is done under the supervision of the Retention Coordinator and the Retention Advisory Group by in-house personnel or an outside consultant. **Selection Criteria:** current profitability, longevity, and profit potential, as well as use of the Shapiro customer classification matrix (Figure 4.1).

3C. Series of videotaped focus groups with best customer groups conducted by an outside moderator; two sessions per best customer group as determined by analysis in Step 3B; focus group questions geared to discovering a predictive model for customer retention. **Examples:**

   a. "What makes a customer think about leaving?"

   b. "Are complaints an early warning clue to customer defection?"

   c. "What are the key points of contact between the customer and Retention Inc.? Which of these are critical to the customer's 'Grow, Go, or Status Quo' decision about the company?" (*Grow*—customer adds business or refers another customer to Retention Inc.; *Go*—customer leaves; and *Status Quo*—customer decides to stay but doesn't make any additional purchases.)

   d. "What is the cycle of a customer's relationship with Retention Inc.? At what points in this cycle is the relationship evaluated by the customer, that is, at what points does the customer make a 'Grow, Go, or Status Quo' decision about Retention Inc.?"

3D. Series of one-on-one interviews with clients who have left Retention Inc. over the last two years; interviews done by an outside researcher; questions geared to understanding why these customers left. **Examples:**

   a. "What made you decide to take your business away from Retention Inc.?"

   b. "What led to your decision to leave Retention Inc.?"

   c. "Where did you go (i.e., to which competitor) and why?"

   d. "What could Retention Inc. have done to have kept your business?"

   e. "Would you ever consider bringing your business back to Retention Inc.? If yes, under what circumstances?"

3E. Telephone survey to statistically quantify the results obtained in Steps 3C and 3D; survey done by volunteer Retention Inc. staff trained and supervised by an outside research agency.

3F. A workshop for peer-elected reps across all job levels and functions within Retention Inc. (Workshop 3.1) with the following **objectives:**

   a. To review results of customer focus groups, interviews, and surveys; and compare with employee homework from Step 3A. Focus on exposing the "gap" between what customers say and what employees think.

   b. To create a vision for Retention Inc. compatible with what's been learned about what makes customers stay or bring more business. Vision to be used as a focus for all Retention Inc. efforts including the "People-Powered Retention" problem-solving teams (introduced in Step 4).

   c. To begin the formulation of a predictive model for customer retention at Retention Inc. This model will be developed in subsequent steps and will eventually include:

     (1) Early warning signs of imminent customer defection. **Example:** in the banking industry, two early warning "flags" for customers at risk of defection are customer complaints and a sudden decline in average balances of more than 20 percent.[12]

     (2) Critical contact points in the customer relationship cycle where the customer makes a "Grow, Go, or Status Quo" decision about Retention Inc. **Examples:** (i) the first six months of a customer's relationship with Fidelity Investments is critical as to whether that customer will end up as a long-term client; (ii) Xerox customers tend to turn over their office equipment on a three-year cycle.

     (3) Key customer bonding opportunities, e.g., cross-selling possibilities. **Example:** Computer-generated "red flag reports" at Manitoba-based Great-West Life Assurance Company provide cross-selling signals for the company's agents. Such a report might reveal the impending maturity of a client's

savings certificate, suggesting that a courtesy call from an agent with information on investment options for the released funds might be in order.[13]

3G. Copies of videotapes and summary report of customer and staff sessions made available to all 46 Retention Inc. employees through internal marketing vehicles recommended by the Retention Advisory Group formed in Step 1.

When?

Months 4 and 5.

CHAPTER 5

Empowered Employees: Your Greatest Asset for Keeping Customers

---

Most of what we call management consists of making it difficult for people to get on with their jobs.

Peter Drucker[1]

A remark made by several employees at the lowest rung of the 15,000-person ladder at United Services Automobile Association (USAA) touched off a series of events that led to the development of 40 separate marketing projects. Approximately twice a month, customer contact personnel from the San Antonio–based insurance company's Property & Casualty Division get a chance to interact directly with company executives in a forum called the Professional Development Day. For part of that one-day session, management sits up front as a panel and fields questions or comments from the floor. Not all employees feel comfortable on their feet addressing the top brass, so questions are written on cards and passed forward. Roundtable discussion is also on the agenda, with employees gathered into small groups of eight to ten individuals. Each table is assigned a topic, the idea being an exchange of information. Assistant vice president of Corporate Quality, Beverley McClure, provides an example: "One table might know how to best handle an abusive customer and they share how they're doing that."

It was at one of these forums that front-liners identified inequities in the company's handling of its various markets. USAA caters to active and former U.S. military officers ("members") and their adult, former dependents ("associate members"). Our employees believed that associate members weren't getting equal treatment, says McClure. "This got our attention." A series of 40-odd programs evolved as a result, including an "Associate Member Master Plan" that called for a new company magazine, *Under 25*, which appeals to the younger set, and a "membership card" that lists USAA services and emergency contact numbers, sized to fit nicely into a teenage driver's wallet. "This became an important issue [which was] identified by very low-level employees."

A company's best ideas can come from its most humble constituents. It only makes sense that those closest to the customer may know a thing or two about customer needs and wants. "The further you are away from the work," contends Sam Malone, Project Manager, Corporate Communications at Xerox Corporation, "the less concrete [the] knowledge you have about the process used to get that work done." Consultant and business professor Robert Kelley estimates that leaders contribute no more than 20 percent to an organization's success while others in the company are responsible for the remaining 80 percent.[2] This runs counter to popular management doctrine that those at the top have all the answers. "That's been a fallacy of management [for] years," claims Rich Bender, director of Sales at Miller Business Systems, and it's a notion not borne out by the facts. Quite the contrary. Work done by Cambridge professor J.E. Bateson in 1989 shows a strong correlation between customer and employee perceptions of customer service. Management's views, on the other hand, were often widely divergent from those of the client.[3] In his book, *The Customer Driven Company*, Richard Whiteley of The Forum Corporation refers to this management alienation as "the iceberg of ignorance." A research group asked a cross-section of people in a large Japanese factory to list all the significant problems known to them. Only 4 percent of problems listed were known to top managers; those next in line knew just a few more, up to 9 percent. Compare that with the 74 percent known to front-line supervisors.[4]

Break the management mold, suggests Laura Adams, vice president of patient services at Parkview Episcopal Medical Center in Pueblo, Colorado. Accept a new role, away from being the generator of all schemes to one of recognizing good ideas from employees.[5] Be a liberator of human ingenuity; manage by walking *away*. A tough assignment, contends Xerox's Malone. "The fundamental problem is most managers today did not get to their position by being participative, by involving their employees. Now, you suddenly pull the rug out from under them and create an environment that a majority haven't had any experience in." By all means, monitor from the top but be aware, say the companies whose stories are told in this chapter; the "customers for keeps" philosophy really starts at the bottom. "We're experts at leading people," says Miller Business System's vice president of Operations, Stan Feldman, "but the true experts are the people who actually do the jobs."

You Lead By Doing

Simon Cooper of Delta Hotels & Resorts sketches an anecdote about a fellow hotel president. Many years ago, Cooper's colleague received a promotion to duty manager from senior desk clerk. Cooper always wondered why one day, as senior desk clerk, he had to call the duty manager to have a $100 check approved but the next day, when he was bumped up the ladder, he was able to sign on his own. What happened overnight when he was sleeping that suddenly gave him the skill he didn't have before?

This is a good question and one that illustrates the somewhat arbitrary rules of power that govern most organizations today. Cooper is a firm believer that the individual facing the guest at the time of crisis A is far more likely to make the right decision than somebody else up the line. Not only that, but for the customer, "a decision made at the time is 100 times more powerful than one made a month later when the thing reaches the general manager or the president and is [finally resolved]." But letting go in favor of the staff closest to the customer doesn't come easily, particularly for the immediate supervisor. "In the old supervisory lingo, these decisions are reserved for us."

Having staff who really do nothing more than control other staff reflects poorly on the organization, according to Cooper. Let's talk about assistant housekeepers, a subject he says is near and dear to his heart. "Their job is to go around and check that the maids are doing their jobs. Having that position is a recognition that we can't hire the right people, can't train them, and can't motivate them."

In an interview with *Inc.* magazine founder Bernie Goldhirsh,

U.S. General H. Norman Schwarzkopf points out that people come to work to succeed, not to fail. This is so obvious yet so many organizations operate on the principle that if people aren't watched and supervised, they'll bungle the job.[6]

The Toronto-based Delta chain has successfully tested going without that first-line supervision. "We've kept a few assistant housekeepers," explains Cooper, "but given them new responsibilities, the training of self-supervised room attendants." Now, when housekeepers finish a room, they don't shut the door knowing there will be a floor supervisor coming behind. "They go out thinking the next person in the room [will be] the guest." That degree of trust has made them far better workers.

What we'll be looking at in this section is the concept of staff empowerment, which is something missing from 90 percent of corporate customer quality programs, according to business management writer Tom Peters.[7] We'll concentrate on why empowerment's so vital for every organization bent on keeping customers—and provide some tips on getting staff powered up for the customer good.

1. *Remember, Employees Can Tell You What Needs to be Done.* And most would like the chance to try, according to an ASQC/Gallup research report released October 1990. When asked to rank ways to increase work performance, employees surveyed put "letting you do more to put your ideas into action" first.[8]

All your people really need is a forum. Consider the case of Air Canada. Faced with losses of $126 million in the first nine months of 1991 and low staff morale in the wake of 4,000 job cuts announced since October 1990, the airline turned to its 20,000 employees for help. A scheme, dubbed "Idea Action," encourages staffers to band together into minibusiness teams and plot ways to save money and work more efficiently. The Idea Action groups get a slice of any savings that result. "The object," claims Michele Monette, who's in charge of the program, "is to make people understand what it is to be an entrepreneur."

One team at the company's Dorval, Quebec, maintenance base submitted a plan to use a different kind of solvent to clean airplane wheel components. The savings for just one year was $12,000. "I've got 12,000 people playing in this sandbox," says Monette. "And it's changing the way the airline does business forever," she claims. "It's opened management's eyes to the skills and ideas of front-line employees."[9]

Another example is from BellSouth Mobility. The hiring system at the Atlanta firm was badly in need of repair. Jim Davis, vice president, Quality at BellSouth Cellular, explains the problem: "It was taking way too long from the time we knew we needed [new] employees [to the time] Personnel was able to source, qualify, and get them on the payroll." And while departments waited on new hires, so often did customer retention efforts.

The process was causing considerable pain throughout the organization, the one criterion used by BellSouth to decide when an issue justifies a "Quality Action Team" (QAT). "We don't try to solve world hunger," says Davis of the team approach to tackling this kind of organizational snag. "We try to delump all these painful areas and address them specifically with the people [they] impact."

To resolve the hiring holdup, the director of Personnel sponsored a QAT and, with Davis's assistance, developed a team mission statement and a membership roster. "We always insist the team be made up of users and department reps," says Davis, "and takes two days of training. The first day, team participants learn problem-solving skills such as process flowcharting; on the second day, we start working on their specific problem."

After the training, reps from Davis's shop stick with the team, but keep in the background. "We go to their meetings but we sit back and are quiet," says Davis. "Unless they run into a brick wall, then the quality counselors lend a hand." Once a quarter, any team on the go makes a presentation to BellSouth's president and vice presidents. "There are two things we look for here. One, what were the team's results; and two, what were the 'learnings'?"

The Personnel QAT at BellSouth began its analysis of the staffing problem by flowcharting the process. Right away, they found a way to shave four days off the hiring timeframe. They reasoned thus: Let's say the director of customer operations signs off a requisition authorizing ten customer service hires. When people are found to fill those positions, he's expected to again supply his stamp of approval. "Get rid of this last step," the team recommended. "After all, approval was given the first time around." "There was no reason to have that step in there," agreed Davis, and out it went.

2. Get Staff to Speak Up. Your people really do want a say in what goes on. Some 1988 research by an American research firm shows that 66 percent of service industry employees said participatory management was very important; only 20 percent, however, believed their employers bought into the idea. Sometimes just giving employees the opportunity to speak up doesn't make that all-important chatter happen. Here are some ideas that might help.

2a. Shut Up Already.   You may be suppressing employee input if you're too intent on hogging the stage. As Lexus Toyota's director of Public Relations, Art Garner, says, "You don't learn anything if you're doing all the talking."

2b. Senior Managers, Set the Example.   Getting middle managers to practice participation happens only if those higher up the ladder do the same. "It's a process that starts with the president and the executive board and goes all the way down," insists Suzanne Brossart, Corporate Communications Manager at Rural/Metro. The emergency services company uses "breakfast with the boss" sessions to get some two-way communication going with its staff. "At least once a quarter, more often if necessary, employees in groups anywhere from 30 to 100 at a time talk issues with senior executives." No topic's out of bounds and "nobody is punished . . . for asking tough questions." Smaller sessions take place monthly between staff and their immediate supervisors.

Weldon Paxton, Fire Chief of Rural/Metro's Fire Department, Maricopa County, provides a few more details about these monthly sessions with the rank and file. The meetings in his district last one or two hours and are attended by representatives elected by their peers. "We don't have the same people there every time. About every nine months we rotate." Usually the first fifteen minutes is a brief overview of what's current and then it's on to questions.

An issue that came out of one of these tête-à-têtes concerned secondary response coverage. "The primary response procedure worked well," the fire fighters said. "But should we be called out a second time, we're not covered." Paxton's follow-up research found that just a few changes to the response guide solved that problem. But it took employees to expose the hole in the system.

2c. Resist the Temptation to "Fix All the Leaky Faucets" Yourself.   It's tough not to leap in and suggest a solution to any organizational problem. But if staff don't build it, they won't buy it, so back off. At

Xerox for example, a manager who identifies a customer issue that needs addressing doesn't automatically overlay his or her own solution on it. "[We] use the process of forming a team and acting as a coach to this team to develop and apply a solution," says Sam Malone.

2d. Act on Employee Input.   Seeing their suggestions take root and bear fruit does wonders for employee willingness to share ideas, insists Miller Business System's Stan Feldman, vice president of Operations. When one of the firm's order-processing teams ("Magilla's Gorillas" to be precise) had an idea to reconfigure a conveyor area that would dramatically enhance process efficiency, the $500 needed to do the job was handed over on the spot. "We had to show them that management was responsive when they asked for intelligent things."

Ninety-five percent of what is recommended by the Texas company's "Employee Involvement Teams" (EITs) is funded; "even those things we, as managers, don't see a whole lot of merit in," says company president Mike Miller. "Especially at the beginning of this program we said, 'Let's just go ahead and do it.' It didn't hurt anything and it helped get people feeling good about what's going on."

2e. Get Some Light Into the Feedback Black Hole.   Even if you can't say "yes" to employee ideas, don't keep them in suspense: tell them just that. It's better than telling them nothing, hoping that no news is good news. Because when it comes to employee feedback it "sure ain't," something AT&T managers found out to their surprise.

At the telecommunications corporation, customer comments overheard by employees have led to a number of great product enhancements, including international and intrastate add-ons for the company's long-distance discount program, "Reach Out America." Getting staff to pass on these comments took some work, according to Janice Colby, division manager of Consumer Market Management.

Before 1990, it fell to visiting head-office managers to solicit customer feedback from employee group interviews. Staff response was pretty tepid, admits Gigi Neff, AT&T's division manager of Revenue Retention and Stimulation. This was primarily because there was no rigorous process to keep track of any input.

"We'd show up one quarter, scribble down their ideas, and head back 'downtown.' Then, lo and behold, we'd be back the next quarter and they'd say, 'Hey, time out, I just gave you all these ideas last time and I haven't seen any new plans as a result. So why should I continue to spend my lunch hour with you if I'm not seeing any kind of response?' "

"They had a good point," says Neff. "We'd resisted telling them what we'd done with their ideas, mostly because over half had been thrown out for regulatory reasons. We thought they'd get discouraged and clam up if they knew so many of their ideas didn't even get to first base. We found that wasn't the case at all. Coming back to them with a rationale so they better understood the constraints [made them] more [not less] responsive." Candor paid off; the volume of employee comments expanded enormously, up sixfold since late 1990.

The company's new quarterly newsletter to customer contact employees also helped encourage AT&T'ers to feed the information mill. "[The] newsletter tells them what has happened in the last quarter," explains Colby, "[and] what their contribution has been to helping us understand the marketplace. We also share success stories like the one that sparked our testimonial ad campaign back in 1989. A comment that a customer made ended up becoming the crux of that ad, about what they hadn't gotten from the competition that they expected from us." The rep involved was well thanked, says Colby. "We gave her a commendation at a special recognition event held in her honor."

The Cooker Corporation, a family-style restaurant chain headquartered in Columbus, Ohio, found a simple but effective way to plug the holes in its system for following up on employee suggestions. Monthly quality circles give staff an opportunity to discuss problems and brainstorm solutions. "We like them to list about 10 each time," says regional manager, Peter Kehayes. "It's possible to up that number, although the limit's 50 per month. They give these to the general manager who has to respond on a [special] bulletin board within twelve days [as to whether] the solution is accepted or not." If not, an alternate has to be posted. More often than not, though, crew member solutions are adopted.

3. *Make It Easy for Your People to Take Power.* Empowerment seems to be one of today's hottest business topics. But too many people see empowerment as a gift to employees, according to Chip

Bell, Dallas, Texas–based service consultant and author. "I happen to believe people have all the power they need." So if the power's there for the taking, why don't employees grab hold? We'll look at several reasons.

3a. Employees Don't See Any Reason to Take the Power Plunge. "People act with power when they are acting with some purpose or mission," claims Bell. It's like the old story about the bricklayer who says he's laying bricks versus the bricklayer who says she's building a cathedral. Make the customer their mission, suggests Delta's Cooper. "Focus [them] clearly on the service responsibility to the guest." Employees shouldn't be doing what they're doing because management tells them to do it, but because the end user wants it that way. Let's say Delta's putting in a new frequent guest program, its "Delta Privilege," and the employee on the front desk asks why. It's very easy for the supervisor to respond, "The company says so," end of story. "I really get upset if I hear those words," says Cooper. "It's got to be put in the context of what the guests want."

3b. Middle Managers Might Get In the Way. Allocating power to the front line usually comes at the expense of the middle-line supervisors. Naturally they're not thrilled with the idea, so they may balk at any change. Pendleton Memorial Methodist Hospital, a private U.S. health care facility, proved that involvement of middle managers can be key to overcoming this kind of resistance. The work of four middle-manager-facilitated teams saved the hospital more than $500,000 and enhanced patient care. In five weeks, one team carved a major slice off patient waiting time in Emergency from 19.31 minutes for an average registration to 10 minutes.[10]

Don't assume that structural groups like middle management or unions will automatically thwart your retention efforts. Be on the lookout instead for pockets of resistance. Joseph Sensenbrenner, ex-mayor of Madison, Wisconsin, calls this "bureaucratic opposition"—for example, ". . . individual managers who . . . resent taking time to reassess tried and true procedures; . . . [or individual] employees who scorn the program as faddish and . . . look on enthusiastic colleagues as management finks."[11] Such sporadic subversion is tough to smoke out and even tougher to smother. It's best to bulldoze your way to customer retention right over these naysayers or find alternative paths around them.

3c. There Are Structural and Procedural Barriers Between Staff and the Power . . . Empowering is more about taking things away than it is about giving things, claims Anthony Putman, consultant and author of *Marketing Your Services.* "You have to subtract the things in the system that are preventing people from being able to do the job right." Like the sign touting the 800 number available to customers with complaints that was removed from Bridgestone/ Firestone stores in 1990. "[These signs] took away the empowerment of the store," says David Dobson, manager of Consumer Affairs. The move didn't eliminate the customer relations department at the auto services corporation, though; it just made it the fall-back position.

Make sure you get it from "the horse's mouth," so to speak. Don't assume on your employees' behalf; ask them. "There wasn't any point in just having myself and my senior managers hobnob about how we can help employees get past any stumbling blocks," claims West Paces' Chip Caldwell. "That's almost a [complete] waste of time." Instead, managers from all departments and all levels at his hospital met in groups of eight or ten and over two sessions and three or four hours brainstormed on process inhibitors. "For example," says Caldwell, "we didn't have anywhere for the [quality improvement] teams to meet. So a room was set aside, equipped with flipcharts and an overhead projector, and put on reserve for that purpose only."

Client contact employees at the investment advisory firm of Fidelity Investments told management there were several barriers preventing them from delivering top customer service. Moving customer reps or "associates" from assignment to assignment, for example, makes for great cross-training opportunities but does zip for proficiency at any one job. "It's also tough," said half the $1.5-billion company's associates, "to track down insiders with know-how," and 62 percent blamed the pressure-cooker atmosphere of speed at all costs for many of their errors.

An example on the last point: Fidelity had been running its people ragged trying to get statement turnaround below 20 days. But this breakneck speed wasn't impressing customers, according to Steve Graziano, vice president of Market Information. In fact, two-thirds of those surveyed in 1990–91 said a 25- to 30-day time frame suited them nicely. "So we'll hold steady at 20 days," says Graziano, "and not make our people jump through any more hoops."

On the heels of a customer expectations survey in 1990 that pointed to responsiveness as key to client satisfaction, Fidelity took a long, hard look at all its policies and procedures. Which of these prevents the company's phone reps from dealing with customer concerns right on the phone, for example? A number of roadblocks became evident; one in particular with the firm's "Automatic Builder Account," which allows clients to deposit a regular dollar sum each month. But that's where the convenience ended with this account; every adjustment to the schedule had to be made by the client in writing. John Post, marketing manager of Retail Services, confesses, "It was ridiculous."

That policy was sent packing and now reps handle any changes on the phone. Not only is timeliness improved, claims Post, "but, because we've done away with the long lead times, so is accuracy as well." Score one for better customer relations too. "We get [a lot] more from a verbal interaction that we would have had they just popped us off a piece of paper."

Following on a 1990 effort to enhance staff interaction with its members, the National Association of Life Underwriters (NALU) also had to get some rules out of the way. It all began, explains Matthew (Matt) Gertzog, assistant vice president of administration and board liaison, with a new quality initiative called "NEXUS!" (NALU Excellence Upholds Success!). A two-day staff retreat explored the quality question, member worth, and employee empowerment. One of the rules that came under fire at this session was the one about signing for incoming packages. "We had this ludicrous rule that any time anyone got a package, you had to sign for it [yourself]. It was ridiculous because things were held up in the mailroom because the person whose name was on the package wasn't there to sign for it." When Jack Bobo, executive vice president and CEO of the 140,000-member association, found out about this policy, he wanted to know why it existed at all. The reason, according to Gertzog: "One time, four years ago, we'd lost one package." That rule promptly bit the dust.

3d. . . . Informational and Emotional Barriers Too. Your employees are rational people, they've seen all kinds of management initiatives coming down the tube. So what's another one even if it does sport a customer retention tag? All they need do is stall for a few months and it will all blow over, yet again. You've got to expect a healthy portion of skepticism and flak from staff; resist the temptation to sweep these under the rug, however. Instead, drag them out to the light of day. It makes for a very bumpy beginning, but it's the only way to get employees on side, and if they're not with you, you're nowhere.

The first few customer care sessions at Burnaby Hospital, a 586-bed institution in western Canada, were a bit dicey. Admits Betty Frenette, director of Admissions, "The initial negative response was pretty devastating." The idea of spending dollars on customer service training in a time of restraint and cutbacks was seen as frivolous at best. "Why isn't this being axed?" was the question. Especially when it was viewed "as a warm fuzzy program," says Anita Lawrence, Radiology director, "and just another one at that."

I was the consultant to the hospital on the project and I vividly recall these first sessions. Staff were anything but keen and if they'd had rotten veggies handy I'd have found a good many coming my way. But this was just the response we wanted. We knew going in that there were legitimate gripes about this program and, if we ignored them, we would do so at our peril. So we opened the floor to criticisms and comments about roadblocks to the program's success. We didn't leave it on a negative note, however; we turned the tables on the objectors and asked for input on overcoming these obstacles.

One problem kept cropping up; people didn't really understand just what this customer thing was all about and what it could accomplish in a health care setting. That made us rethink our training approach. Instead of presenting a series of lectures on customer service theory, we opted to have pilot teams solve one problem apiece. One team, for example, tackled errors in patient dietary forms, wrestling a ten-error-per-week count down to one. Looking back, we'd have been well advised to chart this course from the outset. "If it had been presented right off the bat as a problem-solving method," believes public relations director Ellen Chesney, "They would have bought into it more."

3e. Technology's Been Overlooked as an Empowerment Enhancer. To keep our customers coming back, we have to continually up the ante on service. That means asking more of our people, already "dancing as fast as they can." For example, at Wachovia Bank and Trust the personal touch is a trademark. If you're a customer, there's one special person assigned to your corner, a personal banker who's expected to know every little thing about you and your money. A tall order considering that Wachovia has 750,000 retail customers and only 540 personal bankers. "It's simply impossible for any personal banker to remember everything about a particular customer," notes senior vice president John Ramsey.

There's no need for elaborate memory joggers at Wachovia, though, thanks to a $23-million computer overhaul begun in 1974. Over 3,200 video-display terminals, one at each teller station and on the desk of every personal banker, link employees to a comprehensive customer database. That gives staff access to the complete transactional record of every bank customer, including balances, loan histories, ATM usage, checking and savings withdrawals, even credit bureau ratings. Fifty-four thousand training hours were logged over a four-year period to get staff up to speed on the new system but it was well worth the effort. Personal banking staff can now react quickly to customer queries and complaints over the phone or in person, literally at the touch of a button.[12]

A $26-billion U.S. insurer, United Services Automobile Association (USAA), has similarly empowered its people using technology. In particular, a state-of-the-art electronic imaging system makes customer correspondence instantly available anywhere in the company. "We've got 15,000 employees," notes CEO Robert McDermott, "but every time you call, you're talking to someone who's got your file in front of them."[13]

It's all part of the company's automated insurance environment (AIE), the result of a six-year plan and $130 million, and the cause of a radical change in the way everyone at USAA thinks and works. Take the service representative, suggests McDermott. Thirty years ago, the front line was little more than a sweatshop. "There were people who did nothing but staple and people who did nothing but stuff envelopes. . . . We were giving terrible service and boring our employees." Compare that with the company today where technology gives staff the power to make things happen. "In one five-minute phone call, . . . our service rep can . . . [do] all the work that used to take 55 steps, umpteen people, two weeks, and a lot of money."[14]

3f. No One's Spelled Out Any Power Limitations. Employees are practical enough to know there have to be some of these. "The empowerment process is about boundaries," says Roger Dow, vice president of Marketing at Marriott Corporation, a $8.38-billion hotel chain, but the borders are often obscured by gray areas. " 'What if a guest tells me there weren't enough towels in the room?' a housekeeper may ask. 'Am I suppose to give that person a fruit basket or a free room or should I just say I'll report it; how far can I go?' Or if a customer complains to the waiter about the food, does he just take it off the check or does he have to see the manager?"

Marriott has let its 220,000 employees decide on these limits largely on their own. Each staff unit sits down with the group's boss and decides what they're trying to accomplish and what type of power they have, or need, from their supervisor. "It becomes a negotiating thing," explains Dow. "It's like the bellhops saying, 'If somebody misses the airport van, I can reimburse that person for a cab? Great, now I know.' "

3g. Staff Don't Believe What You Say About Them Taking Over. It'll take some time to convince your people that you really mean them to have more power. IBM Canada knows this only too well. Early in 1989, the powers-that-be in Markham, Ontario issued a proclamation that gave accounts receivable clerks the power to issue customers credit notes up to $10,000 without supervisory approval. The existing process often took weeks and months, says Don Myles. "This was ridiculous."

Management felt much pleased with this show of its ability to loosen the reins but it soon became apparent that the horses had been kept tethered too long. Checking in with employees after three months they found nothing changed, no one had given out any credit notes. Seems staff didn't believe management really meant what it said. "It was an education for us," admits Myles. "We had to say, 'No, we really mean it,' and then feature [the first brave souls] as heroes and give them awards." Gradually the idea took hold.

3h. They Don't See Any Reward in Doing Right By the Customer.
When your people do get this "customers for keeps" stuff right, make sure you make a proper fuss about it so others know this is the way to go. As Barbara Langdon from Digital Equipment Corporation explains, "Make it so visible that this is what goodness is that other people realize this is what I should be doing."

A good illustration of this is the story about a Marriott bellman in Newton, Massachusetts. Two years ago, he was seeing a customer to a cab and casually asked about the man's stay. "Well, to be honest, everything wasn't perfect," the customer admitted. "My breakfast this morning was a little late and it was cold." "I don't think you should pay for that," said the bellman, and ushered the man back into the hotel and up to the front desk. The front desk clerk agreed with the bellman, and pronto, $8.50 was credited to the customer's account.

Dow recalls the bellman's explanation of why he went to bat for the customer. "He said he'd been in this empowerment class and they said he could do this so he decided to see if it worked." The customer was moved to write a letter. "He was amazed, he said; he watched two employees take care of [his problem] on the spot. No manager came over, no two sets of initials, it just happened." Senior management took special pains to recognize the bellman's efforts. It didn't take long after that for word to get around that what this fellow did was the proper way to act.

A final point. Don't expect some fancy mission statement concocted on the executive floor to excite staff lower down. As Bill O'Brien at Hanover Insurance observes, "My vision is not what's important to you. The only vision that motivates you is your vision."[15]

3i. They're Afraid if They Take Power and Pull a Boner, You'll Send Them Packing. Therein lies the true test of any organization's commitment to empowerment, contends Chip Bell. How you react when someone goofs is going to mean the difference between empowerment becoming part of the corporate culture or shutting down altogether. "You can't say to employees, 'We want you to take risks but we don't want you to make a mistake.'" Better the attitude of Andrew S. Grove, chairman for computer chipmaker Intel Corp., whose goal is to have every employee make ten mistakes a month. Go one step further, suggest Canadian Imperial Bank of Commerce managers Gloria Borsoi, Shelley McKay, and Clark Talman, and actually pay incentives for employee errors.

The IBM approach, according to Bell, is illustrated in a wonderful story about Tom Watson and a young executive who'd been in charge of a risky new venture and bombed out. In spite of all his efforts, and in a very short time, the young manager had lost $10 million. Watson, then chairman of the IBM board, summoned the miscreant to New York, who came, knees knocking and heart thumping. "I guess I'm here to receive my pink slip," said the executive to Watson. "Hell no," the chairman retorted, "I can't afford to fire you, I've just spent $10 million training you."

One last illustration on how best to handle risk-taking staffers who shoot themselves in the foot is from David Bray at Quad/Graphics. Some years back, a research engineer at the printing company spent two years and $1.5 million developing a special type of attachment for a press machine, a "pinless folder." The machine was suppose to save money and speed up the printing process. A great idea, says Bray; problem was, it didn't work. "The poor engineer was devastated; he didn't know what was going to happen next."

The project wasn't shelved and the engineer didn't get the boot. In fact, the company threw a champagne startup for the folder that didn't work. At the party, Quad/Graphics president and founder Harry V. "Larry" Quadracci put his arm around the guy and said, "We all make mistakes, this is how we learn. Now go back and start over again and, this time, build me a folder that works." And the engineer did.

4. Let Your People Help With the Real Stuff. Most staff empowerment programs focus on the softer issues, like employee gratification and quality of worklife, missing a golden opportunity for participation in the real issues. "It's not just employee involvement that you want," contends Peter Lazes, associate professor of industrial relations at Cornell University. "You want focused strategic participation in the key areas of the business."[16] These would include contracting out, cutbacks, and corporate restructuring.

Amdhal Canada, for example, opted to use employee brains, not jobs, to reduce operating expenses. Told by head office in May 1991 to hack $1.7 million off overhead, president Ronald Smith challenged his 250 employees to come up with their share of the target—$6,800 per person. The gamble worked. Employees agreed to curtail travel, delay performance review increases, and restructure workweeks to trim overtime. By year-end, more than $3 million had been saved. "It would have been easier . . . to issue a non-negotiable edict," Smith says. "Doing it that way, we would have made the target, but we wouldn't have beat it by 100 percent. And we wouldn't have unleashed creativity."[17]

Xerox has also let staff in on solving the tough stuff. In 1982, the company initiated labor-management cost-study teams to deal with subcontracting issues. Whenever management feels money can be saved by contracting out the services of a particular Xerox department or the production of some component, a team of six union workers and two managers is created. Their task—to find ways to bring the operation up to competitive parity in six months. In every case so far, the teams have saved jobs and money. The first team, for example, came up with a $3.7-million saving. That was $500,000 more than any subcontract scheme would have netted.[18]

5. Unleash Human Ingenuity With Teams. Most organizational structures are ill-equipped to deal effectively with customer retention; primarily because there's so little communication across departmental lines. As author H.J. Harrington notes, "Most companies organize into vertically functioning groups yet most processes flow horizontally."[19] This is especially true from the point of view of the ultimate customer.

Teams of representatives from up and down the organization can accomplish far more than even brillant individuals laboring in isolation. Something magical happens when you get people to work together, claims former CEO at Ford Motor Company, Donald Petersen. "No matter what it is you're trying to do, teams are the most effective way to get the job done."[20] Adds Betty Frenette at Burnaby Hospital of her organization's successful employee action teams, "It was good to see how people . . . could put their heads together and solve problems they couldn't solve on their own!"

5a. Make It Goodness to Work Peer to Peer. Stepping across, or heaven forbid, above the hierarchical ladder to get something accomplished for the customer is a definite no-no in most organizations. In fact, the very thought of such mutinous behavior can throw most managers into an apoplectic fit. Yet, as Gene Amdhal, founder of Amdhal Corporation, so colorfully puts it, "If you only deal with yolks or just with whites, it's pretty tough to make an omelette."[21]

At Digital Equipment Corporation, quite the reverse is the norm. "You don't want to go through your management chain; you want to resolve as much as you can at the peer level," says Mary Schoonmaker, U.S. Channels Marketing. "It's goodness to work peer to peer." And, in case you're thinking that this must be some kind of penny-ante operation where such casual attention to structure can do little harm, think again. The Digital workforce surpasses 26,000 and the network computer systems company netted $12.9 billion in 1992.

The more commitment you can garner across structural lines for any work project or task at Digital, the better you look. "That kind of cross-functional work is very highly valued," explains Marilyn Rutland, U.S. Direct Marketing and Merchandising Manager. For example, nominations for Digital's highest marketing award, the "Marketing Leadership Award," can only come from the vice president of a unit other than your own. In fact, odds are if you aren't taking this approach you'll soon find your salary and promotion prospects dwindling. "If you can't work effectively cross-functionally, you cease to be promoted," insists Rutland.

How is this judged? Through an interesting technique called "salary planning." Once a year, all managers in a multifunctional area get together and evaluate each other's direct reports. Everyone at the same seniority level is evaluated as a group and ranked by all these managers. In illustration, Rutland is appraised by her manager but also by her manager's peer group. "My raise is influenced by how well I feed across the organization. It makes you very conscious of not just what you do from a delivery perspective but qualitatively how do you do it; do you involve the right . . . people?"

But how do you know whom to involve? You learn by doing, says Schoonmaker. You "work the chain." A marketing manager, Barbara Langdon, develops the concept. Let's say you've done some homework on what the customer needs today and you've hatched a new product concept. You then look for individuals or groups within the Digital network with a vested interest in whether that product's a go—the marketing people or the folks in the field, for example. "You tap groups that [you know] you will impact with this new idea," says Langdon. You show them the opportunity, the potential return on investment, the resources you'll need to make it happen. Then you work on getting them behind you. "Maybe [through] a letter, money, or a commitment of resources." For example, when Angela Cossette, a group manager with the U.S. Channels Business Development unit, was developing a new customer retention program called "The Gold Key," she bounced the idea off the marketing people early on in the process, including Langdon and Schoonmaker.

Digital's also built in some other checks and balances to ensure that cross-functionalism is alive and kicking. Products slated for inclusion in the customer catalogue produced by Rutland's unit, as an example, have to first pass inspection by two insider groups. "We have two groups who have veto power over what goes in the catalogue," says Langdon. If the technical support group hasn't been trained on the new product or the direct order takers can't find a price listed, they have the right to say "no." "This partnership enhances the value of what the customer receives," she insists.

5b. Establish Cross-Functional Working Units. At the Texas office products firm of Miller Business Systems, staff are also encouraged to cut across departmental lines if that's what needs doing to get the job done. For example, if an employee work team, called an "Employee Involvement Team" (EIT), runs into an issue that affects more than one department, a "Corrective Action Team" (CAT) is formed. Say for example if the EIT in the Records Department at the company's warehouse finds the problem they're wrestling with has somehow been created by the way the Purchasing EIT places orders, then a CAT team is set up that comprises both teams. Together, they're empowered to recommend a resolution to management. This is what the "North Dallas Salespeople" did when they teamed up with an EIT from Accounting.

Typical of sales staff everywhere, members of the sales team at the North Dallas Miller branch didn't fancy themselves as money collectors; yet, at the $68-million firm, Account Executives follow their customers through the complete sales cycle. "They are responsible for selling, servicing, and retaining the account," explains Ron Journagan, general manager of the Dallas office, "for handling any problems and making sure we get paid." The Dallas team proposed a solution, which ran thus: create two teams in the accounts receivable area and assign each Account Executive to one of those teams. "It's a win, win, win proposition," they said. Less pressure on the Account Executives for the billing side of things, a personal accounting contact for the client, and a foot in the customer's door for Accounting, tightening the firm's grip on that account just a little bit more. Don't stop at teams that cut across functional lines either. Make a "diagonal slice," that is, get people up and down and across the organization involved in solving retention problems.

6. Focus Your People On Doing Things. Because of the inherent risks in putting a customer retention process in place, organizations can often find themselves stymied by "paralysis through analysis." Inevitably though, you're going to have to take the plunge, or as Peter Drucker puts it, "Sooner or later all the thinking and planning has to degenerate to work."[22] Swallow hard, then, and go for it. After all, as Foremost's Rebecca Spratlin says, "Most decisions [wrong or not] are not irreversible."

The action-oriented emphasis of the Burnaby Hospital customer program was key to establishing its credibility with hospital staff, insists public relations director Ellen Chesney. "So many organizations pour a lot of money into heavy training and don't see any results." That's hard to swallow even for the people who accept that a customer focus has to be a gradual transition. And what about those poor folks who are destined for the tail-end of the training program; what do they use for enthusiasm in the meantime?

Burnaby Hospital took a simple approach to training; they didn't do any, at least not right off the bat. "We pulled together individuals who were involved with particular issues, say the switchboard paging system, and asked them to make some improvements," explains Chesney. "We didn't overwhelm people with jargon. We kept it focused on people sitting down and thinking of better ways of doing things." Why not give the troops a little know-how to get them going? People at Burnaby weren't going to buy into a lot of theoretical jargon, Chesney contends. The only way to get them onside was to keep it simple and focused on solving specific problems.

The Admitting Team at Burnaby, as one example, took a small, but significant, bite out of its communication problems with the hospital's nursing wards. A computer printout on bed status, once only seen by Admitting staff, was made available to Emergency and ward personnel. It caused a major drop in the number of frantic phone calls trying to find out when, and if, any beds would be available for incoming patients. One ward alone saw its usual 15-calls-per-day frustration slashed to a third.

There are a number of facets to this "just do it" approach that I'd like to explore in a bit more depth.

6a. Divide and Conquer. As frustrating as it may sound, you're never going to get everyone on board on customer retention upfront. You need to accept this harsh reality, latch onto those who are favorable, and get them to worry their associates into following suit. As Sandra Walczak, assistant vice president at West Paces Medical Center says, "Some of your people will have been waiting for something like this and they'll become your champions. Others are middle-of-the-roaders and, when they see this is going to stick around, [will] get on the bandwagon."

At Burnaby Hospital, the customer care team found it had set itself an unnecessarily difficult task by trying to wow the entire staff all at once. "You're so keen yourself," says Betty Frenette, the head of the team that spearheaded the Admitting project at the hospital, "you assume everyone else will share your enthusiasm." And that, sad to say, never happens. Don't be too disappointed at this, she advises, and don't waste your time on the naysayers. "Keep on rolling and the people who don't buy in will stick out like stumps. Eventually, they'll have nobody to talk to and they'll buy in or leave."

With 20/20 hindsight, Frenette and her cohorts would have taken the divide-and-conquer route. "We didn't recognize that hot buttons vary across different groups within the organization," admits former hospital medical/surgical consultant, Isabel McLeod. "We didn't analyze the differences between department heads and line staff, and across individuals." In the opening sessions of the program, quality of work benefits were stressed with a word or two added about recruitment and retention pluses. This message appealed to some. The medical and financial minds in the group, though, would have found references to improvement and problem-solving more to their taste, McLeod believes.

Anita Lawrence, the hospital's administrative director of Radiology, agrees and feels a better strategy might have been a multipronged approach to communicating the program's potential benefits. "Pick out the pragmatists and the pie-in-the-sky people and give [each of] them what they need to hear. Get right back to 'What's in it for me?' "

6b. Take It One Chunk at a Time.   Customer retention issues need to be digested one morsel at a time; otherwise, there's danger of choking on too big a slice. After all, the journey of a thousand miles must begin with a single step, as a Chinese philosopher once observed. At IBM Canada, the customer relations department got off to a purposefully slow start. No one could tell the fledging unit just how many calls to expect and they didn't want to risk a circuit overload. "The worst thing you can have in a complaint department is your telephone lines plugged so no one can get in," insists former department manager Gerry Webert. So we opened the dykes very slowly, telling only three switchboard operators initially. Now the center's 800 number is posted everywhere and generates 325 calls per day.

This chunking alternative is also best for your own people. You have to expect people to balk at any change, insists Foremost Insurance Group executive Richard Wettergreen, and take things one step at a time. "Resistance comes from the standpoint of the limited resources everybody's faced with. 'How's this going to fit into my routine and what's it going to cost me in terms of time to change this procedure or that process?' " With this in mind, he's easing his company through a radical revision of its customer contact materials, particularly contract policies, now "your standard insurance ugly." "We're trying to make this a rolling change where the impacts are minimized so, operationally, it's as invisible as possible."

Wettergreen proposed a whole new look for the company's policies that included the use of color and simpler language. "I said, 'Let's start with a blank piece of paper and redesign forms purely from the standpoint of the customer. Can the customer see, read, and understand this stuff?' " The policy is now written in English instead of "Insurancese," as he calls the traditional techno-jargon, and product literature includes cartoons that depict the various kinds of coverage policyholders may have. "If they'd bought collision coverage, for example, there'd be a little cartoon that says, 'Hey, you're protected for collision.' "

Wettergreen knew a lot of Foremost people would balk at the change so he took things a bit at a time. Project execution was laid out in two phases, each pretested with employees and customers—first graphic redesign, then language simplification. "We didn't want people to have to totally uproot some established process or procedure." Wettergreen also took a phased approach to the idea's introduction. He tackled senior management, and then, when they were onside, began working his way through the hierarchical layers to the front-liners. "I gave them a strong sales pitch," he says, complete with visuals and hard statistics. I showed them that just one point change in our retention is worth over $1 million in revenue."

The operational people were particularly skittish about the new look, he recalls. He assured them he wasn't looking to change the way they did business. "If you need information on the form," he told them, "we'll find a way to put it [there]. We're just redesigning it so the customer can relate to it."

But why even rock the Foremost boat at all? The logic for it is inescapable, Wettergreen claims. "We have an intangible product here and in order to make that product distinctive in the marketplace we have to find a way to tangibilize it. And if you're going to be different, you have to be a lot different. A little bit of difference isn't going to be noticed."

6c. Get Some Small Victories Quickly . . .   "Success breeds success," goes the adage and it's never been more apt than when applied to customer retention. Start small and chalk up some early victories; then move on to bigger and better things. That's a strategy John Post at Fidelity Investments adopted to persuade his reluctant co-workers to move toward a more customer-friendly way of doing business. "It took us a long time to put the idea into practice." His marketing team thought a few months would do the trick but they had to think again. It wasn't so much that Fidelity folks don't buy into the idea of doing well by their customers; rather, they were intimidated by the enormity of the task. By jumping in and accomplishing one small task, a consistent look to Fidelity's account authorization forms, Post and a team of other early converts were able to convince others that all was possible.

Customer-signed forms authorizing Fidelity to do any number of things, such as change account ownership or authorize another to trade on your account, varied across the company. "It was crazy," admits Post. "Everyone had their own tailormade form; some were asking for more information, some for less." His group standardized the form, making it easier for the customer and for Fidelity employees. That lead to an 80 percent reduction in error rates and opened a lot of eyes to new possibilities. "People saw what you could do with a little work, that there weren't [such] big hills to climb."

6d. . . . Because Memories of Mistakes Can Linger . . .   Watch that you don't bite off more than you can chew; the memories of past indiscretions can linger a long while. This Leslie Burns at Au Bon Pain knows only too well. In January 1990 a company scratch-card coffee giveaway, dubbed the "Lunch in the Sun" campaign, was a major miss. "Every card won a free coffee," explains Burns. "At the time, we had no idea how frequent our customers were. We gave away more coffee than Juan Valdez has seen in his life!" The idea was that customers would trade up and buy a muffin or something else with the coffee freebie, but it just didn't happen. "Our [store] managers were not happy. In their opinion, it was a complete disaster. [Marketing] lost a lot of credibility because of that."

There was an upside to the promotion, says Burns. "Our sales went through the roof," but managers were blinded by their coffee giveaways. "We did lose an amount of money for a certain period but we picked it up in the tail. But, at that particular point in time, these guys were giving away ten cups of coffee a day to almost all their customers. That's all they could see."

6e. . . . And Results Are the Best Convincer. Not talk, but action, is what it will take to convince any retention nonbelievers in your neck of the woods. For example, Gerry Webert, formerly with IBM Canada, found his group's initial customer satisfaction reports did little more than collect dust in department head offices. "For the first year or so, we think they used them for paperweights." Oddly enough, one of the last to buy in were the Marketing people. They believed they already retained customers quite nicely, thank you very much. Webert's group wasn't so sure. "We felt in our gut that was not what was happening." The thing that finally got these skeptics onside was something even Webert hadn't anticipated—qualified customer leads.

Often, clients call into the Customer Relations department with a problem and the solution is an IBM product. This came as quite a surprise to everyone. "No one thought we would generate marketing leads here." Yet in 1990, 6 percent of the calls to Webert's unit were marketing leads, and good ones at that. He offers this example. "We sent 40 leads to one branch, 20 wanted a sales rep right away, two even developed into a sale in just 90 days, and the average sales overall was over $100,000." And that's when Marketing decided it was well worth their while to get into this game.

6f. But Get the Most Bang for Your Buck. If you can do only a little, do what will generate the best return. That's why a $475-million Atlanta-based staffing services company opted to design a comprehensive customer feedback survey as one of its first retention projects.

One thousand Norrell customers were surveyed in 1990 on what they'd like for every contact they had with the company. It was a long wish-list, explains vice president Stan Anderson, which couldn't be fulfilled overnight. "There were 14 things [customers] wanted in the order fulfillment state, for example." Some prioritizing was required and Norrell used a value/difficulty matrix to sort this out. "The first seven or eight things we worked on were in the high-value, easy-to-do category," Anderson explains. One of the larger of these was the creation of the customer feedback system called IRIS, which stands for Integrated Research Information System, now used on each employee after every customer transaction.

6g. Nurture the Ripple Effect.   Participation in a hands-on retention exercise will hook even the most skeptical staffer. In the words of poet John Keats, "Nothing ever becomes real until it is experienced."[23] That's certainly how it's worked for Norrell Services. "The people who contribute get the passion," says Bruce Reeks, a quality facilitator. "They get the fever."

With her branch design team, Georgia Connors, vice president of Customer Service for Norrell, started with only a few that, with time and the ripple effect, touched a lot. "From two people we built up to a group of 24 design analyzers who worked with associates at each of the 12 branches, pushing the number involved up to 68. Then, 14 more branches began implementation based on the initial results. That put us up to 100. But those 14 also roped in many more recruits when they took what they'd learned back to the company's 200[+] branches."

7. Employees Learn Best from Their Peers.   Best-case scenario is when management takes a back seat and the lesson's taught by the peer group. That's how it works for Lexus Toyota's dealer quality circles. Once a quarter, three or four managers from the national office in Torrance, California, along with area and district managers, act as meeting facilitators for eight to twelve dealership people. The sessions are used to bring key quality issues to the dealers' attention, such as how to diffuse a bad situation with a client or a training update on warranties. But the main office keeps well off center-stage at these gatherings. "We're not there to teach or show them how to do things," insists John Dulzo, service planning manager. "They're not going to listen to us, they're going to listen to other successful dealers in the area."

"For example," continues Dulzo, "the topic of an appointment system might come up because our research tells us that getting in and out quickly is important to the customer. We'll say, 'Let's talk about appointment systems; how do you handle [that] at your dealership?' One person will say, 'I've never had much luck with appointments and I don't believe in them.' Then four other service managers will say, 'I use [an appointment system] and it works great, this is how we do it.' They learn a lot from their peers."

Employees also relate best to their own when it comes to customer retention spokespersons. The two-branch pilot of a computerized branch operating system called "BOSS" at Norrell Services is a good example. "We purposely picked branches that were doing a lot of orders just to find out where the bugs were in these things," explains Georgia Connors. That lent more credibility to the results.

And when it came time to go beyond the pilot phase, a video was shot with two key participants in a roundtable discussion with Norrell's president, Douglas Miller. The idea was to mail out this tape to every branch as its number came up on the BOSS implementation schedule. That way, employees there could see what was coming their way. "One of the things that made that video so effective was the reputation of the two field people in it," claims Stan Anderson, general manager of Eastern Division. "There was a great deal of respect for their knowledge [and because] neither of them was a person who'd do things just because somebody told them to." These two individuals talked candidly about the project. "They didn't whitewash the deal. They pointed out what the problems were and the hours they put in." Pilot participants also took over from information systems people on BOSS training in the branches. They came across as a lot more reliable to branch employees, says Connors, than an MIS person who's never set foot outside the Business Support Center before.

8. Don't Be Afraid to Trust Your People. They won't bet the farm, honest. The auto service chain, Bridgestone/Firestone, wasn't convinced of this until after its management took a dramatic stance on customer complaints in 1990. Up until this point, any money spent to resolve a customer problem was charged to the manager's profit center. For every $100 laid out to keep a customer happy, $10 of that was at the manager's expense. "They were reluctant to spend $90 of company money even though we wanted them to do it because they didn't want to spend $10 of their own bonus," says Sunil Kumar, vice president of Retail Operations.

So we made a very bold and very risky decision, he says. "We gave the store managers the authority to fix customer complaints in a separate account that would not affect their books. As long as charges remained within 1 percent of total store sales, we told them they could handle customer complaints on their own, without any other organizational approval."

The Bridgestone/Firestone executive team took this message on the road to its 1,600 managers, face-to-face, explains Kumar, and with great success. Not only were managers delighted with the new strategy but so are customers. "Our customer complaints were down 23 percent in 1992 compared to 1991, while at the same time, customer count increased. We'd also gambled that managers would show restraint and not empty the cookie jar. We were [hoping] that people who were free to spend wouldn't spend." Any fears they may have had were groundless, fortunately. "People are not using it as much as we were afraid they would; it's just one-half of one percent."

The customer won't usually take you to the cleaners either. At BellSouth Mobility, for example, employees are taught to ask disgruntled customers what it will take to make their problem go away. Invariably, notes Annette Loper, manager for Strategic Market Planning, what the customer comes up with costs less than what you think.

9. Take an Empowerment Test. Take the following test to see how far along the empowerment spectrum your organization is at the moment.[24]

Level 1	Managers make decisions on their own, announce them, then respond to employees' questions.
Level 2	Managers usually make the decisions, but only after seeking the views of employees.
Level 3	Managers often form temporary employee groups to recommend solutions to specific problems.
Level 4	Managers meet with employee groups regularly to help them identify problems and recommend solutions.

Level 5   Managers establish and participate in cross-functional employee problem-solving teams.

Level 6   Ongoing work groups assume expanded responsibility for a particular issue, such as cost reduction.

Level 7   Employees in an area function with minimal direct supervision.

Level 8   Traditional advisory roles do not exist; all or most employees participate in self-managing teams.

The Practice—Making It Happen, Part I—Step 4

What?

An introduction to the power of people to retain existing customers through the setup of "diagonal-slice" (up and down and across the organization) employee/manager problem-solving teams called "People-Powered Retention Teams."

Why?

Your people hold the key to customer retention and the best way to tap that potential is through teams—"No matter what it is you're trying to do, teams are the most effective way to get the job done," says Donald Petersen, former CEO at Ford Motor Company.[25]

How?

4A. A participative work session (Workshop 4.1) for the Retention Advisory Group facilitated by an outside consultant. **Objectives:**

   (1.) To explain the setup process for the People-Powered Retention Teams.

   (2.) To begin the selection of team issues and in-house facilitators (through internal marketing vehicles all Retention Inc. employees are able to contribute ideas here as illustrated in Figure 5.1).

Coordinating the "People-Powered Retention" (PPR) Process

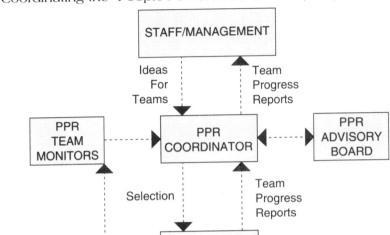

FIGURE 5.1 Your people hold the key to customer retention and the best way to tap that potential is through employee/manager action teams. This figure illustrates how such teams are set up and coordinated.

(3.) To clarify the role of the Team Monitors selected in Step 2.

   a. **Issue Selection Criteria:**

      i. Relates to a central theme, that of customer retention.

      ii. Follows from Retention Inc.'s customer retention vision developed in Step 3Fb.

      iii. Triggers passion for Retention Inc. employees, i.e., is something they really want to get their teeth into.

      iv. Solvable in three months or is a significant *measurable* improvement in one chunk for larger-scale issues.

      v. Can be accomplished with people power and elbow grease with cash influx only as a fall-back option.

vi. Follows from the predictive model for customer retention at Retention Inc. introduced in Step 3Fc.

vii. Focuses on best customer groups.

b. **Facilitator Selection Criteria:**

i. Is willing to "champion" an issue.

ii. Has strong people skills.

iii. Has credibility in the organization.

iv. Is able to commit time and effort required.

c. **Team Monitor Criteria:**

i. Has credibility in the organization.

ii. Is able to commit time and effort required.

iii. Is comfortable with number-crunching.

d. **The "People-Powered Retention Team" Process:**

i. Teams work through the process generally outlined in Figure 5.2.

ii. *"Just-in-Time" Training*—includes three workshops. Content includes meeting skills, process mapping technique, etc.

(1) For team facilitators-in-training—Phase II teams are initially facilitated by an outside consultant with in-house facilitators-in-training observing; final sessions are facilitated by trainees under the direction of the consultant.

(2) For Team Monitors.

(3) For team members with their facilitators-in-training.

iii. *Problem-Solving Process:*

Team Objective—to tackle one specific retention issue, analyze just why this issue is a problem, come up with a solution using only people power and elbow grease, implement that solution, and be able to show a *significant* and *measurable* improvement in the issue in three months.

Team Meetings—each of the teams meets for six sessions over a three-month period. In between these "formal" sessions, team members tackle specific "homework" assignments.

The "People-Powered Retention" Team Process

Meeting	Time	The "Formal" Part	The "Homework"
1.	1-1/2 hours	Who are our customers? What part or "chunk" of this issue will our team tackle in this 3-month period? What's our baseline measurement?	Surveying our customers. Establishing a baseline. Breaking off a manageable "chunk."
2.	45 min.	Why is this issue a concern? Who's doing what on this elsewhere?	Monitoring the whys behind the issue; process mapping. Internal and external competitive benchmarking.
3.	45 min.	Identifying where the process falls down— "the pinchpoints." What's the solution?	Monitoring the whys behind the "pinchpoints" to find the solution.
4.	30 min.	How do we implement the solution?	A test implementation of the solution.
5.	30 min.	Progress report on solution. How do we know how we're doing?	Measure our success, i.e., comparison with baseline.
6.	30 min.	Critique of issue success and team process. Where do we go from here?	Establishing process standards (making sure what's solved stays solved).

FIGURE 5.2 Teams made up of employees and managers up and down the organization work through a process outlined in this figure. Their goal: to select a customer retention issue, carve off a manageable chunk, solve this chunk, and measure their own success over a three-month period. Each of the teams meets for six sessions over a three-month period with "homework" assigned in between, as illustrated in this figure.

4B. Copies of summary report of staff session in Step 4A made available to all Retention Inc. staff through internal marketing vehicles recommended by the Retention Advisory Group formed in Step 1.

When?

Month 6.

CHAPTER 6

Internal Customers: Building Success from the Inside Out

We say, "If you're not serving a customer, then you better be serving someone who is or you better stop what you're doing."

Gerry Webert, former Customer Relations Manager
IBM Canada

When asked what stood in the way of improved customer relations, health-care professionals attending a service training session at Burnaby Hospital, a Canadian facility, overwhelmingly pointed to staff cutbacks as the problem. "Just give us more workers," they said, "That's all we need and we'll solve any customer care crisis in short order." But it's not that simple.

Let's look at this problem from the perspective of what's really important to the ultimate hospital client, the patient. Take the example of pain medication delivery to a patient's bedside; that was right at the top of key concerns among discharged patients researched by Hospital Corporation of America (HCA), notes Eugene Nelson, director of Quality Care Research. The nurse's response to a call from a patient in pain, however, is just the end to a rather long story, he says. The actual delivery process starts with the physician writing the medication order; then the order's forwarded to Pharmacy to be filled, then it's put on carts moved by Transportation staff, and finally it finds its way to the nurse's station on the ward. "There's this long process [behind] what ends up being reflected in a patient checking a box [on a survey] about the response time being excellent-to-poor." And it's only at the very end of this journey that new nursing hires could make any difference at all. To get those painkillers to the patient more quickly, the whole process needs to be speeded up, one link at a time, from internal customer to internal customer, and finally to patient. (Figure 6.1[1])

If you have aspirations of customer retention, you're best advised to start the process at home. What any company outsider sees is actually a reflection of what employees in that organization get from management and from one another. Or as Aleta Holub, quality director at First National Bank of Chicago, says, you can create the most knowledgeable customer service reps, make them all warm and cuddly. But, if no one else in the organization comes to their rescue when it's customer satisfaction time, you've just blown your investment. "We realized if we kicked them, they would eventually turn around and kick the customer."

Research by management professor Benjamin Schneider confirms that employee satisfaction with the way they're treated is directly related to customer satisfaction.[3] "That can lead to a cycle of failure," says Leonard Schlesinger from Harvard's Business School.[3] Consultant Frederick Reichheld of Bain and Co. agrees, "Customer retention and employee retention feed one another."[4]

How customer complaints are handled at American Express provides a case in point. At one time, any one customer complaint touched nine different reps, with each employee performing a separate function in the complaint-handling chain. That made the process slow, the error rate high, and the customer irritated, to say nothing of the effect on employee morale. Today, just one rep works straight through until the problem's resolved. That takes

The Concept of the Internal Customer.
Internal Customers

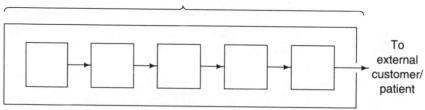

FIGURE 6.1 Internal ("immediate") customers need to depend on one another to be able to serve and retain external or "ultimate" customers. "Everybody's somebody's customer", notes Michael LeBoeuf.[2]

just six days now compared with 35 before, and it's made customers very happy. It's also brought down employee turnover 30
percent in a mere three months.[4] The undisputable conclusion:
customer retention, like charity, begins at home.

So how do you go about getting your own house in order? This
chapter provides the answers in a series of tips.

1. Preach the Gospel of the Internal Customer. At United Services
Automobile Association (USAA), a San-Antonio insurer, employees are treated with the same respect afforded paying clients.
That's because they are customers, or members to be precise,
exlains Michael Patterson, senior vice president of Marketing with
USAA's Investment Management Division. "Our creed gives an
employee full member privileges," he says. "Our employees are
part of our market [and] that market manages the company."

This is an excellent example of the employee as the company's
customer. But what of employees as each other's customers? As
HCA's Nelson notes, "Unless the internal customer chains are
working right, the external customer won't get what he or she
wants, at least not efficiently."

Xerox found it useful to get those links into a circle rather than
along a chain. In its pre–"Leadership Through Quality" days, the
assembly-line design process reigned supreme. Lou Marth, product manager at Xerox's New Build Operations in Webster, New
York, says of this bygone era, "The designer would finish a project
and just hand it over to the plant manager, in effect saying, 'It's all
yours, I'm going to do something else.' "

Today, Xerox designers, engineers, marketers, even company
buyers, work together in new product development teams. In fact,
75 percent of the company's workforce is organized into more than
7,000 quality teams. These 8- to 12-member "family group" units
work with little or no supervision and staff formerly holding
supervisory titles are now referred to as advisors.

Merely bunching people into groups, though, wasn't enough to
make Xeroxers buy in to serving one another or even the end user.
The company sank $125 million into getting 110,000 staffers up to
speed on customer coddling techniques. A good chunk of this
went into 30-hour modules of basic service education. One key
example: workers are trained to find out what happens to a
component after they've worked on it and whether users down the
line are satisfied. It's working; in 1989, customer satisfaction at

Xerox was up 38 percent and the product failure rate had dropped from 30,000 to 425 parts per million.

2. *Identify Exactly Who the Internal Customer Is.* It's not always easy to identify who links up with whom in any organization. At First Chicago, the customer is intentionally defined as "the recipient of your work." "So you're either serving an external client," explains Holub, "or an internal colleague." Keypunch operators in data processing, for example, run tapes for the bank's product areas on behalf of external clients. So data processing's customers are the product people.

On an annual basis, each group and each individual in the bank maps out what they do, why they do it, who the recipient of the work is, and what expectations that recipient has about what's being done. To continue with the data center example: they sit down each year and work out service agreements with each of their internal colleagues, including such things as precise tape transmission schedules.

It all sounds pretty straightforward, doesn't it? Well, it isn't, insists Holub. A lot of employees don't really know what they do or whom they do it for. Identifying these internal linkages can open a lot of eyes. "Just going through the exercise is major progress in itself."

3. *Include Internal Customer Evaluations in Performance Appraisals.* Okay, so now you know who is going to receive your work. Good for you, but not good enough. If you're serious about satisfying your internal customers, let them evaluate you on that directly, something First Chicago has been experimenting with since early 1991. Vice president of marketing Jody Bonneau acted as one of the first test cases for this program. The manager of the bank's product development area, a key internal customer of Bonneau's department, contributes 15 percent of Bonneau's annual performance review. "We are considered internal consultants," she explains.

Of course, Bonneau's boss is an important internal customer for her. There's nothing new in having him evaluate her on how well she's met his expectations; but the other way around, now that's different. "We're trying to turn the organization upside down," she says. "I have more input into my boss's review than he has to mine." Bonneau also has employees, so she's not off the hook on this kind of evaluation either. In fact, once a year, her 10 subordinates use a ten-question survey to size up the Bonneau boss act, and that input forms another 15 percent of her appraisal.

The questionnaire used with Bonneau's employees was structured around specific outcomes that staff needed from management in order to get their jobs done. The idea was not to elicit specific suggestions from employees on how managers could improve but rather on where they needed to improve. That's the difference between outcomes and skills, says Bonneau. She asked bank staff what they'd want to talk to their managers about if they could call the shots. "It boiled down to a few basic principles. They said, 'I would want to talk to them about being fair, are they treating me the same way as anyone else, are they trying to get us to work cooperatively, are they supporting me, are they developing my skills, and are they giving me good insight?' "

Jack Baratta in the sales division of Digital Equipment Corporation also fills out surveys on his internal suppliers, such as the order-processing representative. "He takes all the orders from the account that I work with and gets these into the system," explains Baratta. "He is to supply me with management information. If I feel he's not doing a good job, I get an opportunity to feed back into a customer satisfaction survey [on him]." Baratta responds "yes" or "no" to a series of questions, such as "Are orders being processed in a timely and accurate way?" and is free to add any comments as well.

In a similar fashion, Digital's U.S. direct marketing and merchandising manager, Marilyn Rutland, is graded once a quarter on how well her group meets internal customer expectations, such as whether or not the product catalogue was on deadline and on budget. Ditto across the entire Digital organization, nearly 126,000 souls, says Barbara Langdon, CSO Marketing Programs Manager for U.S. Channels Marketing. "Key linkages" are spelled out for each individual at the beginning of the year. Then, when that person's direct supervisor writes his or her performance review twice a year, managers from all units within the company who are customers of that employee are canvassed for opinions. "We're rated on a scale from one to five," explains Langdon, "one being exceptional; five, not cutting the mustard."

For two years in 1989–90, Langdon and Rutland took this process one step further. "We had a single job plan," Langdon notes. "Two people from totally different organizations reporting to two different vice presidents with one job plan. It was a revolutionary working relationship."

4. Start Your Retention Efforts From the Inside Out. You can strike the building of sophisticated customer satisfaction measures off your immediate to-do list. Start instead with an upgrade of internal service. This may sound a tad drastic but there are compelling reasons for such an approach. First, you'll save yourself *mucho dineros* upfront. Plus you'll get the bulk of your staff involved quickly; that'll ensure you a much better crack at getting their all-important commitment. Too many people in your company don't see themselves as having much, if anything, to do with the external user; they can get their minds around the idea of being a customer of someone else internally. So that's where you start.

This is what Burnaby Hospital did with its first employee customer care teams. The issue any of these teams tackled had to pass some pretty stringent criteria, including: (1) it had to be solvable in three months (some measurable improvement in the right direction sufficed for larger-scale projects); (2) it had to result in internal service improvement, but only if the hospital's external customers gained some benefit along the way; and (3) it had to be accomplished with elbow grease and people power.

The internal focus at the 586-bed health-care facility was as much a matter of necessity as it was of design. There just wasn't any money for extensive patient satisfaction surveys; even the funding for the customer service sessions had to be scrounged from outside sources and in-house bake sales. Putting the hospital's own house in order could be done without cash, and, equally important, could generate concrete results quickly. "We had to get past the 'we've been here before' attitude fast," says Anita Lawrence, director of Radiology. Burnaby veterans had seen too many "one-day work-shop wonders," adds the hospital's director of Admitting, Betty Frenette.

Even from such a shaky start, the Burnaby experiment worked. "It gave people a forum to see there were human beings in other departments and they could negotiate and compromise with those people for everyone's benefit," says Isabel McLeod, formerly the hospital's medical/surgical consultant. One team, grappling with ways to reduce food errors on one nursing ward, found that folks at one end of the tray delivery didn't have more than a vague clue who the folks at the other end were, much less what the others did.

One member, a rep from the Dietetics Department, admitted her contact with ward nurses up to that point had been limited to shouting matches over the phone. "Now [that] I understand what they do, we don't fight anymore." Her response is typical of what the program produced, notes Grace Chandy, Director of Health Records. "It broke down barriers between departments and people."

Naturally, you don't want your people tinkering with things that don't mean anything to your end users; that's a useless exercise. But nine times out of ten your people already know a great deal about what's going on in the customer's mind. Studies by a U.S. research organization prove that front-liners can predict almost 90 percent of cases where customers will have complaints.

The Practice—Making It Happen, Part I—Step 5

What?

An introduction to the concept of the internal customer as the logical starting point for tackling customer retention issues at Retention Inc.

Why?

Customer retention, like charity, must start at home.

How?

5A. A participative work session (Workshop 5.1) for the Retention Advisory Group facilitated by an outside consultant with the following **objectives:**

a. To introduce the concept of the internal customer. **Example:** Selling additional products and services to an existing customer is a solid retention strategy. That's the *external* customer issue. However, if front-line staff don't get good training from the company's human resource experts, effective cross-selling just doesn't happen. That's the *internal* customer issue.

b. To illustrate the need to start from the internal ("immediate") customer and progress out to the external ("ultimate") customer when addressing retention topics. **Example:** A Burnaby Hospital team, grappling with ways to reduce food errors on one nursing ward, found the folks on either end of the tray delivery were not really clear on how the process worked. As homework, the team followed a tray from the kitchen to the patient, discovering along the way a whole series of internal customers who needed to be serviced first in order for there to be any reasonable expectation of keeping the patient happy.

c. To drive home the concept of progressing from the inside out using a series of hands-on exercises. **Example:** "Pick one key process at Retention Inc. that touches your customers, e.g., a customer calls the office and gets the receptionist. Who within Retention Inc. serves that receptionist and how well?"

5B. Copies of summary report of staff session in Step 5A made available to all Retention Inc. staff through internal marketing vehicles recommended by the Retention Advisory Group formed in Step 1.

When?

Month 6.

PART II

Building Organizational Commitment to Customer Retention

CHAPTER 7

To Err Is Human: Recovering Lost Customers

---

*It's not the size of the remedy that satisfies the
[complaining] customer but rather the promptness,
responsiveness, and clarity of the actions taken and
explanations given.*

Linda Lash,
The Complete Guide to Customer Service[1]

In early 1991, Fidelity Investments' 400 pension plan clients were
asked to rate their satisfaction with the company on two levels.
First, they were queried on their basic requirements; in other
words, what would it take to keep them from being dissatisfied?
This was level one, the satisfaction level. The most important
question, on the second level, came next: what would Fidelity have
to do to make customers feel a sense of advocacy, a willingness to
promote the Boston-based firm?

Some unexpected answers resulted from both these questions,
particularly as they concerned the process of coming on board with
Fidelity. This implementation process, as it's called by insiders, is
time consuming and difficult as glitches and delays often seem
around every corner. Clients who offered themselves as advocates
of the company, however, could find little fault with the process,
consistently giving Fidelity's performance here high marks. Satis-
faction-level clients, on the other hand, were not so lavish in their
praise. Unraveling the reason behind these differences proved a
revealing exercise.

The clients in the advocacy level said they all knew what to expect from the implementation process; there were no surprises for them. So whatever pitfalls did befall them during implementation, their satisfaction levels never wavered. Only one-quarter of the other customers could claim such foreknowledge. What's the moral of this story? "Set their expectations early," suggests Steve Graziano. "Tell them what the problems are, keep them informed, and you'll have a satisfied client."

Errors are inevitable, losing customers as a result is not. Mark Beauvais, formerly at America West Airlines, believes your organization's reputation with a customer is built up over time, so it can only be torn down over time. Customers will stick with you through some bad times, he contends, "One bad experience will not necessarily cause them to say goodbye." That's the premise behind the stories and the tips in this chapter.

1. There is Life after Blunders.   Aleta Holub, the quality expert at First Chicago Corporation, tells a tale about a major product glitch a few years ago that threatened the bank's relationship with an important corporate client, a paint supplier to such major corporations as Sears. All initial attempts by First Chicago to smooth things over had miscarried. With a first-class crisis brewing, a "swat team" was brought in to pick up the pieces, and that doesn't happen unless the client's ready to walk. A solution was finally found and First Chicago quickly forgiven its transgressions. When the company next tendered bids for service, the midwestern bank found itself again on the short list. Yes, there is life after blunders.

It's not the problem that's the problem for customers like the paint supplier. It's the recovery, or the lack thereof in most cases, that really sticks in their craws. Holub and First Chicago know this and don't spend an inordinate amount of time beating themselves up when things go wrong. Hassles like the one in this story do occur; the trick is to get by the problem and get on with the solution. "We had a product [problem] to be sure and it needed fixing," admits Holub. "But there was no failure because the customer had brought the problem to our attention," and the bank had a system in place to deal with that problem.

2. Train Your People to Get Past the Error and Onto the Recovery.
Most customers are pretty reasonable if you happen to fall down

on the job. They're not stupid, contends Holub, they know you're not perfect. "Customers understand that things occasionally break down because they do in their own shops." There are limits to their good nature though; they don't want a song and a dance about why you screwed up; they want the problem acknowledged and a solution found but quick. The bottom line: they don't want a reaction, they want a recovery.

Yet too many times, we focus on justifying the problem or redirecting the blame instead of just accepting that the error occurred and channeling our energies into getting it fixed.

"Most customer complaints," contends David Bond, vice president, Marketing and Public Affairs at the Hongkong Bank of Canada, "are caused by people who are unwilling to admit they've made a mistake or who can't ever imagine themselves being the customer." He asks employees to think about the last time someone bungled the service they received as a customer in a restaurant, and then to add up the damage they did to that establishment's image when they complained to all and sundry. "Every time [customers] walk away disgruntled, it's costly. It takes a long time to erase that." Yet it's amazing, claims Lisa Moore, a Royal Bank of Canada manager in London, Ontario, how just two little words—"I'm sorry"—can make such a difference. "Clients appreciate it when you own up to mistakes."

Studies done with Harvard Business School show that more than half of all efforts to respond to complaints actually reinforce any negative customer reactions.[2] That kind of bungling can really hurt. A 1981 study by Technical Assistance Research Programs, Inc. (TARP) for the Coca-Cola Company concluded that bad complaint handling is *four* times as important in stopping sales as good complaint handling is in creating them.[3]

Getting red-faced employees to believe the actual blunder isn't the critical issue takes a bit of doing, however. At the Royal Bank, staff are taught that taking ownership of a problem and solving it quickly is one of the best ways of further cementing the client relationship. "There's a lot of grounding work that goes on . . . in explaining to staff that people are not yelling at us personally, that these are really opportunities." And they're opportunities for all staff, not just the folks on the front line. A 1989 retail banking study by the Raddon Financial Group discovered that respondents were twice as likely to complain about operational problems as about service issues.[4]

The training department at Foremost Insurance Group has found a way to build up staff confidence to deal with the unexpected. Customer service reps, for example, go through practice sessions with company people before they're "let loose" on the general public. Between 10:00 A.M. and Noon on any practice day, the neophyte telemarketers can expect a call from a Foremost volunteer who's been supplied with a call script. Rebecca Spratlin, a five-year veteran at the Michigan insurer, offers a few examples. "We've had people who pretended to have a hearing impairment or to have some [other] disability; I had a practice script which positioned me as a retired widow who was out to make sure no one tried to get anything past me." She recalls with a laugh her own and her colleagues' performances as surrogate customers. "We had no pity."

When a new computer came online at Foremost, a test crash of the system was added to the training agenda. Just as well, according to Spratlin, as the very first call made live by the reps was done without benefit of automation. "Suddenly the system was down and the screens went blank." Thanks to their test training, though, the reps remain poised and were able to cajole customers through the crisis. "And most customers are patient with that."

3. Unleash the Power in Customer Complaints. A customer with a complaint is a customer considering the competition. Most employees, however, don't welcome a sullen shopper with open arms; they see this as a problem heading their way, not as a stroke of luck. Yet research by TARP proves that soliciting customer complaints improves the chances of repeat business even if the complaint is handled poorly. Handle the complaint well and your unhappy patron is at least five times more likely to grace your door again.[5] In fact, TARP figures for returns on investments made to answer complaints, mainly the costs of setting up telephone complaint departments using 800 numbers, range from 15 percent to 400 percent.[6] In the financial services industry, notes Royal Bank of Canada president John Cleghorn, that return is 170 percent.[7] But if you don't actively encourage complaints, research by another U.S. firm, A.C. Nielsen Co., suggests only 2 percent of your disgruntled trade will bother to let you know they're dissatisfied.[8]

So find a way to get customers to speak up. A good example here is the Royal Bank of Canada's guarantee to resolve statement errors within 24 hours or the next month's service charges are on them. Quality manager Rob Edwards wants to impress on customers that his bank wants to know if there's a problem. "We don't want them to just walk out of here mad at us and go somewhere else because we screwed up; we want to correct it." Figure 7.1 offers a few facts and tips on customer complaint management.

Once employees realize that most customer problems aren't their fault, they can begin to appreciate the opportunity afforded by a customer complaint, contends Simon Cooper at Delta Hotels & Resorts. He uses the example of a recent call from a hotel patron at the chain's Whistler, B.C., location to illustrate. The guest had booked a five-room kitchenette and wasn't entirely satisfied that she was getting enough for her $250-a-night payment. "She said, 'There aren't any skillets in the room and the toilet paper is set too far back from the toilet,' " explains Cooper. "I said, 'You're right, I'll see what I can do.' " One hour later, after the hotel had delivered a complete set of cooking utensils, Cooper called her back. "I'm sorry," he told her, "but I can't do anything about the location of the toilet paper today. She was delighted with our response," he quips, "so she'll talk us up around the cocktail circuit 'till the cows come home."

At Delta, customer feedback is encouraged through a three-tiered process of comment cards plus a hotline to the president's office. The secret of success with both, insists Mandy Holland, marketing coordinator, is consistency and follow-up. She explains the cards first, A "stage one" card comes from a guest who's experienced some small irritation or inconvenience, such as no newspaper being outside the door in the morning or slow room service. "We answer that one and say, 'Thank you for taking the time to respond and sorry you didn't get your newspaper.' We phone the front office manager if [the customer's] on file and ask them to note the file and next time [the guest] comes into the hotel, do a room upgrade or [provide] some sort of compensation such as a cheese tray or fruit basket."

If the guest's had a bad experience but is willing to give Delta another try, that's considered a "stage two" and warrants a personalized response on behalf of the hotel's president, Simon Cooper. This is really a form letter, admits Holland, "but I always

Unleashing the Power in Customer Complaints—Some Facts

Upside of Complaints
- TARP studies show that only 9 percent of customers with a problem but who didn't complain will rebuy whereas 54 percent of those whose complaints are handled properly would rebuy, 95 percent if the complaint is handled quickly.[5]

Downside of Complaints
- For every irritated customer who complains, 36 do not. Silence is not golden![9]
- Customers with problems may not complain to the company but they do complain to others. On average, an unhappy customer tells 9 or 10 others; 13 percent tell 20 or more.[10]

Why Don't Customers Complain?[9]
- Lack of knowledge about, and frustration with, the complaint procedure.
- Too much trouble to complain.
- Nothing will happen as a result anyway.

Who Complains?
- The more expensive the problem or service, the more educated the customer, and the higher the customer's income, the more likely he or she is to complain.[11]

Complaint-Handling Tips
- Make it easy for customers to complain, e.g., well-publicized customer service telephone lines or preaddressed postage-paid cards. **Why?** Because the U.S. Office of Consumer Affairs found 800 numbers to be invaluable in reducing complaints and retaining customers.[12] **Example:** An updated customer complaint booklet complete with an easy-to-fill-out form pushed complaints up threefold in just two weeks at the Royal Bank's Ontario district.
- Structure the complaint-handling process, e.g., provide a form that's completed by staff who receive a complaint.
- Make sure there's a human being on the end of the complaint line. **Why?** Because a 1989 study by U.S. research firm Raddon Financial Group found that customers overwhelmingly prefer an assigned person to handle complaints.[13]
- Make sure all employees know that complaints are everyone's business. **Why?** The 1989 Raddon Group retail banking study discovered that respondents were twice as likely to complain about operational problems as about service issues.[4]
- Follow through; remember, no complaint is resolved until the customer says it is. **Example:** For the last four years at the Royal Bank of Canada, customer complaints have been followed up with a mail questionnaire. There's been a nice bonus to this approach. When asked whether or not they'd recommend the Royal to friends, 60 percent of the once-unhappy patrons said they would. It pays to poke for problems.
- Monitor types of complaints, e.g., by type and by branch. Keep this regular, e.g., every 90 days.
- Have complaints handled at a top level in the organization, because "customers want top management to address their problems."[14]

FIGURE 7.1 Research proves that soliciting customer complaints improves the chances of repeat business even if the complaint is handled poorly. Handle the complaint well and your unhappy patron is at least five times more likely to grace your door again. So get your people focused on the potential, not the problem, of customer complaints. This figure illustrates some tips in this direction.

try to make it personal [based] on each person's comments." The general manager of the offending property is expected to follow suit. The final level is called "hot"—"that's when they've had a terrible stay and they're not going to return." Those cards are faxed forthwith to the general manager who responds with a phone call or letter immediately, as does Cooper. For the hot cards, compensation is in order, a brunch for two or a complimentary stay at the hotel.

For guests who'd like to vent in a vocal manner, there's the 1-800-Talk line into the corporate office, the hotline to the president. Of course, Cooper's not glued to his desk 24 hours a day, so when he's unable to answer, say late at night, the call bounces to a 24-hour reservations operator. Details are taken there and the next day a letter is faxed to the general manager who gets on the phone right away, if the guest's still in the hotel, or sends out a letter with a follow-up call otherwise. "The general manager usually takes care of it during their stay at the hotel," says Holland. "It's better if it's answered right away; they leave the hotel with a positive impression."

4. Put Processes in Place that Flush Out Problems. Find ways to force problems to the surface; otherwise, they may fester undetected. The three-year "Total Satisfaction Guarantee" that Xerox introduced in 1990,[15] for example, does more than satisfy customers, contends co-designer James Miller; it gives the company the means to expose any organizational problems. "We looked at it as a catalyst for change. If we weren't good enough to live up to the guarantee, we'd have to get good enough quick."

The guarantee at Cooker Corporation also serves to smoke out difficulties at its twelve restaurants. Customer satisfaction standards are backed by the company's 100 percent guarantee or the meal's on them. For example, explains Glenn Cockburn, vice president of Food Services, "If lunch takes more than fifteen minutes to prepare, we automatically buy your food." Cooker accepts that bloopers are inevitable; the guaranteed refund gives staff the opportunity to make it right and thereby "make a customer." "We make mistakes all the time, we burn chicken, we put the wrong vegetables on the salad. But we have an opportunity to make [customers] happy even though we've screwed up."

The 1,500-employee firm goes to extremes to prove its commitment to customer retention. In 1990, for example, it dished out nearly $600,000 (about 2 percent of sales) under the guarantee program. Restaurant staff aren't passively waiting for quibbles to pop up either, contends Peter Kehayes, the company's regional manager; they practically worry guests into complaining. "It's not only a reactive guarantee; it's proactive. The guest isn't managing it for us; we both manage it." Sometimes, zealous employees find themselves in a tug-of-war with patrons over bill refunds, chortles Cockburn. "We have people say, 'If you buy me anything else, I'm not going to come back.' "

How the guarantee money gets spent is detailed in a daily report from each store. Expenditures are itemized by category, of which there are twelve. President and chairman Arthur Seelbinder elaborates, "We get a breakdown of how they spent each of the dollars, whether it was a misquote [of waiting time] at the door, bad food, or cold food." The report alerts the corporate office to problems at the store level. "It's a good feedback system for [those of] us who aren't in the stores every day." But the system is not meant to be punitive; rather, Seelbinder sees it as a supportive tool. "It gives us the ability to reinforce certain things they might need; [for example], help in the kitchen or coaching at the door."

5. Directly Enlist Customers to Finger Problems. Get customers to do some of your "dirty work," like they do at Northwestern Mutual Life Insurance Co. Every year since 1907, five policyowners descend on the Milwaukee headquarters of the $40-billion life insurance company and begin to ferret out all that is right and all that is wrong. From a list of nominations, many put forward by the firm's 7,000 agents, the board of directors selects four; the fifth participant is a holdover chairperson from the year before. "We try to get a mix of people from different businesses so there's some exchange of ideas," says chairman and CEO Donald Schuenke. He looks for prominent people such as George Dickerman, president of Spalding Sports Worldwide, or Sherwood Smith, Jr., chairman of Carolina Power & Light.

The five-member "Policyowners Examining Committee" sets its own agenda, which may include interviews with trustees, employees, agents, or auditors. After five days of concentrated snooping, with nothing and no one off limits, the committee is ready to sum up its impressions and recommendations. That document appears, unedited, in Northwestern's annual report, which has a circulation of 2.3 million customers. Talk about exposing your assets. It's well worth any risk involved, insists Schuenke. "It keeps us on our toes." It does a great deal for customer loyalty as well. Ninety-five percent of Northwestern's policyowners renew their coverage compared with the industry standard of around 65 percent.

The company has adopted many of the committee's recommendations over the years. In the mid-1960s, for example, the committee took a look at the insurer's strategic planning process—actually, the absence of one. "The upshot of that was the formation of a corporate planning department," says Jim Ericson, president and C.O.O. He offers another example from a decade later. This time the committee's attention was focused on the firm's modest advertising budget, which was concentrated in the print arena. " 'Expand it five times,' was the recommendation, 'or get out of the ad business altogether.' We went to a national television strategy." That was also the time the firm adopted the slogan, "The quiet company." The exercise of being consistently challenged by its customers is one Northwestern management sets great store by. "[We see] it as a healthy management exercise."

6. Target for Early Detection of Problems.   Organizations do foul up with customers, it's a law of nature. The trick is to have a process in place that catches the miscue before it becomes any worse. At First Chicago, a performance measurement system developed from customer interviews in 1981 uses 650 charts to track the weekly progress of every bank product (500 for commercial products, the other 150 for retail). For example, turnaround time for letters of credit or inquiries is monitored. Other measures include how quickly telephones are answered, the number of customers who hang up during a prerecorded message, and the speed at which the bank transfers securities. Deviations from preset performance measures, called "Minimum Acceptable Performance" (MAP) standards and derived from research on client needs, are rehashed at weekly problem postmortems.

Every Thursday afternoon, all product area supervisors meet with their department heads and other members of the senior management team. Barry Sullivan, the bank's chairman and CEO, pops in as often as he can, as do the executive vice presidents and managing partners. How each section shapes up against its MAP standards is presented, shortfalls discussed, and solutions suggested. "They talk about what went wrong and what they can do to ensure it doesn't happen again," explains vice president and manager of quality Aleta Holub. "The objective of this is not just to measure . . . but to improve performance."

First Chicago has added a unique twist to these Thursday sessions—customers and suppliers are invited to join in. Holub admits the bank takes a little flak from competitors on its unorthodox decision to let customers in on its secrets. "They say, 'I can't believe you air your dirty laundry like that in front of customers.' " But customers do appreciate a first-hand look at the bank's process for dealing with screwups. "They're impressed we have an early warning system in place so we know immediately when we have a problem. And we have the right sense of urgency about getting it fixed." It also gives the company a way to show off its culture as one that puts the customer squarely on center stage, a culture, by the way, that has not gone unnoticed by the customer starmakers. In 1988, First Chicago became the first financial institution to win the International Customer Service Association's Award of Excellence.

7. *Customer Behavior Can also Signal Trouble Ahead.* Disenchanted clients invariably send out signals of dissatisfaction long before they put on their walking shoes. They often stall on project approvals for example, claims Michael Walsh, senior vice president and media director at Ketchum Advertising. "An early warning signal I see is when it's getting increasingly difficult to get approval for the work you're doing. Somehow, there's a disconnect in communications." His colleague, Thomas Miller, former president of Ketchum's New York office, adds another sure-fire sign of discontent among ad industry patrons. "Your clients begin to poke around for unsolicited ideas from other agencies." When that happens, a red flag better shoot up the pole, he says, because the relationship's on shaky ground.

The cleaning corporation ServiceMaster counsels its people to watch for telltale "pivotal points" that indicate you're at a crossroads with your customer and, if you don't pull up your socks, you may lose your shirt. Chuck Stair, president and CEO of Service-Master Management Services, offers a case in point. A switch in area manager for its New England district several years ago caused the loss of an important corporate client. "All of a sudden, we got a termination notice and everybody was surprised."

The client gave lack of funds as the reason for its decision but Stair and his colleagues guessed at the real reason. The new man on the job hadn't had time to foster a relationship with the customer and his boss, the district manager, hadn't picked up the slack. ServiceMaster scrambled to respond but, by then, the client was committed to another course. "The lesson there was we were too late in listening. We have to be watching for those vital signs and not taking anything for granted."

Employees on the residential side of ServiceMaster's business are also drilled in how to sniff out client dissatisfaction. Customers are often reluctant to express displeasure, claims Carlos Cantu, president and CEO of ServiceMaster Consumer Services, so service reps need to be sensitive to clues that signal a slip in satisfaction. For example, when a service technician calls to confirm a maid's appointment, a customer may hedge on a specific date. "Unless the customer gives us another time right away, it's a signal that things are not what they should be." That sets in motion what Cantu calls "a callback process."

The supervisor or service manager gets on the phone with the customer and tries to determine exactly what the problem is and if it's fixable. There's a fine line here, admits Cantu, between tenacity and hustling. "We tell our people not to give up too easily; at the same time, we need to be careful not to be perceived as pushy." One way ServiceMaster employees keep on the gentler side of this line is by keeping the conversation short, not more than two or three minutes. A few simple questions are put to the customer and if the answers are consistently in the negative, it's time to hang up and file that customer's name for a three-month follow-up call. "We ask if our people were courteous, if the billing was a problem, and if it would be convenient if we called back within a week. A 'no' answer to those questions is indicative that the relationship is strained; at that point, we just back off."

One strong indication that customers are rethinking their relationship with your company is when they opt not to renew any service contract or cancel partway through, contends James Miller, a manager with Xerox's U.S. Marketing Group. "It should be a red flag." In the past, the Rochester corporation might not have recognized this danger; things aren't so slack nowadays. A new customer contact program put in place in early 1990, for example, gets service reps on the phone with customers 90 days before a service contract or warranty is due to expire.[16]

Authors Mark Hanan and Peter Karp provide a capsule look at customer danger signs in their book, *Customer Satisfaction*. They contend there are three key stages here: "slowdown," when customer approval of your proposals comes more slowly; "putdown," when access to upper-level customer managers decreases; and finally, "shutdown," when plans for any future work with you are delayed, reduced, or cut altogether.[17] Figure 7.2 illustrates customer behavior warning signals.

8. Consider an Automated Tipoff to Potential Retention Problems. Technology as a tool is a theme that pops up occasionally in support of other concepts throughout this chapter and others. It's important enough, though, to warrant a special mention on its own, with the following example in illustration. A special computer program at one U.S. bank analyzes customer transactions, contrasting historical data with weekly account activities. The system automatically flags those relationships that show significant deviations from the norm, for example, a sudden decline in a customer's balance of more than 20 percent off his or her normal level. These flagged accounts are referred to a "Business Retention" team for evalua-

---

Summary of Customer Behavior Warning Signs

- They cancel service contracts midway through.
- They don't renew service contracts.
- They delay approval for work in progress.
- They hedge on future commitments.
- They begin checking out the competition.
- If it's a corporate customer, they cut you off from communication with their upper levels.

FIGURE 7.2 Disgruntled customers invariably send out signals of dissatisfaction such as these long before they put on their walking shoes. These should be red flags for retention follow-up.

tion. Bank "Relationship Officers" whose customers have been identified by the Retention team as being "at risk" of leaving then take over. Customers are called, areas of dissatisfaction explored, and a retention plan implemented.[18] The Hongkong Bank of Canada intends using its new relational database in a similar way. Marketing head David Bond illustrates with an example. He asks the system to tell him all the cases where they've had problems with their "Peak Performance" checking account; have these changed over time?; are they centralized in one branch?; and so on. "It'll serve as a great indicator of problems."

9. Go One Step Further and Anticipate Problems. Even before a problem comes to your customer's attention, it should come to yours. Notes Xerox's James Miller, manager of Reprographics/ Facsimile, Product Marketing, "If you sit back and wait for complaints, you can kiss off 25 percent of your customers."

A computerized tracking system, "CLAIMS," keeps First Chicago one step ahead of customer dissatisfaction. Leased from an outside vendor, the CLAIMS application monitors client activity across all product lines including inquiry tracking and error reporting. "We try to use that information to be proactive," contends Kathleen Stevens, a bank vice president. In one instance, tracking the volume of photocopies produced for a large corporate customer showed that much of the volume was due to repeated requests for copies of the customer's checks. "We now generate microfilm for them so they can pull information on their own [without] having to contact us."

Perhaps CLAIMS' greatest claim to fame is in the area of error analysis. The bank was able to identify a check-encoding miscue, for example, and nip it in the bud before the customer was even aware there was a problem. Says Stevens, "We don't wait for the client to complain."

At Xerox, staff are compiling a database of potential dissatisfiers to use in predicting customer complaints before they happen. Broken calls, as one example, are almost certain to rile clients, says customer marketing vice president Paul Cahn. "When a service rep doesn't fix a problem on the first call, that's one of our largest causes of complaints. Whenever we have a broken call, a flag comes up, and somebody from Customer Relations calls the customer before the customer calls us."

Xerox also relies on technology to anticipate product and customer relations breakdowns; some of its machines can literally call for help when they feel a problem coming on. Available on most of the company's high-volume copiers, duplicators, and electronic printers, "Remote Interactive Communication" (RIC) is a self-monitoring system that continuously checks performance against operating standards. Should a machine fall short of any benchmark, an exception report is zapped across telephone lines to a central dispatch area, ultimately triggering a customer call from a Xerox customer service engineer. The diagnostic system also monitors copier usage, freeing customers from the onerous task of filling out monthly meter cards and keeping billing errors down as a result.

With RIC and its other proactive efforts, the 1989 winner of the Malcolm Baldrige Award hopes emergency maintenance calls will soon go the way of the dinosaur. Cahn believes it's the wave of the future. "Directionally, we're moving from being reactive to being predictive."

10. Get to the Root of the Problem.   As Kathleen Stevens from First Chicago admits, it's good to be able to respond quickly to solve a problem, but a customer soon tires of facing the same error over and over again. At the bank, errors are traced to the source using the automated system, CLAIMS, mentioned earlier. "With CLAIMS, we can focus in on correcting the problem as opposed to just fixing it." She provides the example of a corporate client who'd been experiencing problems with the company's lockboxes. A three-month monitor using the CLAIMS program pinpointed the problem. This exercise had some nice spillover benefits for all the bank's lockbox customers, bringing error rates down from one in every 4,000 transactions to one in every 10,000.

Many organizations rely on their customer relations departments to field customer complaints. But, at IBM Canada, the customer relations department is viewed as a second line of defense only, "a safety net." That's why every time a call comes into this shop, the customer relations people question why that poor customer had to call them at all. All incoming calls are therefore coded as to root cause and the IBM unit that should have solved the problem in the first place is put on alert. The following story is a good case in point.

About three years ago, an IBM customer was traveling in Europe when his four-month-old portable computer bit the dust. It was still under warranty, at least it would have been had he been in Canada, the rules said. He'd taken the machine into an IBM outlet but had been told nothing could be done. He phoned customer relations and one of the reps took his call. "This warranty system stinks" was his sentiment and she agreed, authorizing its repair in Europe at no cost to the customer.

The IBM rep didn't rest on her laurels just yet. She sent an electronic message to the brand manager of that portable, requesting that something be done about this, and kept at him until it was. "He did the legwork, she did the monitoring," explains the former department manager, Gerry Webert. "It's interesting to note," says Webert, "that when a new portable computer was announced in 1991, it came with an international warranty."

This particular problem took four months to completely resolve as it involved the design of a new policy; generally, the customer relations team targets for a 24-hour turnaround. Every month, a printout of such root problems is channeled back to function managers using the company's "Systems Query Language," just one more leg in this closed loop.

11. Don't Give Up. It takes considerable intestinal fortitude to keep hacking away at what seems to be an endless parade of problems. Gerry Webert believes there is light at the end of this tunnel and offers the following story to support his conviction. More often than he liked, calls came into his customer relations center from people adamant that they'd never do business with IBM again. "My people [would] say, 'Can I work on why you're not going to buy from us again?' [The customer] normally would answer, 'Sure, go ahead, but I'm still never going to buy from you again.' " IBM Canada's customer relations people would then work through the problem, 90 percent of the time before the end of the conversation, but at worst, within 24 hours.

To make sure no loose ends are left dangling, a follow-up survey is always mailed to each caller. Now we get to the good stuff. Although these hardliners were dead set against IBM at the outset, a good 60 percent felt the complaint-handling process now made them *more* likely to do business with the company in the future. All things are possible.

A last note of caution about digging in and digging out corporate problems. Make sure it doesn't sap too much of your people's motivation. "One has to be careful it doesn't become too much of a negative," says William Pollard, chairman and CEO at ServiceMaster. "Organizations need victories, not failures."

The Practice—Making It Happen, Part II—Step 6

What?

The setup of the first "People-Powered Retention Teams" to tackle specific issues relating to early warning signals of customer defection and nongrowth, specifically customer complaints.

Why?

This is the first building block in the formulation of a predictive model for customer retention introduced in Step 3Fc.

How?

6A. **Homework** assigned to members of the Retention Advisory Group as follows:

a. "Monitor complaints registered by Retention Inc.'s best customer group over the past month, six months, year, two years. Is there a pattern?"

b. "Research unspoken complaints, i.e., what leads a customer to consider registering a complaint?" Remember, statistics show that less than 10 percent of your unhappy customers will even bother letting you know they're ticked off. **Example:** at Xerox, if a customer requests equipment servicing and the Xerox technician doesn't show or botches the job, referred to by company insiders as a "broken call," it's a safe bet that customer will give serious thought to complaining.

c. "Research other early warning signals of customer defection or nongrowth." **Example:** customers considering a move to the competition at Ketchum Advertising drag their heels on approvals for work-in-progress.

d. "Research company errors that particularly annoy best customers." **Example:** at America West Airlines, Chairman Club members hate finding they've deplaned more quickly than their luggage.

6B. Analysis of best-customer research gathered in Step 3 by in-house personnel under the supervision of the Retention Coordinator or an outside consultant. **Objective:** to back up early warning research done by Retention Inc. staff in Step 6A.

6C. A participative work session (Workshop 6.1) for the Retention Advisory Group facilitated by an outside consultant with the following **objectives:**

a. To review homework and company analysis from Steps 6A and 6B.

b. To select up to four issues for the first People-Powered Retention Teams relating to key early warning signals of customer defection and nongrowth. **Selection Criteria:** highlighted in Step 4Aa with additional details following: (i) *Issue:* Possible options also ranked on a matrix presented in Figure 7.3.[19] (ii) *Number of Teams:* The smaller the organization, the fewer the teams: i.e., just one team at a time is on the go for Retention Inc. (iii) *Facilitator:* Use outside consultant with in-house "facilitators-in-training" observing process. (iv) *Team Membership:* Team members selected based on this criteria: "What groups need to be represented on this team so any team solution sticks?"

6D. Preparation by an outside consultant or the Retention Coordinator of a summary report of Workshop 6.1 and distribution to all Retention Inc. staff through internal marketing vehicles recommended by the Retention Advisory Group.

Retention Issue Selection—a Matrix of Comparison

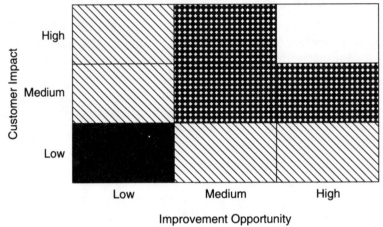

Fɪɢᴜʀᴇ 7.3 This chart provides a simple way to ensure your People-Powered Retention teams focus on the issues that'll give you the most bang for your buck. The "x" axis represents the opportunity for improvement, that is, how easy is it to solve this problem given current organizational resources and constraints? Customer impact, low to high, is represented on the "y" axis. H. James Harrington; Business Process Improvement: The Breakthrough Strategy for Total Quality, Productivity and Competitiveness, (New York: McGraw-Hill Inc., 1991), Figure 2-3, p. 41, copyright 1991, reproduced with permission of McGraw-Hill.

6E. Teams selected in Step 6C work through the People-Powered Retention process introduced in Step 4Ad and developed below.
   a. *"Just-in-Time" Training*—includes three workshops:
      i. **For team facilitators-in-training**—training concentrates on tools for guiding the team process including the following: (a) running an effective meeting (detailed in Chapter 2, page 31–33); (b) collecting data using a "checklist" (Figure 7.4[20]);

Tools for Guiding the People-Powered Retention Process— Check List for Recording Customer Complaints

Customer Complaints	October				
	Week 1	Week 2	Week 3	Week 4	Total
Error on statement	ЖН ЖН ЖН ЖН I	ЖН ЖН ЖН ЖН IIII	ЖН ЖН ЖН ЖН ЖН I	ЖН ЖН ЖН ЖН I	92
Late statement	ЖН ЖН	ЖН I	ЖН	ЖН II	28
ATM not operating	ЖН ЖН ЖН ЖН ЖН ЖН ЖН	ЖН ЖН ЖН	ЖН ЖН ЖН ЖН ЖН ЖН ЖН II	ЖН ЖН ЖН ЖН ЖН ЖН	117
Total	66	45	68	58	237

FIGURE 7.4 To use a check-sheet form like the one in this figure, follow these steps: (1) Have everyone who will be collecting data agree about what is being counted, i.e., specific customer complaints such as late statement or error on statement; (2) Determine the time period over which observations will be made, e.g., the month of October; (3) Develop an easy-to-use format such as the one illustrated here; (4) Collect data carefully; and (5) Tally up event occurrences.[21]

(c) identifying causes of retention problems using a "cause-and-effect diagram" (Figure 7.5[22,23]); (d) mapping, evaluating, and establishing performance standards for a retention process using "process maps" and process evaluation charts (Figures 7.6,[24] 7.7,[25] and 7.8[26–27]).

ii. **For Team Monitors**—training concentrates on tools for customer surveys and interviews.

iii. **For team members** with their facilitators-in-training—**Agenda:** *introduction* by senior managers; *morning session*—training on team concepts and tools with all teams; and *afternoon session*—team-

Tools for Guiding the People-Powered Retention Process—Cause-Effect Diagram: Late Letter to Customer

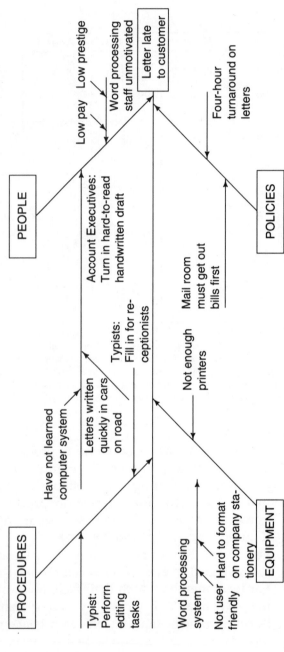

FIGURE 7.5 To use a cause-effect diagram, such as this one, follow these steps: (1) State the problem briefly in the box at the right of the diagram (i.e. "Letter late to customer"); (2) Write the four main factors that may be causing the problem in the four other boxes, i.e. in service companies, use "policies", "procedures", "people" and "equipment"; for manufacturers, substitute "manpower", "machines", "methods" and "materials"; (3) Generate probable causes for each factor by brainstorming; and (4) Continue working your way through the chain of causes by asking 'Why . . . why . . . why?'.[23]

Tools for Guiding the People-Powered Retention Process—
A Blank Form for a Process Map

Key Process: _____	Improvement Target: _____

→ — → — → — → — → — →Time — → — → — → — →

Functions	Sequence of Activities and Measures

Date: _____

FIGURE 7.6 See Figure 7.8.

specific sessions in breakout rooms focusing on thrashing out specifics of team issue (chunk of issue to tackle) and team membership ("Who needs to be represented on this team to make sure any solution sticks?"), as well as clarification of member roles and responsibilities.

b. *Team Process*—highlighted in Step 4Adi with additional details below.

i. **Customer Survey Homework:** teams use team/customer group sessions to gain a better understanding of retention issues through their customers' eyes. Sessions initially facilitated by an outside consultant; ultimately, this role taken over by the Retention Coordinator. **Example:** at New York–based Chase-Lincoln First Banks, branches pick client brains at "close to the customer" sessions.[28]

ii. **Chunking Homework:** teams slice off manageable chunks of their issues, slices that can be analyzed, implemented, and measured within a three-month time span. **Example:** a team at a Canadian provincial agency dedicated to encouraging exports by local businesses, B.C. Trade Develop-

Tools for Guiding the People-Powered Retention Process—A Completed Example of a Process Map

Key Process: PRODUCE A DOCUMENT(CURRENT PROCESS) **Improvement Target:** _____

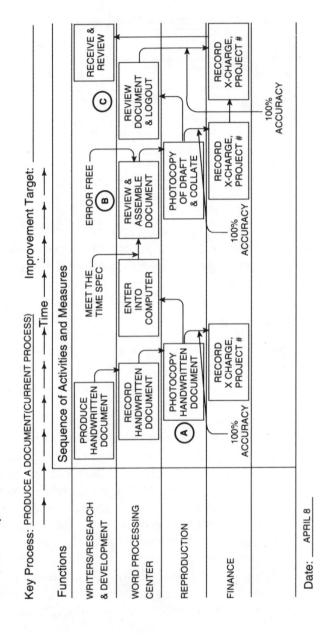

Figure 7.7 See Figure 7.8.

Tools for Guiding the People-Powered Retention Process—A Completed Example of a Process Evaluation and Standards Development

Process: PRODUCE A DOCUMENT   Date: APRIL 28

For the most problematic steps of the process ("pinchpoints"), complete the following evaluation:

PROCESS STEPS

Factors For Evaluation	(A) PHOTOCOPY HAND-WRITTEN DOCUMENT	(B) REVIEW & ASSEMBLE DOCUMENT	(C) REVIEW DOCUMENT & LOGOUT/DONE		
Actual Performance	4 HOURS	IN THE QUEUE A LONG TIME- 6 HOURS	THE DOCUMENT USUALLY DELAYED FOR 2 HOURS		
Desired (Standard) Performance	1 HOUR	2 HOURS	NO LOST TIME- 30 MINUTES MAXIMUM		
Difference	3 HOURS	4 HOURS	TIME-1 1/2 HOURS		
Probable Cause	REQUIREMENT TO COPY EVERY NEW DOCUMENT	SUPERVISOR REVIEWS EVERY DOCUMENT	NO PROCEDURES CURRENTLY IN PLACE		

FIGURE 7.8 These three figures illustrate the techniques of process mapping and process evaluation. To create a process map: (1) Develop a process-map worksheet like Figure 7.6; (2) Identify the key process to be mapped; (3) List the work units involved in the process on the left-hand side; (4) Enter the starting point at the far left side in the row of the appropriate function; (5) Move to the right, entering the activities associated with each function. Make sure you are mapping the process *as it really is, not as you think it should be*; (6) Connect activities from supplier to immediate internal customer using arrows; (7) Finally, identify current measures that exist for each output. eg. "100% accuracy." To create a process evaluation: (8) Build a process-evaluation chart as in Figure 7.8 using the information from your process map. ie. Figure 7.7; (9) Choose the most problematic steps and record them in the boxes immediately under the label "Process Steps"; (10) Enter current performance for each step in the boxes to the right of the label "Actual Performance"; (11) Enter desired performance for each step in the boxes to the right of "Desired Performance"; (12) Enter the differences between actual and desired performance next to the label "Difference"; (13) Record, in the boxes to the right of "Probable Cause," what you believe may contribute to any performance shortfall. Be sure to focus on the underlying problem, not the

ment Corporation, wanted to deal with the issue of interoffice communication. Much too large a task to be tackled all at once, though, so they carved off one important slice—new employee orientation—and improved that first.

iii. **Competitive Benchmarking Homework:** teams look in-house first to see who among their colleagues is doing a great job handling the issue under analysis. **Example:** Boston research firm, Bain & Company, has created a tally of "best practices" for customer relationship development in the financial services industry. On the list are high manager visibility in the branch and employee knowledge of customer names.[29]

c. *Team Progress Monitoring*—done initially through four channels as indicated below. Ultimately, this monitoring function will be integrated across the organization during the final phase of this model (see Chapter 13).

i. Team progress reports, called "storyboards."

ii. Success measurements by the teams themselves. **Example:** a team at the B.C. Trade Development Corporation on Canada's West Coast measured the success of its efforts at improving new employee orientation using a skill-testing questionnaire. New staff not exposed to the team's improved orientation program averaged a dismal 9 on the 20-question survey. The lucky newcomers who received the upgraded orientation, on the other hand, fared much better with an average score of 15.

iii. Team Monitors (introduced in Step 2) who follow team progress and present an objective report of team successes at the end of each phase.

iv. A final progress report presented by teams to Retention Inc. staff and management at the end of the three-month period.

6F. Copies of summary report of team progress made available to all Retention Inc. staff through internal marketing vehicles recommended by the Retention Advisory Group.

When?

Months 7, 8, and 9.

CHAPTER 8

Keeping In Touch: Customer Retention through Customer Contact

> *Any customer contact is an influence over retention.*
>
> Richard A. Wettergreen
> Vice president, Corporate Communications
> Foremost Insurance Group

Customers like to know your company is eager to talk to them, especially those high-income earners who frequent dealer showrooms at Lexus, the luxury division of Toyota Motor Sales, U.S.A. Group vice president and general manager, J. Davis Illingworth, Jr., knows this first-hand. Awaiting him one Monday morning not long ago was a cryptic message from a customer. "All it said was please call at 1:00 P.M., Monday, BMWR." When Illingworth followed up that afternoon, the customer said he'd just been testing the auto company's responsiveness. "He said, 'I was thinking of buying an LS 400 and I called to see if you returned phone calls.' "

Lexus people don't just return calls, they initiate them. All head-office personnel are given a list of seven customers each month. Their mission: to call one per week. "That way we keep in touch with what the customer is thinking," says Illingworth, "and that includes me." This effort's tracked and woe betide anyone derelict in duty. "I got a note several months back from my team captain," Art Garner, public relations manager, admits, "that reminded me to pick up my pace a bit."

Illingworth admits others like Garner haven't always scored top marks on customer contact. In fact, in January 1991, only 68 percent of customers surveyed said someone from the dealership had been in touch to see that all was well. These results propelled Illingworth to take action. He penned personal letters to all dealers stressing the importance of sales and service follow-up. His staff also took this message on the road, chatting up dealers and making examples of the best of those to encourage the laggards.

To ensure the contact process doesn't become onerous, the service planning group headed by John Dulzo has designed a series of quick questions dealer staff can use on the phone with the customer. His associate, customer satisfaction operations manager Marjorie Crosby, provides a few examples of these. "[We asked] questions like, 'Was the work performed as promised?' or 'Did you receive the car when promised?' " Within six months, the callback rate doubled to 90 percent.

The 2,000-employee auto company even uses its bloopers to make contact with clients. A recall on the LS 400 model in December 1990 turned out to be a blessing in disguise, believes Illingworth. While dealers hustled to get the problem under control quickly, he wrote to every one of the 9,000 customers affected. "I personally signed each letter, thanking the customers for working with us, and telling them if they had additional problems to please call." This cloud did have a definite silver lining. "It allowed our dealers and us, as a manufacturer, to bond with our customers and show them we did sincerely put their concerns first."

The Lexus anecdote, along with the others in this chapter, exemplifies the need for organizations to put themselves out in order to keep close to the customer, an effort that doesn't happen by osmosis, but takes process and commitment. It's a labor not without its reward, however. By staying in contact with insurance policyholders, for example, 87 percent will say "yes" to more insurance, claims Albert Sheridan, vice president of the Life Insurance Marketing and Research Association. Of the customers left languishing, though, only 50 percent will purchase again.[1]

1. Don't Wait to be Asked. Action is the order of the day for keeping closer tabs on your existing customers. Don't wait on their good graces; invent excuses to touch them. An obvious strategy but often not done, claims consultant Anthony Putman.

That customers don't always want to make the first move, for example, came as a great surprise to the partners at Manning Jamison (MJ). Yet, a 1990 focus group and follow-up survey confirmed that clients want proactive contact from their accountants. They wanted us to let them know when it was time to add more services, says Michael Corney. That shouldn't have come as such a shock, he admits. After all, "that's what we should be doing if we're looking out for all their interests."

For a company like Foremost Insurance Group, which is largely dependent on outside agents to commune with the customer, proactive contact programs are all the more important. "Our company is often invisible to the ultimate customer because the dealer or the independent agent may not make a big deal that this is a Foremost policy," says Richard Wettergreen, vice president of Corporate Communication. So in 1988, the company created a triplet of customer communication materials nicknamed the "Welcome/Thank-You Program." The program design evolved from an earlier one, "Living Trends," which had been canceled in the mid-1980s primarily due to cost but also to some difficulties in execution. "We discontinued that because the response was not adequate to support it; we had a difficult time getting it followed up by the agents." Why the resurrection? Frankly, it's getting tough all over, says Wettergreen. "We're facing a static market and new business is harder to come by."

He has learned from the past though, the Welcome/Thank-You Program was designed with help from agents, making them more comfortable with the notion of Foremost having a direct line to their customers. Mindful of the ever present concern over costs, Wettergreen has kept the number of new communications to three versus the original six issues of Living Trends. The three work in tandem as follows. Just after a new customer comes on board with the company, a welcoming package including a plastic ID card is mailed. Then, twice during that policy's renewal cycle, one at midcycle and the second just before renewal time, a copy of a follow-up newsletter called "Your Place" finds its way to the customer's doorstep. Finally, when an existing customer renews, a thanks-for-the-business letter is dispatched and the cycle of newsletters continues.

The principal intent of this program is to get the customer to renew, claims Wettergreen, and it's certainly done that. "We're seeing retention rates that are up to 10 points higher compared to control groups. You're looking at a substantial jump." Plus, at a cost of approximately $1.50 per customer, the program is a good bit less expensive than the $20 or $30 Wettergreen estimates it costs to snag a new Foremost customer.

2. Make Use of Systems You've Already Got. Discovering ways to keep the customer relationship fresh needn't be the onerous task you might expect at first glance. Often, there are already points of contact built into your administrative systems and in the way the customer does business with you. These are generally looked upon as paper-pushing exercises, says Rebecca Spratlin at Foremost, but they're really missed contact opportunities. Every time the company structure does touch a customer, that opportunity must be pounced on, claims Xerox's manager of Service Marketing David Spindel. "We have to use things like the service contract and the supplies sale."

Don't settle for simple awareness of these vital contact points; develop a list of customer evaluation criteria. For a financial institution, for example, two key customer/organization junctures are teller lines and the account statement. The Canadian credit union, Richmond Savings Credit Union, researched customer tolerance for bank lineups and found seven minutes to be the magic number. At Fidelity Investments, a statement turnaround of between 25 and 30 days was deemed adequate by clients. Below are a few more examples.

• *Customer cancellation reports.* On a monthly basis, Foremost's computer kicks out a list of insurance policy cancellations, a document that used to be summarily noted and filed. "What a waste," says Spratlin. "These are existing customers who have given up on us; let's see if we can't coax them back and save ourselves the cost of replacing them."

The existing cancellation report at Foremost wasn't all that helpful for this new challenge, however. For one thing, the primary reason cited for cancellation was often given as nonpayment. "That doesn't tell us anything. People don't pay their bills for a number of reasons. They might think we were rude or we didn't explain the coverages or it could be they received their social security check late." Her team of service reps now make a follow-up phone call to each of these departing patrons, try to identify the real reason for the cancellation, then work with the client to save the policy.

Sometimes, customers are confused about coverages and prices and, while in this hesitant state, are lured away by a more persuasive agent from the competition. "We can recoup that loss," says Spratlin, once explanations without insurance jargon have cleared the air. For customers whose fixed-income checks have been tardy, a new payment schedule is set up and they're brought back on board. In many cases, the client's simply forgotten to make payment. For them, a notation's made that the cash is on its way, and in ten days, the computer pops out that customer's name for a follow-up check. "If the account's still in arrears, we'll call again," notes Spratlin. That's only if the customer hasn't indicated an intent to cancel, though. "If they say, 'No, we have no intention of continuing to do business with you,' we will try to find out why, and then do our best to overcome their objections, but we certainly are not going to badger them."

• *Your billing system.* Foremost's Welcome/Thank-You package, discussed earlier, is also driven off an existing company operation, the billing cycle. "The same system that bills customers generates the list we use," explains Wettergreen. New customers make a selection from a number of payment choices: annual, quarterly, or a ten-payment option. Once they're in the system, the Foremost computer automatically tracks and monitors the life of the policy and, at certain points in the cycle, issues a bill if it's a multiple-payment plan, or a list of policies due to expire. Wettergreen coordinates the mailing of his materials with this billing sequence.

He illustrates how this is done for one of the customer retention pieces, a client newsletter that is mailed just before the policy expires. "The March expirations will come up and we'll break that into two groups. [For those expiring] the first 15 days of the month, we'll get one list processed and drop them in the mail on the first of the month. We'll have a second drop in the middle of the month for the second [group]." Foremost uses this existing renewal system to get into 50,000 customer homes each month.

• *Automatic contract renewals.* Xerox Corporation was also missing out on a chance to touch base with its customers through a computerized renewal system for contracts and warranties. When renewal time rolled around, a reminder letter automatically went to the customer. No news was interpreted as good news and the contract renewed. And that was that. Paul Cahn, vice president of Customer Marketing, offers this story to show the lack of customer contact inherent in the system.

Customer X is called by a Xerox service rep who introduces himself. This was the customer's response: "I was wondering when you guys were going to call me. You send me a letter every year saying your service contract's due. I don't notify you so you renew it. That's the sum total of my relationship with Xerox." Not good enough, the company realized in 1990 and implemented a new program called "Customer Loyalty." Now, on a daily basis, a list is generated of all contract expirations coming up over the next 90 days. Someone from Xerox immediately gets on the phone and gives those customers a call. "This program ensures at least once a year [someone] is touching the customer."

• *Tap into an existing customer cycle.* Research shows that office-equipment customers typically go through a three-year cycle with their machines, at the end of which they're itching to buy something new. "We know from experience that once you hit three years, customers start turning over machines progressively in greater and greater numbers," says Xerox's James Miller. The warranty expiration date for a convenient copy cartridge, designed by Xerox in 1986 for the smaller of its copier lines, caused a predictable decision point for customers that the company could follow through on. "We could then have a conversation with them that might result in an upgrade," says Miller, "or, at the very least, might give us a chance to make sure they're happy."

3. Capitalize on Client-Initiated Contact. In the previous chapter, we talked about the opportunity inherent in customer complaints, that a quick and satisfactory response here can persuade up to 95 percent of unhappy customers to buy from you again. Not all customer-initiated contact involves complaints. The same study cited above shows that 50 to 90 percent of all such contacts are requests for information or order placements.[2] Don't let any of these contact opportunities pass you by.

4. Don't Hoard Customer Contact. Don't restrict customer contact to the traditional trench troops because sometimes these people aren't available when the customer comes calling. Anyone who's ever tried to call his or her stockbroker knows full well the irritation of being told that person's tied up and there's not another soul around who knows anything about you. It's an experience that was all too familiar to dealers of WordPerfect Corporation before 1990. Sales representatives for the $531-million business software company were just too hard to get hold of, says Joel Patrick, senior manager of Channel Marketing. "They said, 'Can't you figure out some way to make it easier for us to get in touch with [our rep]?' " A rep assistant program filled the gap. In fact, assistants are usually able to field most dealer calls immediately and, at times, have developed a client rapport greater than the rep's. "Customers love it."

Make connections beyond the customer's front line as well and get yourself known to the movers, shakers, and influencers at all levels in the customer's organization. For instance, in health care, says ServiceMaster's Chuck Stair, your primary contact may be a vice president, who may report to a senior vice president, who takes orders from an executive vice president, and so on up the line. If you hear the story only from your contact level, you might find that person has misinterpreted the decision maker's true wishes and you're history.

The multilevel approach is an integral part of the ServiceMaster strategy. Take the case of a school board in a public education district. Even though the last word on a cleaning supplier rests with board members, usually the business manager gets first right of refusal on any proposal, then onto a superintendent who also needs to feel comfortable with the contract. If it passes inspection here, the school board finally gets a peek. "We have to have relationships with all these people," says Stair. "If the local restaurant owner is on the school board [for example], our manager and spouse are going to be there having dinner once in a while and getting to know that person."

5. Use Research as a Contact Point. In Chapter 3, we highlighted the notion that doing research doesn't just put you in the customer know, it gives you yet another opportunity to build a relationship. One more suggestion on this score. Branch out in your research to hit, and bond with, several levels in your customer's organization. Just such a consideration prompted Xerox Corporation to revamp its survey series, the "Customer Satisfaction Measurement System" (CSMS). "We recognized the need to more accurately capture inputs not only from key operators but from decision makers," explains Peter Waasdorp, business planning manager for Xerox's U.S. Marketing Group.

The new surveys get input from three levels: key operators are queried on equipment reliability and service support; satisfaction with invoicing and billing error correction is the focus for administrators; and decision makers are asked to comment on account and sales support. In total, the company audits a quarter of its customer base, over 55,000 accounts, every three months, rotating survey lists to ensure at least one annual contact per customer.

6. *If You Can't Get Personal, Go for Dialogue.* It isn't always a piece of cake to get your digs into the top levels of your customer's organization. Former president of Ketchum Advertising's New York office, Thomas Miller, can relate to this. "We had cases," he notes, "where, despite all our efforts, we'd had trouble getting to know an account's senior management. That's frustrating because you're very vulnerable when you don't have those relationships." On the advice of an outside consultant who said, "When you can't build a bond, build a dialogue," Ketchum pooled together a number of in-house informational pieces. "The one thing all clients are interested in is useful information," claims Miller.

Grouped by topic (food pieces for the food clients, for example), the material was shipped off to a selective list of reclusive customers, with a covering letter from Miller. In January 1991, unsolicited, the first in a regular mailing to this "President's List" went initially to just five customers. Since then, the roster's been expanded to include another 20.

Control Data's president was one of the first managers on the Ketchum list. "Regular contact with this [man] had been difficult, sporadic at best," recalls Miller. Yet the sending of this material allowed Miller to build a rapport with this client. "He has called me to tell me how much he enjoys receiving it." Control Data's response wasn't limited to words of praise either. The company reinstated a $150,000 advertising program it had abandoned for some time, and Ketchum got the nod. Miller believes the experience with this list underscores an important point: "We underestimated the degree to which clients want to have a dialogue."

A client newsletter, whether it's just a repackage of existing materials like the Ketchum "List" or a more formal affair, is a much overlooked retention aid. At the small accounting firm of Manning

Jamison a bimonthly client newsletter was thought to be mere fluff by staff. Not so in the clients' eyes; in fact, they wanted more. That reaction caught Bob Jamison and his partners off-guard. "We'd actually been thinking of canceling it."

The rules of a good client newsletter are pretty basic. Make sure the content's meaningful, the style readable, and the look attractive. Let customers tell you if you're on track on these. Buttonhole one individual to assume production responsibility while encouraging input from across the organization, as well as from patrons.

7. Anticipate Needs as a Contact Excuse. By being just a bit ahead of the game, the Pittsburgh-based ad agency, Ketchum Advertising, was able to keep, and indeed grow, a large account. In 1985, Ketchum managers sensed some shakiness in their relationship with the company's second largest client, Coty. A low-end mass marketer of fragrances, Coty was, more and more, shopping other agencies for new product ideas. "There were undercurrents; they saw their future in new products," exlains Ketchum's former president Thomas Miller. "The more new product agencies they talked to, the less our chances of hanging onto this business." Since 1980, Ketchum had enjoyed great success promoting existing Coty brands, particularly Lady Stetson, but hadn't ventured into new products. With over $1 million at stake, it was time to change that. "We weren't asked, but we decided we were going to try to get into that part of their business."

Using its own research resources, Ketchum discovered a hole in the fragrance market it believed could be nicely filled by a Coty product. "They were without a brand that appealed to very young ladies," explains Miller. "There's a huge market missed there because girls from 15 to 25 buy truckloads of this stuff. So we made it our business to help them with that niche." An exhaustive competitor analysis and a series of focus groups with these young gals paved the way for a new perfume proposal—"exclamation! Make a statement without saying a word." The idea for the name and theme line came from Ketchum's research. "Young girls buy fragrance to make a statement about themselves; they goob it on to be noticed."

A new company hire, a creative director with expertise in this area, fleshed out the concept, and it was ready to present to Coty's executive. "They just loved it," claims Miller. "We got them excited and they jumped in and began to work with us." A fragrance was created to match the promotion and launched in 1989. Today, exclamation! is the number one–selling fragrance sold through mass merchandisers, such as drug and department store chains. And it totally changed the complexion of Ketchum's relationship with Coty. "It moved us from [being] an existing brand agency to [being] a totally involved supplier."

8. Try Education as a Customer Touchpoint. Inviting customers to an educational forum of some sort offers a subtle opportunity to make contact. Forget the sales pitch, though, that's a sure way to blow the connection. Quad/Graphics' "CAMP/Quad" provides a good example of this. Twice a year, 26 clients from a kaleidoscope of backgrounds attend a two-and-a-half-day introduction to the printing process. "We have six to eight sessions in the spring and the same in the fall," explains Carl Bennett, vice president of Administration.

President Harry V. "Larry" Quadracci starts the sessions off with a brief introduction to Quad/Graphics and an overview of a print operation. That afternoon, attendees are exposed to the "delights" of stripping and platemaking; the next day, it's on to press, and finally finishing. But it is in the evenings that Quad/Graphics staff really get a chance to brush elbows with the customers. A sit-down dinner with the officers of the company forms the usual routine for the first evening, while the second night's a more informal cook-out. "The clients have dinner [the second night] with the people who taught the classes, their customer service reps, and the other managers of the press room."

It's not always the technical people who end up attending CAMP/Quad either; administrative staff such as those in the Accounting department are also on the guest list. This policy has some nice spin-offs, notes Bennett. "In the industry we're involved in, people move from [one] publisher or cataloguer to another. If they had a good experience at CAMP/Quad and then move to [a new company] we're not doing business with, we know we've got someone there who will eventually help us."

9. Keeping In Touch Needn't Take Lots of Time . . . Finding time to touch base with your clients may sound like the impossible dream but it doesn't need to be that way. Michael Corney, a partner with the accounting firm of Manning Jamison, discovered it's mostly a question of taking advantage of contact opportunities placed in his way. The first such happy chance came in the form of a 1991

Canadian regulation that allows individuals to top-up their Registered Retirement Savings Plan, a tax-advantaged retirement vehicle. Eight thousand dollars was the sum in question.

In theory, all working Canadians could take advantage of the change; in practice, though, only a few fortunates had that kind of cash lying about. Of Corney's client list, just six individuals met the bill. A quick memo to each, enclosing a copy of an article covering the details of the pension change, was all it took and six happy clients parted with $48,000.

What the government giveth, though, it also taketh away. Enter the much-maligned Goods and Services Tax (GST), a new consumption tax that came into effect in Canada January 1, 1991. Now, even service and small operations had to be party to taxing the consumer and passing that on to Revenue Canada. Free enterprise lobbyists did manage some concessions, though, including a $1,000 rebate for small businesses. There were strings attached to this miniwindfall (naturally) and applications had to be made before the end of 1991. So, for the first part of that year, Corney, together with his assistant, divided up the clients this affected, phoning between 10 and 20 each month. And, again, it was a phone contact much appreciated by his customers.

10. . . . But It Does Take Process. Just telling managers or employees to get on the blower to customers or to pop over to see them doesn't happen by osmosis—you've got to give the process a shove. "You need to have standard operating procedures that make sure you are communicating and interacting with your customer," believes Anthony Putman, author of *Marketing Your Services*. For companies like Xerox, who make products that last years, it's all too easy to lose touch with customers, particularly the smaller ones, claims James Miller. "These people almost fall out of view if you don't have a conscious program to go back and touch them." That's why Xerox designed the copy cartridge for use in its smaller copiers, mentioned earlier. The cartridge carried a three-year warranty which, on expiration, gave the company a natural in to the customer.

At Miller Business Systems, sales managers are encouraged to touch base with their 25 strategic accounts at least once a quarter. That contact's not left to chance, however. Managers identify their key accounts by volume and strategic market position. Then, four times a year, they're expected to turn in a sheet detailing key account contact including contact names, how any discussions took place, opportunities for new sales, and what, if anything, needs working on. Vice President of Sales and Marketing, Bud Mundt, admits the occasional tweak is necessary to keep these reports rolling in. Still it's been well worth the effort. Against an industry average for retaining important accounts of less than 60 percent, the Miller 96 percent record looks mighty fine.

11. Make Contacts Count. All too often, even when we do get the chance to face off with the customer, we don't really make the contact personal. One of the simplest ways to do this is to use the customer's name during the encounter. At Cooker Corporation restaurants, special incentives and training encourage employees to work guest names into the conversation. Peter Kehayes, Regional Manager, illustrates: "They say, 'Carla, your table is ready,' and to the hostess taking you to your table, it's, 'Please take Carla to her table.' The next time you come in it's, 'Carla, it'll be 15 minutes for your table.' We demonstrate to staff how guest recognition drives up restaurant patronage," continues Kehayes, and as patronage comes in, so do the tips.

The family-style chain also throws a bit of whimsy into the works with its "name games." Front-door hostesses, as well as bartenders, maintain a rotary file, noting customer names in it, with little descriptive notes as memory jogs. "The people who know the most names [in any month] get $1 per name," says Kehayes. For the servers, it's the "Friendly 5s." "If a guest says how friendly they are and they know them by name, they get $5."

Even Cooker managers can get in on the fun. Each store has seven or eight managers, with two or three working at any one time. Every time a guest comes in and is recognized by one of the managers, that person will introduce the guest to another manager on duty. Next time the guest drops in and the second manager can remember the guest's name, a dot is put next to that manager's name on a large race poster. Build up a nice row of dots and you'll soon find yourself across the finish line and a few dollars to the good.

Staff are also taught to "engage the customer," that is, chat a bit to guests as they lead them to the table or bring a meal, making sure to punctuate any dialogue with guest names. This is not just friendliness, or "high woo" as Cooker inmates coin it, but something that can be taught, says Kehayes. This means remembering to walk with and talk to customers as you direct them to a table, rather than silently escorting them, keeping a respectful 10 feet ahead.

If employees aren't engaging their clients, it falls to the manager to coach them back on track, and then, most importantly, to follow-through. If the crew member does respond and begins to chat up customers, the manager should make a big deal out of such efforts. "Hey, you're engaging the customer, that's exactly what I want you to do, that's great" should be the manager's attitude, says Kehayes.

A few dollars might also accompany the pat on the back. Cooker sets aside 0.7 percent of annual sales, about $12,000 per store, for just such crew incentives. Cooker's guests do respond to these recognition programs, averaging two or three visits per week versus a norm of one in six weeks. Not bad for a company that doesn't spend a lick on external advertising. "We don't try to catch one fish with 800 hooks," quips Glenn Cockburn, vice president of Food Services.

12. Keep Costs Down. Keeping tabs on customers can rack up a tidy bill after awhile. With a little help from technology, and some ingenuity, you can keep these costs down, as in the following Marriott story. Every month, Marriott does a newsletter drop to members of its frequent guest program, "Honored Guest Awards."[3] "But with 4.5 million members and growing, we'd soon go broke if we mailed to everyone on the list," says marketing head Roger Dow.

Not all people on the list are active travelers at any given time; after all, schedules and lives do change. So if the hotel chain hasn't seen hide nor hair of you in two months, the computer flags your name and out goes a letter saying, "Dear Carla, where are you?" Still no response and your name is dropped from the list. However, show up at a Marriott property again, any time in the future, and bingo, you're automatically reactivated and receive three mailings. Should you fall off the wagon yet again after this triple set's come and gone, you're back to the deactivation-and-holding pattern.

13. Don't Overdo It. In your zeal to keep in touch with customers, be careful you don't wear out your welcome. It is possible to get too much of a good thing here as elsewhere in life. Some contact efforts can be pretty darn intrusive. According to Michael Patterson, senior vice president of Marketing with USAA's Investment Management Division, "You can't keep battering them; it's offensive and irritating." One tenet of the San Antonio insurer is that customers need protection not just from roving competitors but from the company itself.

Every two years, a USAA survey goes out to customers asking about their marketing channel preferences. Even though over the years the company's toyed with the idea of adding outbound telemarketing to its traditional direct mail communication, it's always been cut off at the pass by customers in this survey. "Consistently, our members come back and say, 'When I want information from you, I'm going to pick up the phone. When you want to tell me something, send me a letter,' " explains USAA Federal Savings Bank marketing boss Daniel Gibbens. And, at any time, members can call and say, "no," to more solicitations on any USAA business line. And that puts an end to the paper trail to that customer's mailbox.

USAA is gung-ho on understanding everything about its customer base, pumping close to $3 million into research every year. Even here, though, the company is careful not to come to the tap too often. "We try to make sure that not more than once every three years will a member get surveyed," says Tim Timmerman, executive director of Corporate Research. A computer tick is placed next to customers selected to receive the company's annual general survey; that gets them off the hook for any other research contact. When it comes to phone surveys, USAA is even more circumspect. "We don't like to call them unannounced," says Timmerman, so a presensitization letter goes out first.

Besides, not all customer contact is profitable. Foremost Insurance Group, for example, found follow-up phone calls to customers receiving its Welcome/Thank-You package (mentioned earlier) didn't result in any significant improvement in awareness. Seventy-two percent of a control group who received neither package nor phone call said they were aware of Foremost. That percentage jumped to 84 percent for the-package-only sample but only edged up to 89 percent for the full treatment (package plus call). "This was not significantly more," says Rebecca Spratlin, vice president of the AARP Business Division. "That told us as a corporation to continue the package but that the telemarketing call on the back end really isn't necessary."

The Practice—Making It Happen, Part II—Step 7

What?

The setup of the second series of People-Powered Retention Teams to tackle specific issues relating to customer contact for Retention Inc.'s best-customer group.

Why?

This is the second building block in the formulation of a predictive model for customer retention introduced in Step 3Fc.

How?

7A. **Homework** assigned to members of the Retention Advisory Group as follows:

    a. "Determine the nature of the best-customer relationship cycle with Retention Inc., i.e., what time period does it span and which part of the cycle is the most critical for retention?"

    b. "Monitor the points of contact along this cycle. Map these out in as much detail as possible. Which of these are company initiated and which client initiated?"

    c. "Learn which customer contact points are the most critical in the customer's evaluation of Retention Inc., i.e., when the customer makes a "Grow, Go, or Status Quo" decision. Analyse what the customer uses to evaluate each contact point and determine how Retention Inc.'s efforts here measure up."

7B. Analysis of best customer research gathered in Step 3 by in-house personnel under the supervision of the Retention Coordinator or an outside consultant. **Objective:** to back up best customer contact research done by Retention Inc. staff in Step 7A.

7C. A participative work session (Workshop 7.1) for the Retention Advisory Group facilitated by an outside consultant with the following **objectives:**

    a. To review homework and company analysis from

Steps 7A and 7B.

b. To select up to four issues for the first People-Powered Retention Teams relating to best-customer contact. **Selection Criteria**—highlighted in Step 4Aa with additional details provided in Step 6Cb. Step 7 teams facilitated by in-house facilitators-in-training under the guidance of outside consultant.

7D. Preparation by an outside consultant or the Retention Coordinator of a summary report of Workshop 7.1 and distribution to all Retention Inc. staff through internal marketing vehicles recommended by the Retention Advisory Group.

7E. Teams selected in Step 7C work through the People-Powered Retention process introduced in Step 4Ad and detailed in Step 6E.

7F. Copies of summary report of team progress made available to all Retention Inc. staff through internal marketing vehicles recommended by the Retention Advisory Group.

When?

Months 10, 11, and 12.

Customer Encounters of the 4th Kind[1]: Keeping Customers through Multiple Relationships, Cross-Selling, and Customer Partnerships

> *A lot of companies talk about service but they also set themselves up in a competitive role with the customer.*
>
> Michael Patterson,
> senior vice president Marketing
> USAA, Investment Management Company

For want of a little relationship bonding, the Pittsburgh-based Ketchum Advertising lost a $15-million client. The advertising agency had acquired this account, along with a number of others, through a 1987 merger with a New York firm, Hick & Greist (H&G). That same year, the new boss at Scherring Co. streamlined its operations and wanted to do the same with its advertising agencies, a group that included Ketchum. When the agency whittling was over, Ketchum was out.

Ketchum might have considered chalking this failure up to the executive shuffle at the Scherring account but for a comment from H&G's ex-president. "It was his observation," says Thomas Miller, former president of Ketchum Advertising in New York, "that we had not really built deep relationships with our clients." With only two contacts at Scherring (and one of those got the boot when the new man arrived), Ketchum had no one rooting for them. The advertiser's work was never in question; that was always deemed top notch. "In the final analysis, I believe we lost that account because the other guys had multiple and top-down relationships with these people."

From that point on, every one of Ketchum's most senior people was assigned a cadre of customers, each level in the Ketchum hierarchy responsible for building personal relationships with counterparts at the account. "That meant social bonds, building friendships, more than just [getting] accolades for good work," explains Miller. This was something many Ketchum managers felt to be the frivolous end of the business. But clients want, and expect, their suppliers to take a personal interest, says Miller. Without these kinds of relationships, you're at a distinct disadvantage, he contends, and illustrates his point with another lost-account story.

In mid-1991, an error in judgment cost the agency the public relations portion of its account with R.D. French Co. Had a strong bond been there, Miller believes, the company would have let the agency off with a slap on the wrist. Instead, Ketchum was shown the door. When push came to shove, there was no one for this client to go to on a personal level and talk the matter out. That's been rectified. "We took immediate steps to correct that right from the top down. The vice chairman [for example] made a point to become close to this client on a personal level." This exemplifies the need to immerse yourselves in a customer's business and organization. "The glory days when you could build an agency on the brilliance of your creativity are gone."

Too true, Mr. Miller; today's competitively beleaguered organizations are opting for fewer and fewer supplier relationships. Xerox cut its production vendor list from 5,000 names in 1982 to just 400 in 1989. And it's not always the designated buyer in a corporation who has the final say about who's on and who's off the bid list. There's many an administrator who has quashed a deal to say nothing of the scores of other employees capable of influencing any decision. So when the music stops, the vendor prize will go to those who've insinuated themselves at all levels in the customer's organization.

In this chapter, we explore ways to tighten your hold on your existing customers using multiple relationships, cross-selling, and customer partnering.

1. Make Your Customer Links Many and Deep . . . Rural/Metro's Clint Vardeman explains the importance of this concept using the example of his company's typical hospital account. I can take the hospital administrator to lunch, he says, and talk about Rural/Metro's great response time on emergency transports but, when it comes to a decision about who to call for an ambulance, the staff floor nurse at the hospital calls the shots (no pun intended), not the administrator. And it's the company's paramedics who see the nursing staff day-in and day-out, not Vardeman or any other manager. "These are the guys who are going to make the difference."

2. . . . But Get Rid of Any Go-Betweens if You Can . . . Watch that your multiple links to the customer don't mushroom into a bureaucratic nightmare. At the Defense Logistics Agency (DLA), a U.S. government group, they're careful not to have the unit's marketing and customer contact people act as go-betweens, or more accurately, bottlenecks, claims Mary Albright, associate director. "We want direct contact between our employees and the customer." That way, customers have access to immediate information and the first-hand customer contact gives agency staff greater commitment to the project's success.

There's no need for a string of middlepeople between the customer and the person in your organization actually doing the job, insists Jim Rudek, sales manager at Quad/Graphics. "Rather than have [a customer's] mailing person deal through the print buyer, through me, and [then] through the printer, we hook up that mailing person on their end with our mailing experts [directly]. I've got a number of customers where there might be seven or eight different people on the customer's end dealing with seven or eight of our people here."

All of which is great for business, he maintains, offering the following example. Recently, a new president arrived on the scene at one of Quad/Graphics' best catalogue customers. A new leader likes to make changes and this fellow was no exception. He soon had the Quad/Graphics' contract on the block. Fortunately, the print shop's influence at this company ran long and deep. "There were 30 people in [his] advertising department who let [him] know in no uncertain terms that they did not want to explore [using] a different printer." And that was the end of that.

Quad/Graphics also pays particular attention to making sure the sales and marketing team doesn't control a customer relationship. "Our job in Sales is missionary, we preach the gospel," says Rudek. But once a client's on the hook, it's the salesperson's job to wed the customer's functional staff to their counterparts at Quad/Graphics. "We take their people and our people and have that second and third echelon bond. Once the sale is made, we back away and allow [those people] to build relationships."

These multiple-level customer links could be interpreted as management muscling in on front-line territory, or worse, as a lack of trust in the abilities of the sales executive. Not if the concept's handled well, claims Kathryn Gressett, marketing director at Miller Business Systems. The company typically parcels out key accounts to its top executives, which the sales contacts recognize as a good thing, she contends. "It's not done on an adversarial [basis]." In fact, the sales staff welcome the input with a certain measure of relief. "There's somebody who can be a sounding board for them if they're having a problem, somebody who has a vested interest in the account."

3. *. . . And Build Employee Commitment in the Bargain.* A direct route to the customer does wonders for retention ("there's less of a communications gap," says Rudek at Quad/Graphics) but it also keeps employees on their toes, claims colleague Ron Nash, customer service rep manager. "The people in the plant get to know the customer and the business; hence, they do a better job because they have some personal stake in it."

4. *Begin As You'd Like to Continue.* If you can get your tentacles into your customers' lives and organizations right off the bat, you make it awfully difficult for them to jump ship when a competitor comes calling. "Retention really begins before the marketing process is kicked off," insists Rebecca Spratlin, vice president at Foremost Insurance Group, a Michigan company specializing in insur-

ance for mobile-home owners. Jim Rudek at Quad/Graphics agrees, "We know if we can sell them on these terms, we'll keep them."

DLA also believes in putting your best foot forward from the start. A bungled attempt at designing a series of training tapes for a departmental client taught DLA the value of multiple relationships with any one customer.[2] The agency is now careful to set up introductions between functional people on both sides of the negotiation right from the beginning. "It's a let's-have-my-people-meet-your-people kind of thing," says Bernard Lukco, program manager. For example, in developing an orientation tape in 1991 for a newly formed Defense group, the Defense Contract Management Command, a joint committee of operational representatives from both organizations met well before the work contract was ever signed.

5. Create Customer Dependency Through Involvement. . . The involved customer is the renewal customer, insists Jack Bobo, CEO of the National Association of Life Underwriters (NALU). Vice president of Public Relations Denise Patton echoes his thought: "If we can get members interested in [our] activities and what we, as an association, are doing, they'll hang in there." The NALU takes involvement very seriously as a result. "If I were to look at one single aspect of our thrust that's the most effective," says Bobo, "it would be the fact that we do engage large numbers of people in all our activities, typically [between] 50,000 and 75,000." He lists a few examples: "We have about 30,000 people involved in our legislative advocacy program; 10,000 in public relations, 20,000 in a public service program each year, 450 in our committee structure, [and] our membership department also involves about 10,000 people in a typical annual drive."

• *The earlier the better.* The most fragile point of any customer/company relationship comes early on, so any customer involvement strategy works best if it's started immediately. All this is particularly apt for the first-time NALU member, for example, says CEO Jack Bobo. "[If] we can get them to renew once, we pretty much have them as long as they're in the business." That's why the association's put together a program it calls "The Rising Star Program." Matthew Gertzog, assistant vice president of Administration and Board Liason, elaborates: "The idea behind the Rising Star is that the early time is crucial for our survival as an association. We want those people involved, we want them to grow with [us], so this program is a hand-holding [by existing members] through your first year with the association. What the oldtimers will be doing is sharing their thoughts on the association with the people who are new."

This kind of strategy can work for other organizations as well. The Marriott hotel chain has involved customers in educational forums, with executive think-tanks, and on product design teams. It's kept them involved, and loyal, claims Roger Dow, Marriott's marketing top gun. "Who do you think they're going to call when they book their next meeting?" Just one anecdote from the Marriott annals should suffice to support this point.

From its regular customer forums, hotel management had heard the same refrain again and again—"Clean up that ruddy invoice of yours, we can't make heads or tails of it." "They'd get so overwhelmed," says Dow, "they would let the [bill] sit for four or five weeks; 'I'll tackle this mess when I have some free time,' they'd say." We listened, then brought in customers as part of an action team to solve the problem. 'What exactly gets your goat about this process?' was the first question put to the team. "Sounds silly," Dow admits, but it all came down to some basic reorganization, starting with the paper size. "We [had] big pages, little pages, receipts; [we'd] clip them all together, put a total on and send it."

Everything is now 8 1/2" × 11" and nicely ordered. The total comes first, then subtotals for each portion are grouped with the relevant receipts. For example, "all the room folios are clipped together, the same paper size, all in alphabetical order—Ms. Able, Mr. Bear, Dr. Johnson." Customers are ecstatic about the new package, claims Dow; they finally have a bill they can read and understand quickly. It's also had a positive impact on Marriott's accounts receivable. "Not only is it making our customers happy but we get our money faster."

6. *. . . And Shared Processes Too.* Create customer reliance by sharing more than just your people and your time. Miller Business Systems has created what it calls a "stockless account." That means customers need no longer clutter up their storerooms with vast amounts of letterhead or paperclips. All their supplies are housed instead at Miller's warehouse and are just a phone call away. Such an arrangement frees up a nice chunk of change for the customer, but it also creates those ties that bind. "The buyer has a vested interest in having a strong partnership with us," explains Kathryn

Gressett, marketing director, "because it would be a real fiasco if they had to give up this supply room."

7. Cement the Customer Bond by Cross-Marketing. Research shows the more products or services a customer obtains from your organization, the more committed he or she is to staying with you over the long term. If customers have one product with a bank, for example, there's a 15 percent likelihood they'll stay loyal for five years. With two products, that rises to 45 percent; with three, it's up to 90 percent. Service consultant Laura Liswood calls this the "glue" of cross-selling.[3] It only makes sense when you consider the bother involved in pulling up stakes with a current supplier and moving on to a new one. Most customers opt for that course only if the existing relationship has soured or when there's a minimum of baggage to drag along. And therein lies the secret to the power of cross-marketing.

Although it seems such an obvious strategy, cross-marketing isn't practiced all that consistently by most organizations. For example, at Packaging Corporation of America (PCA), even its best customers don't usually buy from more than one of the company's five divisions, which produce corrugated containers, paperboard, aluminum, plastic, and molded fiber packaging for corporate America.[4] And this rather cavalier attitude to cross-marketing isn't limited to the manufacturing industry. Seventy-five percent of mortgage customers at any bank, savings and loan, or credit union in the U.S., for example, do no other business at that institution.[5]

Most importantly, marketing additional products and services to your existing customers isn't going to tick them off, if you do it professionally. In fact, it's something they'd wish you'd do more often. Clients of accountants Manning Jamison wanted more proactive cross-marketing from the firm. They wanted us to let them know when it was time to add more services, says partner Michael Corney. A survey of U.S. financial consumers revealed that 92 percent of those who had been solicited over the phone by their financial institution found the experience helpful.[6] For a similar direct marketing test, 46 percent actually purchased the product in question.[7]

Let's look at a few aspects of an effective cross-marketing strategy.

7a. Get Your Sales Force Onside. Any cross-marketing efforts that don't have solid support from the sales and marketing units soon sputter out and die. Even though everyone's supposed to be working for the common organizational good, it doesn't really come naturally to do so. Sales staff from one unit probably give little thought to asking questions about a customer's needs for other areas, that is, "unless it hits them between the eyes," laments Chuck Curlett, a regional vice president for PHH, a 44-year-old company that provides vehicle, facilities, and relocation services to *Fortune 2,000* corporations.[8] There are a few tricks to getting your sales staff to buy into cross-marketing:

• *Communicate, communicate, communicate.* To be able to effectively market all the company's products to their customers, your sales staff need to know what's going on elsewhere in the company. Consider regular get-acquainted sessions for salespeople from different units and use in-house organs to keep everyone up-to-date. Maryland-based PHH (originally Peterson, Howell & Heather) relays news about its "Sharing Leads to New Business" program in "PHH Marketplace," a newsletter that goes to all sales, account management, and marketing personnel.[9] PCA boosts interdepartmental communication through bimonthly confabs among "national account/synergy coordinators," high-level managers from the company's five main business groups, from research and development, and from the PCA technical center.[10]

• *Make it worth their while.* Salespeople value their customers and might get testy if they suspect these relationships may be in jeopardy. The challenge, contends Bram Bluestein, vice president at A.T. Kearney Inc., a Chicago-based consulting firm, is to make cross-marketing a win-win scenario for each unit within an organization.[11] Sales reps at PHH, for example, collect a $250 cash bonus if any leads they've qualified for other company units convert into new business. A computer printout keeps reps posted on lead status every two weeks.[12] At PCA, recognition, not reward, motivates the company's lead salespeople who are responsible for marketing the full spectrum of company products to 25 key accounts.[13]

• *Make it easy.* Don't make it tough for sales personnel to do right in the cross-marketing department. Under its "Sharing Leads" program, PHH supplies sales reps and account managers with an easy-to-use booklet that sets up lead qualification questions for all company groups. The booklet also contains duplicate-copy forms called "PHHootprints." The reps keep one copy of the PHHootprint; the other's sent off to Marketing, which passes it on to the right operating unit. The program generated 150 leads and eight new contracts in its first five months. Vice president of Marketing Gene Arbaugh expects the program to bring in an additional $1 million in annual revenue.[14]

7b. But Don't Neglect Your Non-Sales-Contact Staff. San Antonio Savings Association, a U.S. savings and loan, hadn't seen a $600,000-plus goldmine that was right under their noses. Three-quarters of San Antonio's most creditworthy customers, its mortgage holders, were single-product users. Some calculations by marketing manager Russell Cobler unearthed nearly $170 million in potential business. "Now, I'm not greedy," he insists, "so I don't expect to get all these single users to convert over to being multiple users. I'd happily settle for just 10 percent!"

Interviewing these reticient patrons to learn why they limited their dealings with San Antonio was Cobler's next move. He recalls his frustration with their reason. Nobody had ever mentioned that there were other products to be had from the Texas institution. "They thought we were just a mortgage-type company even though we have more branches around than anybody else. I was sitting behind a two-way mirror (during the focus interviews) and I wanted to leap up and shout, 'No, that's not right.' But that is what they think and therefore, that is how it is."

Most of the 13,800 customers in question hadn't seen the inside of a branch since they'd signed up; they just pop their monthly mortgage checks in the mail. Contact was accomplished through a series of direct mailers offering preapproved lines of credit, home-improvement loans, and free checking accounts, resulting in balances of $600,000 from just one mailing.

The company's careful with new mortgage customers not to repeat its previous mistake of being too tight-lipped about the rest of its product line. Customer-service reps are now trained to phone clients with mortgage approval confirmations, taking the opportunity then to suggest related services, such as mortgage cancellation insurance. This simple exercise of getting staff to ask for the business has been a solid success. "In the first 60 days this was in place, 1,100 of our 1,400 new mortgage loans brought in an average of two additional services."[15]

7c. Use Your Computer to Trigger Cross-Marketing Opportunities. This assumes you've built up a solid Customer Information File (CIF) system that integrates all information on any one customer into a single record (see Chapter 3). Once in place, the CIF can be used to pinpoint individuals or groups within your client base who'd be most receptive to a particular product or service offering. Two CIF triggers are most common: a transactional event such as the maturity of a customer's term deposit, or an event in a client's life, such as turning age sixty-five.

7d. Communicate Your Cross-Marketing Message to Customers. Don't forget to let your customer in on the good news about cross-marketing. At PCA, George Bayly, vice president of Marketing and architect of the company's national account program, promotes PCA division synergies in meetings with top brass at the 25 key accounts in the program. The national account program makes it "much more difficult to dislodge us," explains Bayly, who expects the program to result in an annual growth rate of at least 10 percent in key account sales. In 1987, those customers accounted for 20 percent of the company's $1.2-billion revenue.[16]

8. Put Customers on Your Team. More and more these days, companies are seeing their clients not as simple cash cows and profit plumpers but as partners, reliant on one another for success. Benson Shapiro, a marketing professor at Harvard Business School, calls this "strategic partnering" or "close encounters of the fourth kind."[17] Some suggestions follow on how such a collaboration might evolve.

8a. Remember the Obvious Link—Market Research . . . A quick revisit to our old friend and customer-contact opportunity extraordinaire, market research, with an illustration from IBM Canada. For the last four years, managers at the Toronto-based subsidiary of IBM Corporation have relied on feedback from user advisory councils to shift the company's attention from itself to its customers. As with a jury, council members number 12, serve for a specific time period, usually one or two years, and pass judgment on IBM schemes and dreams. The company's entire customer satisfaction survey, for example, was designed in partnership with council participants. "We went to [them] and said, 'Here's what the market research folks told us were the priority things we should be trying to measure. What do you think?' " explains Lee Kea, formerly IBM Canada's director of strategy and business management.

The company also uses its own technology to pick council member brains. A system called a "decision support centre" allows customers to vote electronically on what's tops on their IBM hit lists. For senior executives at a 1991 advisory council, the clear favorite was the need for the company to improve on partnership. "Don't be so standoffish," they said, "Get more involved in our business." "It was unanimous," says Kea. IBM Canada had been experimenting with joint ventures up to this point; to customers, however, this was just the tip of the iceberg. "Work *with* us, not just *for* us; share the risks as well as the rewards or do without either."

IBM took these words to heart, says Kea, illustrating with the following anecdote about a banking customer. To allow him to make better decisions, the client needed a certain turnaround on information from his computer system. A mutually dependent arrangement was struck. "If we exceed the [agreed] timeframe, he pays us a premium. If we don't meet the objectives, however, we pay."

8b. . . . But Go Beyond the Obvious. Don't just ask customers for their input on product design, for example; involve them directly, like Quad/Graphics did recently with a cataloguer located in Colorado Springs who wanted to make its direct mailings a more targeted affair. But that meant mixing and matching the company's catalog and eight different knickknacks to produce four unique bundles, each bound for a different target audience.

When the customer first came to Quad/Graphics with this dilemma, administrative vice president Carl Bennett admits the company was stumped. "We didn't know how to do this." But working in tandem, Quad/Graphics and the customer soon had the riddle solved. Each mix of mail is assigned one of four bar codes, then matched to a particular name and address. As individual address labels are printed, an electric eye reads the bar codes. That's the trigger to fire the appropriate packet of goodies into "polybags." The label's affixed to the bag and it's ready to roll. It seems a bit like smoke and mirrors but it's just progress. And it's been a tool Quad/Graphics has since been able to sell to other clients.

8c. Get Customers to Work for You. In the typical customer/ supplier relationship, the supplier labors for the customer and gets paid in the process, a one-sided working arrangement. A pox on such arbitrary distinctions. Get customers to work for you, and for themselves in the bargain. We're not talking revolution here; after all, ATMs and self-serve gas pumps already dot the commercial landscape. Putting clients on the job can be as simple as getting them to opt for choices that make life easier for you, and ultimately, for them. A perfect example: Delta Hotels & Resorts' daily guest-room newsletter.

Weekends are guaranteed horror shows for most hotels. A Delta hotel, for example, can have upwards of 1,300 customers all clamoring to go home at once. A brief word to the wise on the convenience of video checkouts in the newsletter and that's down 20 percent, says Carel Folkersman, vice president and general manager of the Delta Chelsea Inn in downtown Toronto. Reference in the newsletter to a free extended checkout on Sunday can also ease the mass exodus that morning by as much as 15 percent.

8d. Make Customers Part of the Appraisal Process. If you're really serious about measuring how well your people please customers and you want to keep close tabs on them as well, consider a less circuitous route than the typical satisfaction survey allows. On the corporate side of First Chicago Bank's business, customers like General Motors are asked if they'd like a whack at filling out an appraisal form on the service reps dedicated to their account. Usually clients react favorably, contends Aleta Holub, the bank's vice president of quality assurance. "It's a labor of love for [most of] them."

Admittedly, there are a few who take a dim view of the offer. "They say, 'You've got to be kidding. I have 40 of these to do on my own people that I never get done on time and now you want me to do yours too.' " These folks aren't bothered again. "You make a note in the file that you don't ask them again," says Holub, and look for alternate ways to get some direct input, like a telephone survey. "We want to ensure customers do report cards on us," she says, "that's what keeps them close to us. You can't keep something you are distant from."

8e. Put Customers on the Sales Team . . . Some of your best sales-people are your customers, contends Gary Cartwright, administrative plant manager with Quad/Graphics. This is something his company takes full advantage of. Customers, and prospects, en route to printing trade shows are invited to a Quad/Graphics hospitality suite aboard the company's three-car train, the "Silver/ Rail." On one such occasion, a group of loyal Quad/Graphics clients were up in the dome car playing poker with a handful of noncustomers. The table chatter eventually came around to the subject of printing. "One customer suddenly realized the fellow sitting across from him wasn't a Quad/Graphics customer," says Cartwright. " 'Why not?' he asked, 'What's the matter with you?' He did more selling [right there] than we could have done in months."

Another Quad/Graphics manager, David Bray, adds his tale of the customer as PR and sales agent. Staff at a small account of his, *Spy Magazine*, put in a particularly good word on his behalf with another publication, a bimonthly out of Minneosta called *The Utne Reader*. "They told me point blank that *Spy* gave us a glowing recommendation and that was instrumental in their decision to come here."

8f. . . . Even if They're Not There in the Flesh . . . Your customers don't even have to *be there* to play the role of advocate. Michael Corney at Manning Jamison (MJ) used a customer videotape to convince an existing client, who'd put its audit up for grabs, to stay the course with his accounting firm. The tape was a record of a customer research session commissioned a few months earlier. Participants in this focus group had a good many nice things to say about MJ, and about Corney. "I thought it would make a powerful tool. So I sent along a copy with the new [audit] proposal." This was accepted and still brings a fee of $12,000 into the company every year.

8g. . . . And Reward Their Efforts. At Lee Valley Tools, an Ontario-based mail-order and retail outlet for woodworking tools, customers are rewarded when they spot a problem or come up with a new design. President and owner Leonard Lee sketches the story. A customer came into the Ottawa outlet one day to return a device called a "honing guide." "The little cam roller on [the guide] wouldn't turn," recalls Lee. "As soon as I saw it I knew what was wrong."

Unfortunately, this was not an isolated incident; the four-store firm had over 1,400 guides in the hands of dealers across the U.S. and Europe. Calls to the manufacturer requesting replacements and to the dealers for returns nipped the crisis in the bud. "If those

1,400 honing guides had gone out to customers from our dealers, we would have been in deep trouble," admits Lee. That customer saved the company a lot of money and aggravation, a favor that hasn't been overlooked. "[He's] getting $100 worth of products as a gift." This isn't generosity, insists Lee. "It's self-serving."[18]

9. *Encourage Customer Referrals.* Employees are notoriously skittish about asking for referrals. But done well, referral marketing can really put you in line for substantial business. It doesn't hurt to encourage client referrals through some kind of incentive. For example, Au Bon Pain, an operator of 82 quick-service French bakery cafes, gets its existing walk-in customers to recommend potential targets for the bakery's catering business. Notes advertising and promotions manager, Leslie Burns, "If [customers] refer us to another customer, they get a free lunch at Au Bon Pain." Just one of the ideas Burns has been using over the last few years to drum up more catered customers. It's been working too, she says, pointing to an increase in weekly sales of over $10,000 in less than one year.

10. *Partner Up with Your "Middlemen". . .* On route to the end user many organizations cross paths with agents, dealers, and suppliers. Building partnerships here is every bit as important as partnering with patrons if we want that ultimate customer for keeps. A major dilemma for any insurance company, for example, is to keep independent agents from defecting to the competition, taking their clients with them. Weave a tight web about them at the beginning, suggests a Foremost Insurance Group senior vice president, which is precisely what his corporation did when it successfully lobbied for an endorsement by the Federation of Mobile Home Owners (FMO) in Florida.

Part of the deal struck with the Federation was an exclusive right to place an ad in the association's monthly magazine listing the Foremost/FMO agents. These lucky few could also tour the mobile home parks promoting themselves under the auspices of the association's good name. They knew that if they didn't continue to send business Foremost's way, they'd lose that access.

We're talking paradigm shift in the way we think of our distribution channels, insists Barbara Langdon, a marketing manager with Digital Equipment Corporation. Traditionally, her company viewed its channels as mere carriers of Digital product and the "more of that product they carried, the happier we were. But now we need to work our minds around the idea of them as partners," she contends, "who help us provide computer solutions for end users. [The question becomes] 'How are we going to form relationships with [them] in order to satisfy the end customer?' "

A channel is more valuable to Digital if it brings more to the party with the customer and should be compensated accordingly. In the past, volume discounting was the norm; Digital's reworking that strategy toward a value base. Langdon elaborates: "The more blocks in the chain [to the end user] or the more needs that are satisfied by that third party, the higher our discount."

11. . . . But Keep Their Numbers Down. It's tough to make a go of any one relationship if you've got many on the string, so when it comes to suppliers, keep your numbers few and your bonds strong. In the face of major Japanese competition in the early 1980s, Xerox Corporation, for example, revised its entire approach to suppliers along these lines. There are two key tenets to the new strategy. First: lose that adversarial relationship with suppliers. Don't beat the heck out of them 'til the price comes down; that's counterproductive. Second: focus and foster; that is, cut the supplier roster and promote strong bonds with the few remaining.

Xerox's 1982 stable of 5,000 vendors has been trimmed to less than 400 today. For electronic components, 80 percent of the company's business now rests with only 10 or 12 suppliers. Getting that supplier base down was essential, insists James Sierk, vice president of the quality office for development and manufacturing. "We decided we should be important enough to every one of [our suppliers]—one of their top five to be exact—so they can afford to do things for us," things like early design involvement and Just-in-Time (JIT), an inventory management system.

But in 1982, few of its suppliers had any inkling of what Sierk was talking about so it fell to Xerox to enlighten them. That happened through training, offered free of charge to quality managers, engineers, and manufacturing managers at supplier shops. With the training course under its belt, a vendor could then be certified by Xerox for provision of a specific part.

The result was a dramatic rise in parts quality. A Xerox defects average of 10,000 parts per million (ppm) in 1982 plunged to less than 200 in 1989. But not for all company components, unfortunately. For certain high-tech items, the numbers don't measure up quite so impressively. For subassemblies, for example, the fallout rate is between 2,000 and 3,000 ppm, down from 10,000 in the early 1980s, but still a far cry from the Xerox benchmark of 125 ppm.

This change in attitude toward supplier partnerships has altered the purchasing role at Xerox forever. In 1980, says Sierk, the lobby outside the Purchasing Department was regularly mobbed by salespeople, anxious to ply their wares to Xerox buyers. Now that no one gets on the Xerox supplier list through cold calls, that's all changed. Purchasing is part of the new product development team, which includes a Xerox design engineer, and quality and technical experts from the supplier side. That early vendor development means better quality for the end customer, claims Sierk.

The Practice—Making It Happen, Part II—Step 8

What?

The setup of the next series of People-Powered Retention Teams to tackle specific issues relating to customer bonding for Retention Inc.'s best customer group.

Why?

This is the third building block in the formulation of a predictive model for customer retention introduced in Step 3Fc.

How?

8A. **Homework** assigned to members of the Retention Advisory Group as follows:
   a. "Evaluate the effectiveness of best-customer bonding opportunities currently being used at Retention Inc., i.e., what's being done about referrals or cross-selling?"
   b. "Consider additions and subtractions to current best-customer bonding techniques at Retention Inc. Which should be attempted first and why?"

8B. Analysis of best-customer research gathered in Step 3 by in-house personnel under the supervision of the Retention Coordinator or an outside consultant. **Objective:** to back up best-customer bonding research done by Retention Inc. staff in Step 8A.

8C. A participative work session (Workshop 8.1) for the Retention Advisory Group facilitated by an outside consultant with the following **objectives:**
  a. To review homework and company analysis from Steps 8A and 8B.
  b. To select up to four issues for the next People-Powered Retention Teams relating to best-customer bonding. **Selection Criteria:** highlighted in Step 4Aa with additional details provided in Step 6Cb. Step 8 teams facilitated by in-house facilitators-in-training with supportive backup from outside consultant.

8D. Preparation by an outside consultant or the Retention Coordinator of a summary report of Workshop 8.1 and distribution to all Retention Inc. staff through internal marketing vehicles recommended by the Retention Advisory Group.

8E. Teams selected in Step 8C work through the People-Powered Retention process introduced in Step 4Ad and detailed in Step 6E.

8F. Preparation by an outside consultant or the Retention Coordinator of a summary report of team progress, and its distribution to all Retention Inc. staff through internal marketing vehicles recommended by the Retention Advisory Group.

When?

Months 13, 14, and 15.

PART III
Organizational Integration

Lead, Follow, or Get Out of the Way: Translating the Customer Retention Model into Management Action

Example is leadership.[1]

Albert Schweitzer

*E*ver hear the one about the singing vice president? Well you're about to. In the summer of 1989, BellSouth Mobility, part of BellSouth Cellular Corp., the $1.7-billion cellular phone subsidiary of BellSouth Corporation, committed itself to a customer satisfaction guarantee (see Chapter 2). As part of the guarantee's publicity, the company's Region 2 vice president wrote an article for a quarterly publication distributed to BellSouth customers. He told them, "I'm here and available, call or write if you have a problem," and one Atlanta client took him up on it. The message came across loud and clear. The company had repeatedly sent bills to the wrong address so the customer was not getting them on a timely basis. What he did receive were phone calls from the collection department. He was not a happy customer.

At first blush perhaps a minor problem, but one that could easily mushroom, and a wonderful opportunity to really tighten the company's grip on this customer's loyalty. Why wait until the customer's threatened disconnect before the company acts?

Enter the singing telegram, an apologetic jingle composed just for this occasion and delivered in person by the vice president at the customer's office—"along with a letter of regret and some credit for the error," adds Dilg. "The customer was just bowled over."

That singing telegram did more for internalizing the guarantee concept with employees than any number of memos from the executive floor, insists Annette Loper, manager, Strategic Market Planning. "It was a good use of his time because it did more to solidify what the guarantee meant than a lot of talking could do; this kind of top-down thing 'speaks' volumes."

Mobilizing an organization for the customer retention battle, says Early Davis, BellSouth Mobility's director of customer operations, Region 2, takes overt management commitment, such as was demonstrated by his executive. "The top people . . . have to believe and not just talk the talk but walk the talk." You can't delegate customer care, insists the president of West Paces Medical Center, Chip Caldwell. Too many organizations, he says, try to foist this responsibility onto one specialized department. "There are four or five people who work down there and they study records and look through stuff; the administrator doesn't have the faintest idea what any of those reports say."

Even worse, the upper echelons at most U.S. corporations won't own up to their share of the blame when customer retention takes a dive. They'd rather point the finger elsewhere, as a 1990 Gallup poll commissioned by the international consulting firm of Philip Crosby Associates (PCA) confirms. Forty-three percent of the 401 CEOs surveyed believed inadequate worker skills was at the heart of the problem with 41 percent pointing to lack of employee commitment as the villian of the piece. And a startling 61.7 percent didn't see lack of attention on their part as a roadblock. Nor did they believe that pressure to make a buck in the short run got in the way; 70 percent dismissed this idea outright.

Get a grip, says PCA president Larry Arrington. "When executives look only to the workforce or only react to individual disgruntled customers, they are ignoring the fact that the real problem most likely rests somewhere back up the line, perhaps too close to senior management for comfort."[2] That's certainly true for the banking world, claims an executive vice president at a U.S. savings & loan. "It's a common belief that bank's problems of [customer] quality are caused by workers. In reality, 80 percent are caused by management."

Let's consider a few ideas about managers as hands-on leaders.

1. Flatten the Hierarchy.   Bill Grove, manager/advocate at the Milwaukee firm of Quad/Graphics, believes you need to eliminate management layers until there's just one level—"the people who get the job done." The actual structure at the printing firm contains two strata: teachers and employees. "Once you become a teacher of others," explains manager of Sales Jim Rudek, "you're a manager." No one is being supervised; everyone is responsible for his or her own actions. "You run until someone snaps back your leash," says Grove.

This is not a style of management that's comfortable for either side in most institutions. It's tough for managers to relinquish control but it's also tough for some employees to accept the reins of responsibility. The no-control Quad/Graphics style is an unsettling concept for some, admits Gary Cartwright, administrative plant manager. "The concept of giving up control and letting people do what they do best is very frightening to a professional manager." But it's a style of operation that sits well with this company. Carl Bennett, vice president, Administration, points to the company's phenomenal growth in recent years. "When I started 14 years ago, Quad/Graphics had 100 employees and sales of $10 million. The year ending 1992 we did about $500+ million in sales and we had 6,000 employees."

2. Get Off Your Duffs.   Probably the best way for managers to express firm commitment to customers for keeps is to get off mahogany row and talk to the people on the front line, says Chip Bell, trainer, consultant, and author of *Managing Knock Your Socks Off Service.* "I asked a CEO recently," he adds, "to tell me the last time he'd spent one hour one-on-one with an employee more than two levels below him, or for that matter, with a customer. He sat in his chair and said, 'You're absolutely right, it's been two years since I've done either of those.' " So how could he, or any other executive with the same track record, hope to know anything at all about what's really going on? "Get out of your office and sit and talk with them," counsels Bell. "Prop your feet up on [an employee's] desk [or] have lunch with your customer."

Caldwell at West Paces is just one of many company presidents highlighted in this chapter who has heeded such advice. At the outset of the hospital's customer quality initiative, the "Quality

Improvement Council" (QIC), a staff group spearheading the program, made it clear that Caldwell had to be very visible. "They insisted I spend two hours with every department on every shift, even weekends. It took me four months to go through that and halfway, I said, 'Man, I'm burned out. Somebody else needs to share the load.' The QIC was adamant, 'If it's not you, it sends the wrong message.' "

Caldwell continues to spend 20 percent of his working week enhancing the customer culture in his organization. For an hour and 45 minutes every 14 days, for example, he pitches the service line to new recruits at employee orientation sessions. "There isn't anything more important for the 1,200 employees and 600 physicians who work here [than] to know what their role in improving quality is and that starts with me."

At Northwestern Mutual Life, a $40-billion life insurance company headquartered in Milwaukee, Wisconsin, they're so serious about executive involvement that a year is set aside for the president-elect to get acquainted with the grass roots. His primary responsibility for that year, explains CEO Donald Schuenke, is to travel the countryside, visiting the company's agencies and learning more about the operation and the agents.

But presidential involvement doesn't end when this first year's over. A president's roundtable is convened each quarter with a random selection of 20 home-office staff. A human resources representative keeps track of anything said in this forum that the president needs to follow through on. Scheunke recalls one change that came about as a result of his participation in one of these sessions. The employee suggestion program wasn't working. There was so much process involved in approving ideas that people lost interest. "We changed that."

Consider copying the "adopt-a-zone" program that AT&T has going. Senior marketing managers at the $38.8-billion telecommunications giant each have an "adopted zone" or office, like Kansas City for Janice Colby, division manager for Consumer Market Management. "We establish a relationship with these folks and act as their headquarters ombudsman and general source of information," she explains. Fellow manager Gigi Neff says this form of adoption gets communication going in both directions. "It's like, 'What's hot in the field, what's hot at headquarters?' "

An idea to upgrade the company's "Reach Out® America" long-distance program came through this venue, says Neff. There are a whole host of AT&T customers who live in the north for part of the year and travel south in the winter. "We were charging these 'snow birds' twice for installation of our service," she points out, once at each location. Once we heard about the problem through our adopted zone program, we filed a special tariff to recognize the (unique) dynamics of this set of customers—to allow us to charge them only once.

3. Stand Shoulder-to-Shoulder With Your Staff. "You lead by how you act," insists Lexus vice president and general manager J. Davis Illingworth. "I expect everyone in the division to phone one customer each week, and I don't exempt myself from this assignment. It certainly wouldn't work for me to tell everybody else to call customers if I don't do it myself. You have to do what you ask your people to do; if you're not willing, they won't be."

At BellSouth Mobility, they follow a similar path. Wherever possible, managers take a turn working alongside their employees. "One of their most effective methodologies is to have managers sit in a customer service rep's chair for a day or a week, make them interact with the customer on a daily basis, let them listen to the complaints, see the obstacles," says Early Davis.

"As part of our management by objectives program," adds Annette Loper, part of BellSouth Cellular Corp.'s Strategic Market Planning department, "it is our responsibility as managers to spend a certain amount of time each year doing something outside our immediate job functions. One year, for example, I rode with our service van driver for a full day. I got a flavor of what he goes through driving from one end of Atlanta metro to the other, stopping with individual customers, watching him diagnose the equipment, perform the repair, back on the van [and] on to the next one."

It's only through this kind of hands-on involvement that a manager can ever begin to understand what it's like for the people on the front line, she insists; it won't happen hiding behind a desk in your office. At BellSouth, "this is seen as part of the manager's job."

4. Make Time for the Customer . . . To really understand your customers so you can keep them coming back, you need to talk to them, face to face. To keep its senior folks in touch with customers, Miller Business Systems parcels off strategic accounts to top executives. "We don't want to lose a key account and then find out that nobody in management darkened their door for a year and a half," says president Mike Miller. "That can happen when you get busy."

Several years ago, one of his major assigned accounts in Dallas had a problem with a company sales rep. The people there called Miller and said, "We know where you're coming from, but this guy's from a different planet. Get us someone new." "I was able to change the rep and keep the business," says Miller. "That wouldn't have happened had they not known Mike Miller; that account would have been gone."

Executive closeness to the customer can also be a powerful tool to convince the powers-that-be of the importance of marketing for keeps. These people have got to face off with the customer at some point, insists quality assurance manager Aleta Holub at First Chicago Bank, or they'll never be convinced. That was definitely the case when the bank began its customer quality journey in the early eighties.

"Our culture then," Holub explains, "was such that if we'd hired outsiders to research our customers and the answers that came back pleased our managers, they'd say, 'Yep, see, look at that.' If they didn't like what they heard, they'd have said, 'Those people aren't bankers, they just didn't ask the right questions.' When you're sitting face-to-face with customers and you can see the glint in their eyes, somehow that experience sticks with you more than some data in a presentation."

Now, the bigwigs at First Chicago are expected to keep tabs on a batch of important accounts—twenty each, to be exact. They act as "senior relationship managers" to such customers as General Motors (GM) and attend monthly meetings with "client service teams" for each product or service that GM might purchase from the bank.

5. . . . *Even if it Means Reworking the Structure.*   To get its managers closer to the customer, Ketchum Advertising of Pittsburgh, Pennsylvania, went so far as to create an entirely new client service structure. Traditionally, says Michael Walsh, the agency's media director, this function is handled by three levels of personnel. The account executive's at the bottom of the pyramid and is responsible for the day-to-day business of the account. This individual is supervised by an account supervisor and both these people report to a management supervisor.

That configuration hurt the 1,300-employee advertising and public relations firm in two ways. "The first and most significant of these," says Walsh, "is that it places a lot of the ongoing client contact at the lowest [level] in the agency. Second, it doesn't involve the individuals at the agency who have the most experience and the best ability to ensure projects are being done correctly. It doesn't involve these people upfront [so] projects aren't necessarily going to get off on the right foot; projects were taking a lot longer than they needed to. Ultimately, that would translate out to client satisfaction [and] we were wondering whether we were getting the client bonding that we really need. A twenty-three-year-old account executive is simply not going to bond with a fifty-year-old chief operating officer."

In 1990, Ketchum adopted an hourglass framework for account management, getting rid of the middle layer and hiring more senior-level individuals to fill out the top. What this has done, claims Walsh, is to place our senior people on the front line with clients right at the beginning. "So when a client says, 'I need this particular project done,' the management supervisor can say, 'Let's talk about this some more, maybe we ought to go in this direction.' They're eliminating the [possibility] of this thing getting off course and not [being detected] until much later."

The benefits of the new Ketchum infrastructure have been twofold, continues Walsh. "It's helping us in terms of client bonding and we're better able to manage projects internally. I have seen a marked reduction in my department [for example] of work being done twice."

6. *And Don't Stop There—Be the Customer.* Really walk a mile in your customer's shoes like Digital Equipment Corporation former president Ken Olsen. Occasionally, he likes to pretend he's the customer, says Angela Cossette with the Customer Service department. He frequently has equipment shipped to his house where he'll set it up himself or he tries to load a software program using the customer manual. "It's his way of testing how easy the equipment is to use, how good our documentation is. And you never know when and where he'll strike next," she laughs. One time he insisted the shape of a computer box be changed because it didn't fit through his doorway.

7. *Make Sure Management's Not Above the "Law."* Managers have

to be willing to put themselves on the line, says Rich Bender, director of Sales at Miller Business Systems, and abide by the same rules they set for their staff. As an example, the first brainstorming session he convened with his direct reports after they'd all been through a 16-week course on customer quality centered on areas where he could improve. " 'Okay,' I said, 'Let's discuss what I do well, what I don't do well.' " "Give us a memo board for sales announcements," they told him, "and lay off the memo writing." "I've changed accordingly," says Bender.

8. Walk the Talk.   Don't expect employeess to fall in line with what you say if they don't see any consistency in what you do. Research by Forum Corporation suggests that many industry captains say one thing but, through their actions, signal quite another to their lieutenants.[3] Of 611 Fortune 500 executives interviewed in 1989, the majority (92 percent) of CEOs said customer service in their business was extremely important but just half (51 percent) said the same of financial results. These positions contrast sharply with the views of their middle managers. Only 83 percent of this group bought into the key role of service yet nearly three-quarters (70 percent) were convinced of the importance of financial results.

Just one more indication, says Xerox's business planning manager Peter Waasdorp, that success for any customer retention initiative boils down to role modeling from the top. "People act the way the boss acts. When we began our in-house service training sessions, we made the decision that we were going to start at the top of the house [and] cascade it down." All staff were divided into "family [work] groups" beginning with CEO David Kearns and other top-level executives. This core group then became the service teachers to the next lowest family group and so on down the hierarchy.

9. Promote What You Preach.   Who gets promoted is a critical signal to employees about what's really important to the top echelons. It seems most company managers fare pretty poorly on this score. According to a 1991 survey of 2,400 Canadian workers at all levels by the Wyatt Company, almost 50 percent of employees believe managers are too tolerant of poor performers. And 70 percent believe promotions don't go to the most competent.[4]

At Xerox, executives admit their promotional policies haven't always made the grade. In a 1987 internal assessment of the company's customer quality process, employees complained that not all those people bumped up the ladder were practicing what was being preached.

Now, only individuals worthy of imitation get the nod at promotion time. A new employee appraisal system effectively ties promotion to dedication to the customer cause. Once a year, managers go through a process called the "Management Resources Profile" (MRP), an ongoing performance assessment prepared by the immediate manager and signed off by the supervisor one level above. Five attributes, including quality leadership, teamwork, and business results, are rated from 1 to 3. Sam Malone delineates the process.

"The [bottom 1] rating, 'requires development,' would stimulate a development action plan [on] what needs to be done to turn that around. The second rating is 'competent'; you're probably in the throes of internalization and practicing but you aren't fully on board." The three ratings go only to those "fully on board," individuals "worthy of imitation [as] role models." And it's only those folks who need apply now for any of the corporation's top 200 positions.

The Practice—Making It Happen
Part III—Step 9

What?

The setup of the first group of special teams, called "Team of Teams," which will apply the People-Powered Retention (PPR) process to the issue of management involvement and commitment for best-customer retention.

Why?

"The manager's behavior is the single most important aspect of communicating [customer retention]"—**Sam Malone, Xerox Corporation.**

How?

9A. A participative work session with the Retention Advisory Group (Workshop 9.1) facilitated by an outside consultant with the following **objectives:**

a. To critique current management involvement and commitment to best-customer retention.

b. To determine what needs to be improved regarding management involvement and commitment to best-customer retention.

c. To reshape improvement requirements in Step 9Ab into issues for the first-level PPR "Team of Teams." **Selection Criteria:** highlighted in Step 4Aa with additional details provided in Step 6Cb. **Facilitator Criteria:** facilitated by outside consultant with in-house "facilitators-in-training" observing process. **Team Membership Criteria:** representatives of Phase II team facilitators, senior management, and other employee groups as appropriate.

9B. Preparation by outside consultant or the Retention Coordinator of summary report of Workshop 9.1 and its distribution to all Retention Inc. staff through internal marketing vehicles recommended by the Retention Advisory Group.

9C. Teams selected in Step 9Ac work through the PPR process introduced in Step 4Ad and detailed in Step 6E.

9D. Preparation and distribution of a summary report of team progress to all Retention Inc. staff through internal marketing vehicles.

When?

Months 16, 17, and 18.

CHAPTER 11

The Buck Stops on Everyone's Desk: Staff Accountability for Customer Retention

> *There is no outside; . . . you and the cause of your problems are part of a single system.*
>
> Peter Senge,
> The Fifth Discipline[1]

At BellSouth Mobility, part of BellSouth Cellular Corp., employees are held accountable for any customer problem they happen to discover. "If an employee hears about a problem, they own that problem until it's solved," says Early Davis, director of customer operations, Region 2. "There's no buck passing," even if it's only a derogatory comment overheard by someone from Accounting at a dinner party. That employee fills out an internal document called an "Opportunity to Excel" (OTE), describing what the problem is and what it will take, in the customer's opinion, to put the matter to rest.

Of course, not everyone in the company will know how to get an appointment to repair a phone antenna or credit a customer's bill if that's the problem, admits Davis "They're going to need our help [at customer operations]; we'll work through the solution [with them] but they have to go back and close with the customer." It's a frightening step for many, but those BellSouth employees who've filled out an OTE have been thrilled with the results.

The BellSouth anecdote illustrates the flipside to staff empowerment—staff accountability. If taking power is a tough assignment for most employees, accepting responsibility is doubly so. Unfortunately, for some, passing the blame is a breeze.

Take the example offered by IBM Canada's Don Myles of a branch manager rooting out the underlying cause of product returns and subsequent credit notes. "Everybody 'knew' this was an administrative problem," he says, at least that's what they thought at the outset. A two-week analysis showed popular opinion at that branch needed considerable reworking. Ninety out of 160 glitches in one month had nothing whatsoever to do with the billing system. In fact, over one-quarter of these could be laid at the branch's own door. "Twenty-four had their root cause in the sloppiness of [branch] account reps in putting an entry into the original [client] contract."

Just how do you get your people to accept that the buck also stops with them? Here are a few recommendations on how this can be done.

1. *Let Employees Know They Can't Pass the Buck.* The urge to blame someone else when the customer takes a hike runs pretty deep in all of us. Maybe we're born with it or maybe we learn it along the way. However we come by it, we've all got it, no matter where we sit on the hierarchical ladder. "Everyone points the finger at everyone else," laments Sherril Guthrie, owner of Pulse Consulting, a Vancouver, British Columbia, firm specializing in customer relations.[2] In the last chapter, we saw how adept the guys at the top are in passing the buck. Just one more nail in that coffin, according to a 1990 survey by Pulse Consulting of 1,000 *BC Business* readers, a representative sample of middle and upper managers from a wide scope of industry sectors in the province.

Respondents in the Pulse study weren't overly enamored of service in general from their business peers, 69 percent assigning a "fair" or "poor" grade. They didn't consider themselves as falling down on the job, though. On the contrary, nearly three-quarters generously granted their own organizations an "outstanding" or "very good" rating. Maybe they don't do business with one another.[3]

Buck passing's not a phenomenon restricted to the upper echelons. The IBM Canada anecdote mentioned earlier refutes this notion. Here's another example from a restaurant chain on the Canadian West Coast called White Spot. The results of a summer survey in 1990 revealed a less than stellar evaluation by company customers. Service staff obviously didn't believe responsibility lay at their door; they consistently rated themselves higher than the customers did. For example, staff thought they rated a 4.21 out of 5 in the category "well trained, well prepared, knows products and service." Customers weren't so kind, giving a rating of just 2.92. Concludes Guthrie, "Everyone thinks it's someone else's problem."[4]

Everyone in your organization must be held accountable for retention results, period. Or as Shakespeare's character remarked to his friend, "The fault, dear Brutus, is not in our stars, but in ourselves." Consider the example of a sales management training program at Pioneer Bank in Lynnwood, Washington, that teaches branch managers to take full responsibility for what's going on in the branch, not to blame factors in the organization, the economy, or the competition.[5] Or that of the Royal Bank of Canada where employees are encouraged to "Speak Up" even if their immediate boss isn't all that accommodating. "If you have a boss who doesn't listen," counsels chairman Allan Taylor, "find a way . . . up and around him or her. There are ways . . . you can be heard."[6]

2. Don't Let Your People Get Hung Up on Job Descriptions. It's too easy to get bogged down in job descriptions, says Clint Vardeman at Rural/Metro, like "my role is this and I'm not going to do anything else." Everyone's role is to do what it takes to make it work for the customer, no ifs, ands, or buts. Too often, says Vardeman, young kids come into the emergency medical services (EMS) business looking for the spine-tingling saves, those cardiac arrest victims brought back from the jaws of death. "EMS is not just the glamorous," he tells them. "It's also helping to strip a bed in a nursing home if need be, to market, to be polite, to make sure we retain the business."

Vardeman and his management team lead by example. "They will see me or my staff behind the desk on the phone, sweeping out a warehouse garage, or unloading a truck of intravenous supplies, in a shirt and tie." If management's willing to take out the trash, he tells staff, they ought to be willing to do their part in marketing and public relations on each call. "It's all our jobs to take care of these things."

At Digital, they've really chucked the traditional division of labor out the window. Each individual on special 18-person performance teams is expected to perform all team functions. To manufacture a computer keyboard, for example, 27 tasks are required. There are no supervisors and no quality control inspectors. Employees choose their own hours and plan their own schedules, and they all interface directly with the customer. The payoff on the keyboard example: increased employee motivation, a decrease in throughput time by 40 percent, and a doubling of the number of flawless units produced.

A last comment on job descriptions. If you really must have them, at least ensure the concept of accountability is well entrenched. The Canadian bank, Scotiabank, for example, has made every single employee accountable to the customer, that's stated right in every job description and reaffirmed at annual appraisal time.[7]

3. And Don't Let Them Believe That Money Solves Everything. It's such an insidious conviction, that money can solve everything. People, not pennies, solve problems. No amount of new technology, for example, will clean up a customer retention mess. A study of American financial institutions found that personal service didn't improve with the installation of new computer systems. Seems employees were too busy peering at the screens to notice the customer.[8]

When I first arrived as consultant to the customer care strategy at Burnaby Hospital I was greeted, if you can call it that, with a chorus of "give us more money." One of the first teams looking at ways to improve the hospital paging function, for example, groused about the lack of funds for a systems upgrade. With a little objective research, though, they discovered a good part of the problem wasn't with the equipment but with those using the equipment. A new paging protocol developed by the team eliminated nonessential pages, giving switchboard staff time to clearly repeat all essential messages. Patients and staff now report fewer disruptions. "We've all believed that we can only improve things with money," says Lorna Leckie, a diabetes education nurse who participated in one of the pilots. "Now we're focusing on the idea that we can make changes and improvements that do not cost money. And that's important, because it's clear that health-care dollars have been capped."

4. Remind Employees That They Have a Better Finger on the Customer Pulse. David Bray at Quad/Graphics uses the following story to illustrate this point. At a recent sales meeting, he and his "companions-in-crime" were complaining there weren't enough vice presidents to go to when decisions needed to be made. President Harry V. "Larry" Quadracci, his boss, responded: "If you've got a problem and you come to me with it, I'm going to ask you, 'What do you suggest?' Nine times out of ten, I'll simply say, 'You're in a much better position to know what's best, go do it.' " But what of the 10 percent? We all know in our hearts which decisions lie within and which are beyond our expertise, claims Bray. "Make the decision you personally feel qualified to make."

5. Spell It Out in Dollars and Cents. Sometimes, employees don't really understand the value of existing customers. It doesn't hurt to enlighten them, as the National Association of Life Underwriters (NALU) did in 1991. "Our national member dues are $48 per year," explains assistant vice president of Administration and Board Liason Matthew Gertzog, "so our people thought any one member was worth only that amount to the association." Some statistical analysis on how much members tend to spend on NALU products and services revealed the average member value to be more like $3,000. "That was revolutionary for [our people]," he admits.

Customer retention is a do-or-die proposition for a lot of companies today, and their people better be made aware of this. At AT&T, there was little choice other than to pass along a hard-times message to the troops. The 1983 congressional ruling that broke up the telecommunications giant opened the door to some pretty stiff competition for the first time. "Brand awareness of AT&T in 1984 was only about 4 percent," notes Janice Colby, division manager for the company's Consumer Market Management department. "The competitive threat was new and intense and we needed [our] people to rally around saving customers."

As a result, the company has paid close attention to communicating the importance of the customer to all its contact employees. "We've done it in the context of 'we all have to do this or the customer you talked to today will be somebody else's tomorrow. [And] the more customers who leave, the less of you we need.' " It was a strong message but it worked. In 1991, customer awareness was up to nearly 90 percent.

6. And Hit Them in the Pocketbook. Money talks. So let it convey the message of customer responsibility, for example, with sales reps. Normally, these folks and their bosses are paid, and hence motivated, by revenue, "making their damn quotas," quips Lea Kea, former director of Strategy and Business Management at IBM Canada. That amounts to zip in the customer's book, though. A new IBM "shared measurements" compensation plan is built around the customer's agreement to a mutual set of objectives, 95 percent client satisfaction for the job at hand, for example. If a rep can get a customer to sign off on this objective, his or her bonus doubles. "That cements the relationship and forces a new discipline of consistent measurements with our customer." At first, the field force cast around for ways to beat the system, he admits. They soon realized the only way to do that was to have a happy customer.

For his own direct reports, Kea took this idea a step further. The people in his area now accept the responsibility of rating their own work with validation from their customers. "Don't try to please me as your manager," he told them. "Please your customers. I don't fill out appraisal forms, you do."

Nonsales staff can also get the retention bug if incentives are tied to customer defection rates. At credit card giant MBNA, each department focuses on the one or two things that have the biggest impact on keeping their customers. Achievement targets are set for these, and daily measures taken and posted throughout the company. Should any day's performance top 95 percent of targets, company money's funneled into a bonus pool. That pool is used by managers to award yearly checks that can reach 20 percent of any employee's salary.[9]

7. Let Them See It for Themselves. In her book, *The Manager's Guide to Service Excellence*, author Anne Petite sums up this tip: "If you allow your inside people to go out to meet the customer and see why it's so necessary that your product arrive on time, undamaged, and defect-free, they are more likely to take the responsibility to make it happen, to feel some accountability."[10]

8. Spread the Responsibility. We're all in this together, for good or bad, says Bud Mundt, vice president of Sales and Marketing at Miller Business Systems. Spreading the responsibility lightens the load for everyone and benefits the customer, as this Miller example illustrates. The company had sold its customers on the importance of having their own personal contact in the customer service department. The concept backfired, however. When that person wasn't available to take a call, the customer would end up irritated. "They were under the impression that was the only person in the world who could handle the problem when, in fact, we had a number of people who were competent," says president Mike Miller.

The department was realigned along team lines, five reps to a team plus a manager. Now each account is serviced, not by an individual, but by a group, each with its own unique identity and name, like "Killer Bees," "Silver Bullets," "Fort Worth Stars," "Dallas Diamonds," "Midway Mustangs," or "Top Guns." Account executives are also asked to sign on with one of the teams, making an unbroken line from sales to service. Customers have taken to the idea with gusto, claims Miller. "They're happier because they don't have to wait for so-and-so to get off the phone." In fact, they feel like one of the gang. "One holiday, a customer sent in a cake addressed to the Silver Bullets and a lot of [customers] have requested and received their own team T-shirt."

Good things have come in the guise of better employee morale as well. "Customer Service is no picnic as a place to work," says Miller, "and it used to be a high turnover area for the company. They're the ones who get the complaints, the problems; the phone's always ringing." There's a new sense of worth in this department. "They now feel a camaraderie with their team members and a pride in the customers they serve."

9. Don't Be Afraid to Hold Their Hands For a While. It'll take time for everyone to get used to the idea of shifting responsibilities, so take it in chunks. Leslie Burns, advertising and promotions manager for fast food chain Au Bon Pain, found she had to ease store managers into the notion of meeting her halfway in customer retention. Typically, a store manager would come to his or her district manager and say, "My God, sales are down." The district manager would then call Burns and say, "Sales are down in Kendall Square, help," and hang up the phone. "I was expected to get out the magic promo wand and wave it and everything would be fixed." But keeping customers doesn't work that way; no head-office campaign is going to take off without input from the store level. "I may be in the store once or twice a week but they're there every single day. They are the ones who know."

"We're not asking them to take over the task of dreaming up promos," explains Burns, "that's my job. We are holding them accountable, though, for at least knowing what's going on with their customers and their competitors." She gives an example: "If they want to do a coffee special, 39 cents a cup with a muffin, and Dunkin' Donuts next door is giving away free coffee with a muffin, obviously that's not going to work."

Since 1991, once a quarter Burns and the $48-million company's co-chairman Ron Schaich have met with each regional manager and the head of that district. She calls these exchanges "Marketing Resource Program" (MRP) meetings. At the first session, Burns et al. agonized over customer counts, trying to fathom causes of any underlying problems. They asked questions like, "Is it a matter of not getting enough repeat business or is the store losing customers to the muffin shop down the road?"

For subsequent meetings, a MRP package goes out ahead of time to the district. It's a worksheet, explains Burns, that the manager plugs store numbers into to build a picture of that location and its market. "We knew this was all new to them so we made it dead simple," she insists, "just a matter of pulling numbers from reports they already have." Even so, the new role seems foreign; "it's not like when their oven breaks and they fix it and it works again."

Burns uses general manager meetings, held once every eight weeks, to buck up resolve. "I show them the success stories, 12 out of 15 on the first post-MRP promotions, and tell them, 'You guys came up with these.' " It's been slow going, she admits, but Au Bon Pain's 82 store managers are coming around. "The whole key was to get them to start thinking about [these things]," and not leave it all up to the brainpower at headquarters.

The Practice—Making It Happen, Part III—Step 10

What?

The setup of the second group of special Team of Teams, which apply the People-Powered Retention (PPR) process to the issue of staff accountability for best-customer retention.

Why?

Customer retention is not something that can be dictated from the top or driven from the bottom; staff at all levels must accept responsibility: "A catalyst from the top, energy from the bottom, and solutions from the middle."—**Hal Hoare, Vancouver Community College.**

How?

10A. A participative work session with the Retention Advisory Group (Workshop 10.1) facilitated by an outside consultant with the following **objectives:**
  a. To critique current staff accountability for best customer retention.
  b. To determine what needs to be improved regarding staff accountability.
  c. To reshape improvement requirements from Step 10Ab into issues for PPR Team of Teams. **Selection Criteria:** highlighted in Step 4Aa with additional details provided in Step 6Cb. **Facilitator Criteria:** facilitated by in-house facilitators under the guidance of an outside consultant. **Team Membership Criteria:** as outlined in Step 9Ac.

10B. Preparation by outside consultant or the Retention Coordinator of summary report on Workshop 10.1 and its distribution to all Retention Inc. staff through internal marketing vehicles recommended by the Retention Advisory Group.

10C. Teams selected in Step 10Ac work through the PPR process introduced in Step 4Ad and detailed in Step 6E.

10D. Preparation and distribution of summary report of team progress to all Retention Inc. staff through internal marketing vehicles.

When?

Months 19, 20, and 21.

CHAPTER 12

Recognizing Good Work: Using Employee Incentives for Customer Retention

Think like a customer but act like an owner.
A BellSouth Mobility Precept

In just six years, the Cooker Restaurant Corporation went from zilch to 12 restaurants, 1,500 employees, and $33 million in sales. Not bad for a company that pays nothing for advertising. "We don't advertise outside our front door," says vice president of Food Services, Glenn Cockburn. Yet patrons keep rolling on in, most at a frequency of two or three times a week. Compare that with the typical restaurant's patronage of one visit every six weeks.

So what's cooking at Cooker? Guest recognition for one thing; it's a treat to go where everyone knows your name. You can't get that if your staff turnover rate is through the roof, insists president and chairman, Arthur Seelbinder. "The people who have been here the longest tend to have the highest check averages." Cooker's turnover is enviable, just 74 percent in 1989 versus up to 300 percent for many entry-level service jobs.[1]

What makes a Cooker crew member stay put? The job is demanding—"when you leave work, you've got to be tired," says Seelbinder—but the pay is great. Greed will do it every time. Hostesses, for example, are routinely paid 15 to 25 percent above market rates, many have salaries double the $4.75 industry average. "Superior pay for superior performance," chimes Seelbinder. And that's just the beginning.

Cooker allocates about $12,000 per store each year just for employee incentives like "the friendly 5s," where a supervisor will lay a fiver on a server for a guest compliment. Managers also get a chance to build up their bank accounts through participation in sales bonus plans and contests like the annual race to lower staff turnovers. Plus the company contributes to an employee stock ownership program (ESOP), brought in three years ago this October. Open to all Cookerites, the ESOP is nevertheless weighted in favor of the oldtimers.

A final weapon in the Cooker compensation arsenal is the "Cooker Partner Program." Seelbinder elaborates: "A crew member can become a Cooker Partner by buying company stock through payroll deduction." A special name tag distinguishes partners for both guests and other staff. This last program particularly has been great for keeping a lid on turnover but off revenues. "The restaurants that run the smoothest and are consistently the most profitable are the ones that have the highest degree of participation in the Cooker Partner Program." Never underestimate the power of ownership.

Ditto the power of money to motivate ordinary staffers. This was a notion that always eluded a former boss of mine who could easily understand why a bonus of $30,000 plus kept him on his toes but couldn't fathom how a measly $1,000 could perk up a clerk in the back office. If you really believe in customer retention, why not put your money where your strategy is? At Xerox, claims Peter Waasdorp, business planning manager, "If it's important, we pay for it."

Sales and service people expect that if customer satisfaction is number one, there should be some money in it for them. And why not? There's obviously money enough to go around, at least for those at the top of the heap. In the last decade, compensation for U.S. CEOs jumped 212 percent, while the average factory worker saw only a modest 53 percent increment.[2] According to Graef S. Crystal, a prominent pay consultant, CEOs at the largest American corporations are paid 150 times more than the average worker.[3]

You can't say these numbers are justified by any great gains in corporate earnings. Quite the contrary. A 1991 study by Crystal found that when earnings rose 10 percent a share, CEO salaries and bonuses shot up 13 percent. However, when earnings fell by 10 percent, executive pay still went up by over 4 percent.[4]

Consider this approach. At Zytec Corporation, a Minnesota

power-supply manufacturer, pay increases are identical for everyone. There are no executive perks or bonuses, and the CEO's salary's capped at just 14 times that of the lowest-paid employee. A few consequences of this democratic approach to compensation: New product development costs are down by 50 percent at Zytec, sales per employee are up and, recently, the company won the Malcolm Baldrige Award for Quality.[5]

You take care of your people, says Mark Coleman, formerly at America West Airlines, and "they'll gladly take care of the customer." And why shouldn't seeing one's efforts rewarded be as enticing to folks in the trenches as it is for the grand poohbahs up the line? It's one thing to say, "Work hard and the company does well," claims Coleman. "It's a lot more fun to say, 'If you work hard, the company does well, and so do you.' " Management professor Michael LeBoeuf summarizes: "Rewarding the customer is everybody's job, and rewarding those who reward the customer is management's job."[6]

Cash isn't the only way to get employees excited about customer retention and it may not be the best way either. The latest in motivational theory suggests that today's workers want more than good pay. An American Productivity and Quality Center study concluded that challenge and recognition outweigh pay as motivating factors.[7] A 1992 survey by Conference Board of Canada columnist Peter Larson for *The Vancouver Sun* newspaper found employees in a half-dozen Canadian cities also ranked financial rewards lower on a list of motivators than recognition programs. Of the 1,100 respondents in the *Sun* survey, only one in ten felt low pay was a major source of discontent and just 6 percent thought increasing pay would make them any happier on the job. In fact, recognition of individual contribution was considered 3.5 times as important to job satisfaction as salary hikes.[8]

Those among us with access to the executive washroom have a personal stake in the success of their organizations. For most of their staff, though, there's no reason, other than a paycheck, and often a meager one at that, to be concerned with continued corporate success. In this chapter, we'll take a closer look at some suggestions on making employee reward and recognition work in the customer's (and the company's) favor.

1. Line Up Corporate Objectives with Individual Objectives . . . If customers for keeps is what you're after, reward employees to do that. In the words of Aleta Holub, vice president and manager of quality assurance at the First National Bank of Chicago: "I think any company that is serious about customer service [and retention] has to tie [these] objectives into [employee] performance appraisals, bonus structures; it doesn't matter what it is, whatever you pay for has to be tied into whatever it is you want to happen." This logic isn't commonplace for most organizations, however. In a 1991 survey by the Wyatt Company of 2,400 Canadian employees, only 49 percent saw any link between pay and performance.[9] Staff south of the border aren't any more convinced. Opinion Research Corporation stats from 1970 to 1988 reveal that the majority of employees across job categories saw little connection between effort and subsequent pay raises.[10]

That's not the case at First Chicago, where 50 percent of a sales rep's compensation is based on how well that person maintains and grows existing business. That's because it costs the bank anywhere from 6 to 100 times as much to add an incremental dollar in sales from a new customer as it does to add a dollar of business with an existing client, claims Trish Barr, a vice president in the Cash Management Sales department. Putting out for a customer can also earn a nonexempt employee, one who qualifies for overtime, up to $1,500. Exempt [managerial] staff can look forward to a bonus up to one-third base salary if they go that extra mile.

2. . . . And Watch That Sales Incentives Follow Suit. Getting staff racking up new business by dangling incentive carrots in their paths is great—unless, of course, that new business doesn't hang around; then all that selling fervor has been for naught. Foremost Insurance Group is careful not to fall into this trap. Monthly incentive campaigns for its service reps, who can earn up to $300 a month this way, include some pretty stringent retention criteria. If, for example, an employee sells the most policies but half of these cancel a month later, the retention portion of the bonus is pretty much history, according to Rebecca Spratlin, vice president of Foremost's AARP Business Division.

3. Let Employees Set the Compensation Rules. We talked earlier about how participation breeds passion in team retention efforts. The same holds true for reward and recognition programs. A San Antonio insurer, USAA, uses employee-designed measures to monitor individual and group performance, part of the reason the $26-billion company has a sterling reputation for service in an industry infamous for its indifference to the customer. The "Family of Measures" (FOM) is a continuous evaluation process, tracking five areas: "quality," "quantity," "service timeliness," "resource utilization" (a measure of efficiency), and "customer satisfaction." Every staff member receives an individualized report prepared on a monthly basis. The company looks for progress over time, granting special recognition to those who've made significant improvements in their performance.

Specific measures within the five categories are defined by a representative group of employees, although management does get a crack at some final fine-tuning before implementation. The employee group uses the following four questions as a design guide: (1) "Is the activity under our control?"; (2) "Is it significant?"; (3) "Does it involve some form of data that we can collect?"; and (4) "Can we easily analyze the results?" A vote is taken on which measures to include and on their relative weight in the FOM, both for the group and for individual USAA employees. Individual standards vary with experience and job grade.

Let's look at an example of the FOM in operation using the customer contact or policy service function within the Property-and-Casualty division. The current measure for group resource utilization here is the ratio of hours worked to hours paid; for service timeliness, the percentage of calls answered within 20 seconds. A random mailing of post-service questionnaires yields customer satisfaction ratings. The final two factors, quality and quantity, are weighted 60/40 in this unit. Quality is measured by Policy Service managers through telephone, computer, and correspondence audits. A numbering of phone and business transactions comprises the quantity measure, with the more difficult transactions given more weight. For example, "umbrella" transactions count five times as much as do those for auto policies.[11]

4. *Steer Clear of Performance Measures Employees Can't Directly Affect Themselves.* A direct link between retention performance and employee compensation is hard to beat if you want to institutionalize long-term customer commitment. Instead of an annual or quarterly profit-sharing plan, why not a performance-based system that can contribute to an employee's income every paycheck? A 1987 Council for Financial Competition survey found that predictable, frequent dollar amounts were more powerful than random bonuses in changing behavior.[12] "A quarterly payout is

too far out to motivate individual behavior," notes Michael Crump, a senior consultant with the Boston firm Forum Corporation. "It's not all that meaningful. Employees don't know why they get or don't get a bonus. It's not connected to their own performance."[13]

Tom Sargent, president of $150-million First Technology Credit Union (FTCU) in Portland, Oregon, concurs: "The individual affected by the incentive program has to be able to affect the results." His organization canned a profit-sharing plan in favor of salary adjustments for the credit union's top performers. Even with the potential to earn up to 10 percent of their salaries as a year-end bonus, the old compensation scheme fell flat as an employee motivator. "We found no difference in behavior at all. The high performers still performed, and the unmotivated employees were still unmotivated," Sargent recalls. "The bottom line was it didn't work. The employees came back to us and said, 'That's not the reason we do the things we do.' "[14]

5. Get All Staff Marching to the Same Compensation Tune. To have staff at different levels compensated according to different rules will do little for corporate harmony. At best, it'll be an exercise in frustration, according to Peter Waasdorp, business planning manager for Xerox's U.S. Marketing Group. Senior managers at "the document company" are on the same bonus arrangement as district managers, and "we're migrating the concept down through the ranks," claims Waasdorp. "We started with the district and senior management because they're the ones who really set the tone."

And don't restrict this consistency to the upper echelons. At IBM Canada customer satisfaction forms the basis of measurement for anyone with any customer interaction—"from accounting clerk to sales rep, all contacts and all management teams," says Lee Kea.

6. Use Dollars to Buy Cooperation. There's nothing like being tied to a common pot of gold to make people feel the need to work together. That's the thinking behind Xerox's collective district bonus. In a past life, the company's compensation package for district managers tended to favor the sales side of the business. "We'd say, 'That machine really doesn't fit into that particular [customer's] room, but we need the business, so let's put it [there],' " admits Waasdorp. That's all changed. There are now three equal partners at the district managerial level: one for sales, one for customer service, and one for administration.

"We want this partnership to work as a unit," says Waasdorp, so all three participate in one collective bonus. Between 10 and 20 percent of a district manager's salary is withdrawn on a monthly basis and set aside in a bonus fund that grows as a function of district profit and revenue. If the district fails to meet a minimal level of client satisfaction, however, the money's forfeit, for all three. Participation is voluntary, at present, as is the manager's choice of how much salary to put at risk. "You might, for example, get a 10/10/20 split across the three partners. That's because the service and administrative arms of the partnership still aren't entirely comfortable with the concept," explains Waasdorp.

Let's look at how this partnership fund works in more detail. Say you opted to set aside $10,000 of your annual salary and your district's satisfaction yardstick is set at 91 percent, with minimum being 89 percent. You knock the socks off your profit and revenue targets and that $10,000 blossoms into $70,000. Your satisfaction rating, however, doesn't measure up to baseline. End result: you lose the entire pot—$70,000 out the window. "Conversely," continues Waasdorp, "if you do very well with customer satisfaction and you're at 93 percent, your $70,000 can grow to $100,000." And the target's always moving. Each year, we move closer to 100 percent and the margin for error narrows. In 1991, for example, "if you [fell] short by a point, you [were] in trouble."

7. Let Everyone Have a Piece of the Action. Don't cut off nonsales and service people from taking a shot at making a few more dollars. BellSouth Cellular Corp. preaches that every employee's performance is essential to the company's overall success. The extension of this philosophy is a compensation plan in which every employee is eligible for bonuses.

Employee bonuses reflect two factors: the performance of the company in meeting a specific goal and the individual's performance in his or her job. The result is a bonus in the mail room and install shops as well as in the executive suites.

8. Make More Owners. Nobody gives better service than an owner, claims Mark Coleman, former senior vice president of Sales and Product Development for America West Airlines. This is a truism his company's built virtually its entire existence around. When the $1-billion carrier set up shop in 1983, it was determined to set itself apart from all other airlines. "We started with the premise that it was almost as important to be different as it was to be better," explains Coleman. "We looked for differences that would be meaningful to the business traveler, and we came across employee ownership. Now, that was different; there were no employee-owned airlines then."

The employee-ownership idea was underscored through the first four years of the Phoenix-based airline's life. One of the original ads featured a woman and the caption read, "There's something unusual about Laurie, she owns an airline."

"We use ownership as the factor that makes our claims of better service at fairer prices believable," says Coleman. And travelers certainly notice the difference: "They sense immediately that there's something really different about the people on board."

In addition to the share program, all America West workers partake of a cash profit-sharing plan. "On a quarterly basis, 15 percent of annual pretax profits are allocated across the entire workforce," explains Mark Beauvais, former managing director, Sales & Marketing Programs. Based on the time an employee has been with the company and his or her position, the profit pool is calculated using a five-year time span. Beauvais enlightens us a bit more: "Your salary multiplied by the time you've been with the company divided into the total salaries paid by America West over that five-year timeframe is your percentage. If you made $20,000 a year and you've been with the company five years, your cumulative base pay would be $100,000. That $100,000 would be divided by the gross [dollar value] of all salaries, let's say that's $500,000,000. That would give 0.2 percent, and that's the percent of the profit-sharing pool you would get."

This approach is more objective and less prone to dissension in the ranks, claims Beauvais. It also takes into account any raises or promotions you've garnered over the five-year period and makes for a consistently good service experience for America West patrons. "The enthusiasm, the willingness to do a good job for the customer is motivated by the fact that if the company succeeds, the people succeed."

9. Get Recognition Out of the Closet. Don't stop at cash as a means of motivating your people to keep on the retention straight-and-narrow. Consider the value of recognition. "Money is not always the best incentive," claims marketing coordinator John Wilbur at IBM Endicott/Owego Employees Federal Credit Union. "Money is given and spent, and soon forgotten."[15]

Monetary incentives are certainly much appreciated, admits Cooker's regional manager Peter Kehayes, but what really seems key for employees is the recognition that they're doing a good job. Quarterly crew surveys at Cooker on management's good and bad points always come back to this one issue, as Kehayes says, "the biggest complaint is there's not enough positive reinforcement."

Aleta Holub at First Chicago Bank agrees: "We have learned that the real issue is respect for the individual. It's just amazing," she says, "how a picture with our executive vice president will tickle the troops. He has a hard time understanding why it's important because his own family doesn't have a picture of him on their desks," she chuckles.

And for heavens sake, don't hide this kind of appreciation, says Holub. At First Chicago, the bank's executive used to call a deserving employee into the manager's office, and, with the door closed, hand him or her a certificate for deeds well done. "The poor person didn't know whether they should hide it or not." Get out of the closet with recognition activities, she advises. "You should be out there in the middle of the workforce giving it out, letting people know what kind of performance is recognized." That's just one reason why Digital Equipment splashes the faces of employee customer heroes and heroines across its "I Got Caught" bulletin board and Rural/Metro blows up customer commendations into computer-generated banners. "It's very important to tack a compliment to a crew," says Clint Vardeman, general manager for Rural/Metro's Arizona Medical Transport. "It means a lot to them."

10. Steer Clear of Recognition Programs Unrelated to Real Performance. Watch that your recognition programs don't get too fluffy and unrelated to real retention performance. Before switching to a cash-incentive system for individual performers in 1988, United Federal Credit Union (UFCU), a Michigan credit union, had used the familiar "Employee of the Month" approach to award staffers for being on time and accurate. General manager Vern Lubben admits the program did little to alter performance as the same employees kept winning. It wasn't a distinction much prized at the $67-million Buchanan institution. In fact, many employees found the whole business rather embarrassing. "They were saying things like, 'I don't want to win next month.' " Now UFCU employees earn concrete dollar amounts for specific sales behavior. For example, the program pays $5 for each Visa account opened. This incentive program's been well received, says Lubben, "because [employees] can see it in their paycheck right away."[16]

11. Involve Top Brass. Personal recognition from the top is a lot more powerful than any certificate. A waiter at a Canadian hotel puts it more eloquently: "I'd rather have a pat on the back from my manager than a T-shirt."[17]

Marriott Hotels finds a personalized thank-you for a job well done from the chief really lights its employees' fires. At one location, consistently rated number one by customers over the years, the general manager sends ten such letters every week to his employees' homes. Vice president of marketing Roger Dow provides a few illustrations: "Dear Susan, I just want you to know what a great job you did in the catering setup for the American Medical Association. Their executive director came to me and said, 'Wow, people like Susan make a difference,' and you do. I'm glad to have you on the team," or "Dear Bill, I just heard from Mr. X how you went out of your way to charge his battery in the pouring rain and he made his appointment on time. That's what Marriott is all about. You're terrific, glad you're on the team."

12. Don't Forget Training as a Motivator. According to a 1988 Decima survey, training's what employees would dearly love more of. More than half in that study said they'd gladly trade higher pay for additional training.[18] And research by Benson Shapiro and Stephen Doyle funded through Harvard Business School and the Western Electric Fund confirm task clarity as the principal element in sales staff motivation. Salespeople will work longer hours on the job when they clearly understand the nature of the selling job, the authors contend. "Task clarity was 50 percent more important in determining motivation than personality and nearly three times as important as type of pay plan."[19]

Employees may want training but they don't get much, according to the American Society for Training & Development, an Alexandria (Va.) trade group. Most of the $30-billion a year Corporate America spends on training is accounted for by less than 10 percent of all companies.[20]

So spend some major bucks in pursuit of staff training, like IBM Canada does. Two-thirds of Canadian firms spend no money at all on formal staff training.[21] Contrast this with the IBM Canada 1990 training budget of $48 million for 13,000 employees or nearly $4,000 per employee.

Some food for thought on training. Hold regular staff meetings to brush up on skills and knowledge, and to provide a forum for employees to role play. Provide product and service training for all employees; don't stop at the front line. Much of what customers use to assess an institution's worthiness relates to administrative functions like account statements. Take the training team on the road and into the branches. Not only will staff appreciate the gesture but your training people will experience first-hand what really goes on in the trenches.

The more at ease your people are with the nature of your business, the better chance they'll have at keeping your customers so give them the big picture of the company's raison d'être and how their jobs contribute to that. And keep them up-to-date on changes to company strategy. This is what Richmond Savings Credit Union, a West Coast credit union, did using the employee newsletter "In Touch" to keep staff informed on its new relationship-banking orientation.[22] Finally, make training easy and even fun. John Hancock Life Insurance Company uses an interactive video called "The Marathon Game" to ease agents into the use of a computer keyboard.[23]

Training isn't just about product courses or management workshops; it's also about communication, such as feedback on employee input. (Recall the AT&T experience from Chapter 5.) One final comment: if it's the price tag of training that brings you up short, take note of this quote from Derek Bok: "If you think education is expensive, try ignorance."[24]

13. Finally, Don't Assume You Know What Motivates Your Staff. Even with recognition programs, it's different strokes for different folks. Apply the customer focus here and find out what motivates each employee group and deal with that, suggests First Chicago's Holub. "One unit within the bank's check collection division came up with a lapel pin idea—a shoe with a hole that said, 'We walked that extra mile for a customer.' The staff there loved the idea but it really bombed with the remittance folks," she claims.

That's why her organization surveys staff after every recognition event. "We ask award winners and management for improvement suggestions: 'Is there anything we can do to make it more meaningful, what did you like least, what did you like best?' " One recommendation that came out of this process was the separation of multiple winners from the new kids on the block. Now, up to three wins and your success is celebrated at a special breakfast ceremony; above that and you rate a cocktail party.

The Practice—Making It Happen, Part III—Step 11

What?

The setup of the next group of special Team of Teams which apply the People-Powered Retention (PPR) process to the issue of staff recognition and reward for best customer retention.

Why?

What gets rewarded gets done.

How?

11A. A participative work session with the Retention Advisory Group (Workshop 11.1) facilitated by an outside consultant with the following **objectives:**
   a. To critique current staff reward and recognition programs and policies for best-customer retention.
   b. To determine what needs to be improved regarding staff compensation and recognition.
   c. To reshape improvement requirements in Step 11Ab into issues for PPR Team of Teams. **Selection Criteria:** highlighted in Step 4Aa with additional details provided in Step 6Cb. **Facilitator Criteria:** facilitated by in-house facilitators-in-training with backup support from an outside consultant. **Team Membership Criteria:** as outlined in Step 9Ac.
11B. Preparation by outside consultant or the Retention Coordinator of a summary report on Workshop 11.1 and its distribution to all Retention Inc. staff through internal marketing vehicles recommended by the Retention Advisory Group.

11C. Teams selected in Step 11Ac work through the PPR process introduced in Step 4Ad and detailed in Step 6E.

11D. Preparation and distribution of a summary report of team progress to all Retention Inc. staff through internal marketing vehicles.

When?

Months 22, 23, and 24.

What Works Today May Not Work Tomorrow: Adapting Your Customer Retention Strategy

It's messy but it works.

Roger Dow
Vice President, Marketing
Marriott Corporation

In the early 1980s, First Chicago National Bank's new chairman, Barry Sullivan, was looking for a way to thank staff who had participated in the company's first customer quality team. He hit upon the idea of a cocktail party in the executive dining room, "57." When he saw how delighted ordinary employees were with such a treat, he knew he'd struck gold, says quality manager, Aleta Holub. "It did a world of good for management to see the power of recognition. We stumbled onto this," she admits, "but we reacted properly and did something in terms of carrying it forward as a strategy, not just letting it happen, but replicating it in [other] situations." And that, ladies and gentleman, is exactly the way customer retention often happens; it's more like trial-and-error than an exact science.

Service consultant and author Chip Bell says many senior executives run their organizations with what he calls "administrative logic" rather than "human logic." They control by the rules and manage by the numbers. This makes sense on the surface, but customer service and retention aren't about rules or numbers; they're about people who simply aren't measurable in the quantitative sense. *Marketing Your Services* author Anthony Putman agrees. For these managers, you have to put a number to something or it's not real. But you can't put numbers to what goes on between two people, he insists, you can "only quantify that satisfaction crudely."

Neither of these gentlemen is suggesting you forgo number crunching altogether; nor am I. "Numbers can point you in the right direction, justify or defend some move, or persuade [others]," says Putman. But customers for keeps is not an exact science. "There's a place for measurement, but it's not at the core of things." Most of the time, you're not really going to know for certain that you're on the right track; you'll just have to go for it and see how things turn out. And that's when the real skill comes into play. You need to be able to react quickly to squash what bombs and nurture what blossoms. "Success can only be achieved through repeated failure and introspection," claims Soichiro Hona, founder of Honda Motor. "In fact, success represents the 1 percent of your work which results . . . from the 99 percent that is called failure."[1] That's the premise behind this final chapter.

1. Don't Expect to be Right-On Right Away. Chances are, even with the best customer intelligence, you'll end up making a number of wrong turns; fortunately, there is life after blunders. Your organization's reputation with a customer is built up over time, according to Mark Beauvais, formerly at America West Airlines, so it can only be torn down over time as well. Customers will suffer with you through some bad times, he contends. "One bad experience will not necessarily cause them to say goodbye." We all know that no company is immune to bad experiences, or bad decisions.

Even the mighty Xerox Corporation started down the wrong road initially with its total customer satisfaction guarantee. During the fourth quarter of 1989, the corporation did focus groups with a few of its midsize accounts, "named accounts" as they're referred to. Of key concern to these customers was their perception of the risk associated with purchasing Xerox equipment; they wanted to feel in control of these decisions. "That was where we were the weakest," says James Miller. "We were too quick to pull out the terms and conditions."

A few managers from the U.S. Marketing Group did some brainstorming on this problem and came up with a proposal for a 90-day money-back guarantee. Pats on the back went all around, recalls Miller. "The concept appealed to a lot of our people." It didn't do much for customers, though, as subsequent focus groups and a 600-client telephone survey revealed. "They didn't want a money-back guarantee; they wanted a machine that worked," or at least the opportunity to exchange any faulty equipment for a like machine, "like for like" in Xerox jargon. "It was a lemon-aid kind of law of protection." Customers also wanted the guarantee to span their relationship with the company. "They were thinking they were entering a long-term relationship," says Miller. "So, if it wasn't longer than 18 months, don't bother."

The result was a three-year "Total Satisfaction Guarantee" crafted by a cross-functional team of 30 Xerox staffers. Under the terms of the guarantee, customers with equipment maintained through a Xerox service contract or warranty decide for themselves when it's time for their Xerox machine to pack it in and for an identical or comparable machine to take its place. Effective as of September 1990, the guarantee has met with solid success. In the first six months, for example, research on new buyers showed that, for 35 percent, the guarantee was a key factor in their preference for Xerox. It's also made technical reps at the company very happy. "For the first time, they were going to be out of the middle," notes Miller. But the true test of any new strategy is the reaction of your competition, he claims, and virtually all Xerox competitors introduced some form of guarantee within six months of the Xerox model's debut.

2. *Exploit Your Luck.* Let me introduce this point with an anecdote from Early Davis at BellSouth Mobility. The story concerns an engineering employee who hadn't been long on the job when he found himself up against a serious switch problem. The system was down and a lot of unhappy customers couldn't use their phones. There was no one to turn to—his immediate boss was out of town and unreachable, and the person next up the ladder was laid up in the hospital. He had no authority to repair the system but he did anyway, and he was rewarded by the company for this infraction of the rules. "He did a job that wasn't really his job, one that he was actually prohibited from doing," says Davis. "But he did it because it was the right thing to do."

You're probably saying to yourself that these stories are a dime a dozen and pretty meaningless because such people don't grow on trees. That's true enough but it isn't the crux of this story. The point here is that the managers at BellSouth were astute enough to recognize this disobedience as an opportunity, one that would give them the chance to encourage employee action on behalf of the customer, and then do something about it. As a philosopher once said, "Luck is the juxtaposition of opportunity and effort."

For the last few years, P.A. Bergner, a $1.2-billion Midwestern department store chain has had personal computers (PCs) available in its 68 stores. For most of its managers, these were little more than administrative tools; for a few go-getters, though, the PCs represented a neat way to recognize outstanding efforts by selling associates. Senior vice president of Marketing Ed Carroll fills us in.

Using their own initiative, a few Bergner managers wrote a little computer program that allowed them to print up a thank-you letter to any customer who'd recently made a significant purchase. It also gave them the opportunity to praise the staff involved. A typical letter might read: "Dear Customer, I know you were in the other day and you made a major purchase with us. I hope you enjoy your new wardrobe. If there's anything I can do, fine; if not, I'm sure Sally, your competent selling associate, can."

We come to the moral of the story: Bergner's senior staff didn't just let things go at that—they pounced on this idea and spread it around. "We talked to our data processing people," says Carroll, and put the following question to them: "Can we pick up all the information off our sales transaction sheets, translate those numbers into a customer base file, then print overnight a listing of those customers who made this amount of purchase and in what department?" "Yes, it can be done," was the response, and so it was. Again, a case of capitalizing on a lucky break.

3. Build In Some Organizational Flexibility. If you really want customer retention to happen, you'll have to accept a considerable level of organizational flexibility. To some that spells chaos; to the more savvy, it's a sign of the times and the only road to success.

3a. Rework the Structure to Fit the Client. Sometimes, what works best for those inside the organization isn't all that hot for outsiders. Look at the time-honored tradition in the advertising industry of separating media buying from media planning. This is a nice tidy arrangement, for the agency, that is; not so for clients, claims Michael Walsh, senior vice president and Ketchum Advertising's media director. This is particularly the case for the small accounts who think of advertising as one seamless process and don't care to be bounced around the bureaucracy from one expert to another. "They don't necessarily want, or need, a high degree of specialization."

Three years ago, signs of discontent among its smaller clients made Ketchum rethink the old ways. "It was getting increasingly difficult to get approval for work we were doing. We began to suspect it was our organizational structure that was responsible." Then, one important client broke ranks and threatened to walk. The emotional loss of this account, to say nothing of the financial repercussions, propelled Walsh to action. He put together a team of three individuals to take on both media roles for the small customer accounts. It wasn't really a plum job as these accounts were a distraction from the more sophisticated larger customers and were viewed with some disdain. A successful team venture would mean convincing these three to take ownership of this business. That meant a high degree of autonomy and a new structure.

"We gave them their own direct line of reporting to me; that was radically different from the way we typically manage," explains Walsh. "We created a separate organization within the media department that housed these people, gave them their own separate identity." The fledging group was christened "The Impact Team"—"an acronym we invented that stands for Integrated Media & Promotional Activity Team."

"Do what it takes to keep these accounts satisfied," the team was told, a dictum that effectively gave them a licence to recreate their job function and appraisal. Typically, Ketchum evaluated account success through quantifiable measures, like cost efficiency for media plans. "We have evaluated by our own rules and not by whether or not the client was happy." That changed with the new setup. Clients like Eat N Park Restaurants, a regional family restaurant, no longer had to endure an endless litany of meetings and jargon-riddled documents. It made them very happy, says Walsh, and the new unit very productive. "We were able to reduce the time on this business by 75 percent."

3b. *Say Farewell to the Assembly Line.* The assembly-line approach to most jobs saps whatever ingenuity employees may have. Get rid of it, like America West Airlines did. The airline's customer service employees go through a 17-week training course that gives them the skills to perform any passenger service job the airline has to offer, from flight attendant to baggage handler. Each month on a seniority basis, staff bid on posted "lines of work." For example, as an America West (fully cross-utilized) Customer Service Representative, you might act as a flight attendant for two weeks, then be on dispatch for two more; or you might scoop up a 1/3 : 1/3 : 1/3 split across baggage handling, reservations, and ramp work. Most lines are mixed although there are some that include all reservations, for example.

This cross-utilization strategy benefits the airline in several ways. First, it's a shot in the arm for employee morale. Enthusiasm in the ranks can really take a beating if staff are faced with doing the same things over and over again. And attention to traveler satisfaction also wears pretty thin. Says Mark Coleman, the company's former senior vice president of Sales and Product Development, "By the fifth leg on a three-day trip, they're just another herd of customers coming on." Second, each employee sees the complete customer retention picture, not just their little corner. "They're going to understand this as a business, not just as a position." Finally, the integration across job distinctions gives the airline a lot of flight schedule flexibility. "It's allowed us to get about 10 to 15 percent more productivity compared with traditional airlines."

3c. Keep No Secrets. In many organizations, information is power and so it is handed out in niggardly snippets and only then to selected individuals. Too often, this means the people who need it the most, the people trying to keep the customer, aren't tapped into the information hotline. Financial data is particularly tough to pry out of managers, claims Bonnie Bickel, president of B.B. Bargoon's, an Ontario home-decorating company. Yet, in the absence of the right dollar figures, employees just fill in the blanks with the wrong ones. Besides, once they understand the bottom-line rationale for retention strategies, you'll get them onside that much faster, she contends.

Adopt a no-secrets policy, like Burnaby Hospital did for its customer care strategy. Progress reports were available to anyone in the hospital, and times for the team working sessions were posted and all welcome to drop by. On more than one occasion, input from this audience kept formal team members on the straight-and-narrow, as in the case of the Administration Team, which had taken on the task of improving communication between Administration and the rest of the hospital.

The voice of the three users on the Administration Team was occasionally tentative; they were understandably awed at having the hospital's president and two of his vice presidents as fellow players. Given that tendency, the team often fell victim to intro- spection and contemplated a management philosophy rewrite as the answer to the communication conundrum. "You're way off base on that one," the audience kept piping up. "The real issue is that infernal black hole that swallows up any employee ideas and returns little or no feedback." As a result, the team turned its attention to closing the employee input loop. Several strategies followed; one, an open forum between Administration and all staff, received a 4 out of 5 rating. "It's a long way off from solving the problem completely," admits Burnaby Hospital president Norm Barth, "but at least we're on our way. The general consensus is we're taking a step in the right direction."

3d. Forget the Rules Sometimes. Most of us find solace in rules; they give us a comforting framework. That's a habit that needs breaking as it almost always interferes with your organization's ability to commune with the customer. At First Technology Credit Union in Portland, Oregon, rule breaking is a virtue, if it's in aid of better customer service, and can earn the "Dirty Harry Callahan Award," named after the movie detective played by Clint Eastwood.[2] A little further north, in Canada, Richmond Savings Credit Union fosters a similar attitude toward rules and regulations. They call their program "Cowbusters."

Private ambulance corporation Rural/Metro tries to wean its employees off traditional ways of thinking with an opening exer- cise at employee training sessions. "We give them a deck of cards and tell them to build the tallest structure they can," explains Clint Vardeman. "Almost immediately they're asking for clarifying rules: 'Can I bend the cards? Can I tear any of them?' " The classroom facilitator stays mute throughout and lets them test their limits. "We want them to start thinking, to open up their focus."

Rural/Metro managers have even found themselves caught in the rule trap on occasion. The company's firetrucks have always been lime green. There are sound reasons for this, explains Weldon Paxton, fire chief for the company's Maricopa County Fire

Department. "We paint them that for visibility. The old dark red fire trucks show up as black at night; and, at certain times of the day, such as early morning or at dusk, the white ones [appear] gray or blend into the woodwork." But the board members of Fountain Hill district just outside Phoenix had their hearts set on fire-engine red. Fire trucks are *supposed* to be red, aren't they?

A few years back, admits Paxton, the response to this request would have been a perfunctory, "no," end of discussion. "It was more like, 'This medicine's good for you, take it.' " But some shaky relationships in recent years with a few major contracts like the Fountain Hill one made the folks at Rural/Metro reconsider such rigidity. "Now we say, 'That's okay,' if they want their trucks to be blue or red or orange, it's not a life or death situation." Adds his colleague Suzanne Brossart, corporation communications manager, "We certainly make recommendations, but the customer has the final decision."

Let me end this section with a note of caution on rule bashing from Lord Beaverbrook, a famous onetime Canadian resident who was Minister of Aviation Production for Great Britain's Winston Churchill during the Battle of Britain. "You have to break eggs to make an omelette, but please don't use any more eggs than necessary."[3]

The Practice—Making It Happen, Part III—Step 12

What?

The setup of a final series of Team of Teams, which apply the People-Powered Retention (PPR) process to the issues of organizational integration and adaptability for best-customer retention.

Why?

It's the adaptable organization that will keep the customer coming back for more, but adaptability doesn't mean lack of structure. As Peter Drucker points out, "The only things that evolve by themselves in an organization are disorder, friction, and malperformance."[4]

How?

12A. A participative work session with the Retention Advisory Group (Workshop 12.1) facilitated by an outside consultant with the following **objectives:**

    a. To critique current organizational adaptability for best-customer retention: for example, how do existing rules and regulations enhance or detract from best-customer retention?

    b. To determine what needs to be improved regarding organizational adaptability.

    c. To reshape improvement requirements in Step 12Ab into issues for PPR Team of Teams. **Selection Criteria:** highlighted in Step 4Aa with additional details provided in Step 6Cb. **Facilitator Criteria:** facilitated by in-house facilitators-in-training with backup support from an outside consultant. **Team Membership Criteria:** as outlined in Step 9Ac.

12B. Preparation by outside consultant or the Retention Coordinator of a summary report on Workshop 12.1 and its distribution to all Retention Inc. staff through internal marketing vehicles recommended by the Retention Advisory Group.

12C. Teams selected in Step 12Ac work through the PPR process introduced in Step 4Ad and detailed in Step 6E.

12D. Preparation and distribution of a summary report of team progress to all Retention Inc. staff through internal marketing vehicles.

12E. A participative work session with the Retention Advisory Group (Workshop 12.2) facilitated by an outside consultant with the following **objectives:**

    a. To critique current organizational integration for best-customer retention, i.e., how do we ensure that the gains made in Steps 1–11 aren't lost and additional gains are made toward best-customer retention?

    b. To determine what needs to be improved regarding organizational integration.

    c. To reshape improvement requirements in Step 12Eb into issues for PPR Team of Teams. **General Selection Criteria:** highlighted in Step 4Aa with additional details provided in Step 6Cb. **Issue Suggestions:** (i) the final development of a predictive model for best customer retention; (ii) the development and training of a pool of in-house facilitators for ongoing PPR teams; (iii) the development of an effective system for ongoing customer retention measurement; and (iv) an evaluation of technology as a key customer retention tool. **Facilitator Criteria:** facilitated by in-house facilitators-in-training with backup support from an outside consultant. **Team Membership Criteria:** as outlined in Step 9Ac.

12F. Preparation by outside consultant or the Retention Coordinator of a summary report on Workshop 12.2 and its distribution to all Retention Inc. staff through internal marketing vehicles recommended by the Retention Advisory Group.

12G. Teams selected in Step 12Ec work through the PPR process introduced in Step 4Ad and detailed in Step 6E.

12H. Preparation and distribution of a summary report of team progress to all Retention Inc. staff through internal marketing vehicles.

When?

Months 25 to 30.

Epilogue

The quest (for customer retention) is not always going to be easy; so when there's no wind, start rowing.

Aleta Holub
Manager, Quality Assurance
First National Bank of Chicago

Our summary takes the form of a handy list of do's and don'ts.

1. DON'T confuse service and quality initiatives with customer retention. Retention is the strategy that gives you the tangible results you hoped you would get through a quality approach.
2. DO look at your existing clientele as being "the greatest asset on your balance sheet," as Stephen Brown, professor of marketing and director at First Interstate Center for Services Marketing, Arizona State University, advises.
3. DON'T believe you can make customer retention stick without a complete reworking of the hierarchical structure. You need to get past the notion that those at the top are the only ones who know what needs to be done.
4. DO focus your efforts on the best among your existing customers. Master the few, not the many.
5. DON'T focus on attaining perfection. Instead, get your people to view retention errors and customer complaints as the opportunities they are.
6. DO pay for employee commitment to the customer cause. And I don't mean dollars in dribs and drabs to a chosen few; I mean serious bucks for anyone who really puts out to retain your customers. And don't forget recognition as a critical motivator but get past the T-shirt brigade.
7. DON'T forget the value of simplicity in all this. Techniques notwithstanding, most of what really works is common sense

and a little elbow grease. As Delta Hotels & Resorts president Simon Cooper says, "We can fight our [retention] battles without any of the bells and whistles."

8. DO understand that, if you're serious about keeping customers for life, you're going to have to really shake things up at your place. Challenge all existing precepts, policies, procedures, and people. Customer retention is going to take all the innovation you can muster.

9. DON'T get hung up on analysis and measurement. No matter how well you've done your homework (and I recommend you do the best you can here), still there will come a time when you just have to hold your breath and jump. I like the way David Lloyd George says it: "Don't be afraid to take a big step if one is indicated. You can't cross a chasm in . . . small jumps."[1]

10. DO progress in all your customer retention efforts from the inside of your organization out.

11. DON'T get hung up on traditional ways of looking at management's role. Consider a less intrusive one and focus on providing the right atmosphere to let employees get on with the job of doing right by the customer.

12. DO let your people know that with power comes responsibility.

13. DON'T pick at your people; pick instead at your organization's processes and be sure these make it easy to keep customers coming back.

14. DO institute ways for your organization to touch its customers often.

15. DON'T set yourself up in an antagonistic role with your suppliers or customers; be a partner instead.

16. And finally, DO get on with it. The potential rewards of customer retention are enormous.

Notes

Table of Contents Notes

1. American Marketing Association, "Corporations learning to pay more attention to customers," *Marketing News*, June 6, 1988, p.6.
2. H.J. Harrington, *Business Process Improvement: The Breakthrough Strategy for Total Quality, Productivity, and Competitiveness*, (New York: Mc-Graw-Hill, Inc., 1991), p. viii.
3. Chris Lee, "Using Customer Ratings to Reward Employees," *Training*, May 1989, p. 42.
4. Benson P. Shapiro, V. Kasturi Rangan, Rowland T. Moriarty, and Elliot B. Ross, "Manage customers for profits (not just sales)," *Harvard Business Review*, September-October, 1987, pp. 106, 107.
5. Patricia Sellers, "What Customers Really Want," *Fortune*, June 4, 1990, p. 59.

Preface Notes

1. Quoted in a speech by Jim Clemmer, "Pitfalls and Fatal Flaws of Implementation: A Safety Guide," to the *22nd Annual Conference on Improving Public Sector Efficiency through Total Quality Management*, April 9 and 10, 1992, Toronto, Ontario.
2. Ibid.
3. Frederick F. Reichheld and W. Earl Sasser, Jr., "Zero Defections: Quality Comes to Service," *Harvard Business Review*, September/October 1990, p. 110.

CHAPTER 1.   Customer Retention: The Key to Growth and Profit

1. Frederick F. Reichheld and W. Earl Sasser, Jr., "Zero Defections: Quality Comes to Service," *Harvard Business Review*, September/October 1990, p. 106.
2. Kate Bertrand, "Sales and Service: One Big Happy Family?" *Business Marketing*, December 1988, p. 36.
3. American Marketing Association, "Corporations learning to pay more attention to consumers," *Marketing News*, June 6, 1988, p. 6.
4. Dave Zielinski, "Focus on customer retention is a proven profit strategy," *The Service Edge*, June 1990, p. 1.
5. Council on Financial Competition, "Retail Customer Retention: Strategies and Tactics" (The Advisory Board Company, 1991), p. 17.

6. Customer Service Institute, 1989, cited in a CareerTrack workbook, "Quality, Speed, Customer Involvement, and the New Look of Organizations Seminar," Samuel Boyle (developer) and Alison Peterson (editor) (California: Excel, 1992), p. 8.

7. Laura A. Liswood, "Once You've Got 'Em, Never Let 'Em Go," *Sales & Marketing Management*, November 1987, p. 73.

8. Frederick F. Reichheld and W. Earl Sasser, Jr., "Zero Defections: Quality Comes to Services," *Harvard Business Review*, September/October 1990, p. 110.

9. David C. Jones, "Existing Clients Can Offer a Valuable Market," *National Underwriter Life & Health/Financial Services*, October 24, 1988, p. 46.

10. Robert L. Desatnick, *Managing to Keep the Customer: How to Achieve and Maintain Superior Customer Service Throughout the Organization* (San Francisco: Jossey-Bass), 1987, p. 4. Copyright 1987 by Jossey-Bass, Inc., publishers, and William Bard, "Measuring the High Payoff for Satisfied Customers," *Sales & Marketing Management in Canada*, December 1988, p. 25.

11. Peter M. Dawkins and Frederick F. Reichheld, "Customer Retention as a Competitive Weapon," *Directors & Boards*, Summer 1990, p. 44.

12. Frederick F. Reichheld and W. Earl Sasser, Jr., "Zero Defections: Quality Comes to Services," *Harvard Business Review*, September/October 1990, p. 107.

13. Carla B. Furlong, *Marketing Money* (Toronto: Gage Educational Publishing Company, 1989), p. 210.

14. Frederick F. Reichheld and W. Earl Sasser, Jr., "Zero Defections: Quality Comes to Services," *Harvard Business Review*, September/October 1990, p. 108.

15. Laura A. Liswood, "Once You've Got 'Em, Never Let 'Em Go," *Sales & Marketing Management*, November 1987, p. 73.

16. Otis Port with John Carey, "Questing for the Best," *Business Week*, October 25, 1991, p. 10.

17. Kate Bertrand, "In Service, Perception Counts," *Business Marketing*, April 1989, p. 44.

18. Laura A. Liswood, "Once You've Got 'Em, Never Let 'Em Go," *Sales & Marketing Management*, November 1987, p. 74.

19. Kate Bertrand, "In Service, Perception Counts," *Business Marketing*, April 1989, pp. 46, 48.

20. Quoted in a speech by Jim Clemmer, "Pitfalls and Fatal Flaws of Implementation: A Safety Guide," to the *22nd Annual Conference on Improving Public Sector Efficiency through Total Quality Management*, April 9 and 10, 1992, Toronto, Ontario.

21. Keith Hammonds with Gail DeGeorge, "Where Did They Go Wrong?" *Business Week*, October 25, 1991, p. 34.

22. John A. Byrne, "High Priests and Hucksters," *Business Week*, October 25, 1991, p. 53.

23. Frederick F. Reichheld and W. Earl Sasser, Jr., "Zero Defections: Quality Comes to Services," *Harvard Business Review*, September/ October 1990, p. 110.

24. Peter Lanson "Organizations that Learn By Experience," *The Citizen*, October 5, 1991, p. J1.

25. Author acknowledges independent anonymous reviewer.

26. Peter M. Senge, *The Fifth Discipline: The Art and Practice of the Learning Organization* (New York: Doubleday/Currency, 1990), p. 73.

27. Robert H. Schaffer and Harvey A. Thomson, "Successful Change Programs Begin With Results," *Harvard Business Review*, January/ February 1992, p. 80.

28. Ibid., p. 85.

29. Jim Clemmer, "Public Sector Too Often Falters," *The Financial Post*, August 23, 1990, p. 12.

30. Robert L. Desatnick, *Managing to Keep the Customer: How to Achieve and Maintain Superior Customer Service Throughout the Organization* (San Francisco: Jossey-Bass, 1987), p. 15.

31. Rosabeth Moss Kanter, *When Giants Learn to Dance: Mastering the Challenge of Strategy, Management and Careers in the 1990s* (New York: Simon and Schuster, 1989), p. 43.

32. Quoted in a speech by Gerald Heibert to the Canadian Association for Quality in Health Care conference "Navigating the Quality Journey," May 6–8, 1992, Vancouver, B.C.

33. William A. Band, *Creating Value for Customers: Designing & Implementing a Total Corporate Strategy* (New York: Wiley, 1991), p. 11.

34. Dave Zielinski, "Focus on customer retention is a proven profit strategy," *The Service Edge*, Volume 3, Number 6, June 1990, p. 3.

35. Donald V. Potter, "Success Under Fire: Policies to Prosper in Hostile Times," *Inside Guide*, October/November 1991, p. 46.

36. Juan Gutierrez, presented in a speech at the *1991 Canadian Conference for Credit Union Executives*, Toronto, October 1991.

37. Peter M. Senge, *The Fifth Discipline: The Art and Practice of the Learning Organization* (New York: Doubleday/Currency, 1990), p. 24.

38. Linda M. Lash, *The Complete Guide to Customer Service* (New York: Wiley, 1989), p. 152.

39. Keith H. Hammonds with Gail deGeorge, "Where Did They Go Wrong?" *Business Week*, October 25, 1991, p. 38.

40. Dave Zielinski, "Focus on customer retention is a proven profit strategy," *The Service Edge*, June 1990, pp. 2–3.

41. Robert L. Desatnick, *Managing to Keep the Customer: How to Achieve and Maintain Superior Customer Service Throughout the Organization* (San Francisco: Jossey-Bass, 1987), p. 42.

42. John A. Byrne, "High Priests & Hucksters," *Business Week*, October 25, 1991, p. 57.

CHAPTER 2.   We're All in This Together: Using Cooperation to Keep Your Customers

1. Rosabeth Moss Kanter, *When Giants Learn to Dance: Mastering the Challenge of Strategy, Management and Careers in the 1990s*, (New York: Simon and Schuster, 1989), p. 43.
2. Peter M. Senge, *The Fifth Discipline: The Art and Practice of the Learning Organization*, (New York: Doubleday Currency, 1990), p. 25.
3. Anne Petite, *The Managers Guide to Service Excellence: The Fine Art of Customer Service* (Toronto: Summerhill Press, 1989), p. 57.
4. Rosabeth Moss Kanter, "Why Cowboy Management Is Bad for American Business," *Working Woman*, April 1989, p. 136.
5. Joseph Sensenbrenner, "Quality Comes to City Hall," *Harvard Business Review*, March/April 1991, pp. 65–66.
6. H.J. Harrington, *Business Process Improvement: The Breakthrough Strategy for Total Quality, Productivity, and Competitiveness*, (New York: McGraw-Hill, Inc., 1991), p. vii.
7. For more details on the Xerox customer contact program, "Customer Loyalty," please see chapter 8, pages 149–150.
8. Glenn Lafel and David Blumenthal, "The case for using industrial quality management science in health care organizations," *Journal of the American Medical Association*, November 24, 1989, v. 262:2869–2873, Figure 1, p. 2870.
9. Richard C. Whiteley, *The Customer-Driven Company: Moving from Talk to Action* (Reading, MA: Addison-Wesley, 1991), Figure 8, p. 259.
10. V. Daniel Hunt, *Quality in America: How to Implement a Competitive Quality Program* (Homewood, IL: Business One Irwin, 1992), p. 244 (Fig. 10-6).

CHAPTER 3.   To Know Them Is to Retain Them: Researching Customer Wants and Needs

1. Michael Jackman (editor), *The Macmillan Book of Business and Economic Quotations*, (New York: Macmillan Publishing Co.), p. 388.
2. Customer Service Institute, 1989, cited in a CareerTrack workbook, "Quality, Speed, Customer Involvement, and the New Look of Organizations Seminar, Samuel Boyle (developer) and Alison Peterson (editor) (California: Excel, 1992), p. 8.

3. Carla Furlong, *Marketing Money* (Toronto: Gage Educational Publishing Company, 1989), p. 12.

4. Carla Furlong, "Get It from the Horse's Mouth," *Credit Union Way*, August 1990, p. 26.

5. *Close to the Customer: An American Management Association Research Report on Consumer Affairs*, Don Lee Bohl, editor (New York: AMACOM, 1987), pp. 16–21.

6. Carla Furlong, "Keeping tabs on the competition," *Small Business*, July/August 1990, p. 44.

7. James R. Healey, "U.S. Steel learns from experience," *U.S. Today*, April 10, 1992, pp. 27–28.

8. Carla Furlong, "Focus on focus groups," *Small Business*, October 1990, p. 52.

9. Ibid., pp. 52–53.

10. Ibid., p. 53.

11. Carla B. Furlong, *Marketing Money*, (Toronto: Gage Educational Publishing Company, 1989), p. 9.

12. Ibid.

13. Demetra Takes Osterhoudt, "How Harleysville National is Gaining a Competitive Edge Through Service," *Measuring and Monitoring Service Quality*, (Chicago: Bank Marketing Association, 1988), pp. 3–4.

14. Carla Furlong, "Keeping tabs on the competition," *Small Business*, July/August 1990, pp. 42, 44.

15. Ibid., p. 44.

16. John A. Goodman and Arlene R. Malech, "The Role of Service in Effective Marketing," *Handbook of Modern Marketing*, Victor P. Buell, editor (New York: McGraw-Hill, 1986), pp. 88–6.

17. Peter Dawkins and Frederick Reichheld, "Customer Retention as a Competitive Weapon," *Directors & Boards*, Summer 1990, p. 46.

18. Mark Hanan and Peter Karp, *Customer Satisfaction: How to Maximize, Measure, and Market Your Company's "Ultimate Product"* (New York: AMACOM, 1989), p. 97.

19. William H. Davidow and Bro Uttal, *Total Customer Service: The Ultimate Weapon*, (New York: Harper & Row, 1989), pp. 16–17.

20. A. Parasuraman, Leonard L. Berry, and Valarie A. Zeithaml, "Understanding customer expectations of service," *Sloan Management Review*, Spring 1991, p. 42.

21. George M. Hill, "A New Millennium of Customer Service," *Public Utilities Fortnightly*, January 1, 1991, p. 23.

22. Laura Zinn, "The New Stars of Retailing," *Business Week*, December 16, 1991, p. 122.

23. Chekitan S. Dev and Bernard D. Ellis, "Guest histories: An untapped service resource," *The Cornell H.R.A. Quarterly*, August 1991, p. 34.

CHAPTER 4. Focusing on Your Best Customers: The 80/20 Rule

1. Benson P. Shapiro, V. Kasturi Rangan, Rowland T. Moriarty, and Elliot B. Ross, "Manage customers for profits (not just sales)," *Harvard Business Review*, September-October, 1987, pp. 106, 107.
2. Carla Furlong, *Marketing Money*, (Toronto: Gage Educational Publishing Company, 1989), pp. 47, 49.
3. Benson P. Shapiro, V. Kasturi Rangan, Rowland T. Moriarty, and Elliot B. Ross, "Manage Customers for Profits (Not Just Sales)," *Harvard Business Review*, September/October 1987, p. 101.
4. Ibid., Exhibit II, p. 104.
5. Ibid., p. 106.
6. Ibid., p. 108.
7. Ibid., p. 102.
8. Ibid., p. 108.
9. Carla Furlong, *Marketing Money*, (Toronto: Gage Educational Publishing Company, 1989), pp. 169–170.
10. Laura Liswood, "Focus on customer retention is a proven profit strategy," *The Service Edge*, June 1990, p. 3.
11. Carla Furlong, *Marketing Money*, (Toronto: Gage Educational Publishing Company, 1989), pp. 93, 201.
12. Council on Financial Competition, "Retail Customer Retention: Strategies and Tactics," Volume II (The Advisory Board Company, 1991), p. 61.
13. Carla Furlong, *Marketing Money*, (Toronto: Gage Educational Publishing Company, 1989), p. 168.

CHAPTER 5. Empowered Employees: Your Greatest Asset for Keeping Customers

1. J.M. and M.J. Cohen, *The New Penguin Dictionary of Quotations* (London: Penguin Books Ltd., 1960) p. 128.
2. John A. Byrne, "Management's New Gurus," *Business Week*, August 31, 1992, p. 46.
3. J.E. Bateson, *Managing Services Marketing: Text and Readings* (Hinsdale, Illinois: Dryden Press, 1989), pp. 314–315.
4. Richard C. Whiteley, *The Customer Driven Company: Moving from Talk to Action* (New York: Addison-Wesley, 1991), p. 117.
5. Mary T. Koska, "Adopting Deming's quality improvement ideas: a case study," *Hospitals*, July 5, 1990, p. 62.
6. George Gendron, "FYI," *Inc.*, January 1992, p. 11.

7. Tom Peters, "Sometimes good just isn't good enough," *Inside Guide*, November 1992, p. 10.

8. Erica Wade, Tommy Jones, Paul Eakin, Lucretia Aloi, Vincent Ortiz, Jr., and Ron McGlynn, "The Human Side of Quality," *Fortune*, September 24, 1990, pp. 137–208.

9. Michele Monette, "Troubled Air Canada banks on money-saving employee ideas," *Vancouver Sun*, December 13, 1991, p. D9.

10. Robert Dailey, Frederick Young, and Cameron Barr, "Empowering middle managers in hospitals with team-based problem solving," *Health Care Management Review*, Spring 1991, pp. 55–63.

11. Joseph Sensenbrenner, "Quality comes to City Hall," *Harvard Business Review*, March/April 1991, p. 69.

12. Carla Furlong, *Marketing Money* (Toronto: Gage Educational Publishing Company, 1989), p. 179.

13. Thomas Teal, "Service comes first: An interview with USAA's Robert F. McDermott," *Harvard Business Review*, September/October 1991, p. 126.

14. Ibid., pp. 125, 126.

15. Peter M. Senge, *The Fifth Discipline: The Art and Practice of The Learning Organization* (New York: Doubleday/Currency, 1990), p. 211.

16. Michael A. Verespej, "Partnership in the trenches," *Industry Week*, October 17, 1988, p. 57.

17. Anne Kingston, "Power to the people," *Report on Business Magazine*, July 1992, pp. 16–17.

18. Michael A. Verespej, "Partnership in the trenches," *Industry Week*, October 17, 1988, p. 64.

19. H.J. Harrington, *Business Process Improvement: The Breakthrough Strategy for Total Quality, Productivity, and Competitiveness* (New York: McGraw-Hill, 1991), p. 18.

20. John Hillkirk, "New award cites teams with dreams," *USA Today*, April 10–12, 1992, p. 113.

21. Rosabeth Moss Kanter, *The Change Masters: Innovation for Productivity in the American Organization* (New York: Simon and Schuster, 1983), p. 156.

22. Bruce Rawson, "The PS 2000 task force on service to the public: the chairman's comments," *Optimum*, 1990/91, Volume 21-4, p. 19.

23. Peggy Hewson, "Vertical marketing in the Canadian Parks Service," *Optimum*, 1990/91, Volume 21-4, p. 64.

24. Jack Orsburn, Linda Moran, Ed Musselwhite, and John H. Zenger, *Self-Directed Work Teams: The New American Challenge* (Homewood, IL: Business One Irwin, 1990), p. 30.

25. John Hillkirk, "New award cites teams with dreams," *USA Today*, April 10–12, 1992, p. 1B.

CHAPTER 6. Internal Customers: Building Success from the Inside Out.

1. V. Daniel Hunt, *Quality in America: How to Implement A Competitive Quality Strategy* (Homewood, IL: Business One Irwin, 1992), p. 24 (Figure 2-1).
2. Kate Bertrand, "Sales and Service: One Big Happy Family?" *Business Marketing*, December 1988, p. 37.
3. Leonard A. Schlesinger and James L. Heskett, "Breaking the Cycle of Failure in Services," *Sloan Management Review*, Spring 1991, p. 18.
4. Patricia Sellers, "What Customers Really Want," *Fortune*, June 4, 1990, p. 59.

CHAPTER 7. To Err Is Human: Recovering Lost Customers

1. Linda M. Lash, *The Complete Guide to Customer Service* (New York: John Wiley & Sons, 1989), p. 152.
2. Christopher W.L. Hart, James L. Heskett, and W. Earl Sasser, Jr., "The Profitable Art of Service Recovery," *Harvard Business Review*, July/August 1990, p. 150.
3. Warren Blanding, *Practical Handbook of Distribution/Customer Service* (New York: Traffic Service Corporation, 1978), p. 459.
4. Kathleen Hawk, "Sales Efforts May be Eroding Service Quality," *Bank Marketing*, September 1989, p. 7.
5. TARP, Inc., *Consumer Complaint Handling in America*, U.S. Office of Consumer Affairs, Washington, D.C. 1979, cited in article ("The Role of Service in Effective Marketing") by John A. Goodman and Arlene R. Malech in *Handbook of Modern Marketing*, Victor P. Buell, ed. (New York: McGraw-Hill, 1986), p. 88-6.
6. William Band, "Measuring the high payoff from satisfied customers," *Sales & Marketing Management in Canada*, December 1988, p. 25.
7. John E. Cleghorn, "Write On . . .," in booklet, "Write On . . . Responding to written complaints," part of Royal Bank of Canada's *Quality in Action!* series, November 3, 1988, p. 1.
8. William H. Davidow and Bro Uttal, *Total Customer Service: The Ultimate Weapon* (New York: Harper & Row Publishers, 1989), p. 32.
9. Stanley A. Brown, "Yes, please complain!", *Canadian Banker*, Volume 97, Number 2, March/April 1990, p. 26.
10. From a speech by Carol Krauss, "Customer Satisfaction: A Bottom-Line Performance Indicator" to the 1987 American Marketing Association Services Marketing Conference, San Diego, California, September 27-30, 1987.
11. Milind M. Lele with Jagdish N. Sheth, *The Customer is Key: Gaining an Unbeatable Advantage Through Customer Satisfaction* (New York: John Wiley & Sons, 1987), p. 213.

12. Laura A. Liswood, "Once You've Got 'Em, Never Let 'Em Go," *Sales & Marketing Management*, November 1987, p. 75.

13. Kathleen Hawk, "Sales Efforts May Be Eroding Service", *Bank Marketing*, September 1989, p. 10.

14. Leonard L. Berry, David R. Bennett, and Carter W. Brown, *Service Quality: A Profit Strategy for Financial Institutions*, (Homewood, IL: Dow Jones-Irwin, 1989), p. 119.

15. More detail on the Xerox guarantee is provided in Chapter 13, pages 216–217.

16. For more information on the Xerox customer contact program, see Chapter 8, page 149–150.

17. Mark Hanan and Peter Karp, *Customer Satisfaction: How to Maximize, Measure, and Market Your Company's "Ultimate Product"* (New York: AMACOM, 1989), p. 2.

18. Council on Financial Competition, "Retail Customer Retention: Strategies and Tactics," Volume II (Advisory Board Company, 1991), p. 49.

19. H.J. Harrington, *Business Process Improvement: The Breakthrough Strategy for Total Quality, Productivity, and Competitiveness* (New York: McGraw-Hill, 1991), Figure 2.3, p. 41.

20. Richard C. Whiteley, *The Customer-Driven Company: Moving from Talk to Action* (New York: Addison-Wesley, 1991), Figure 7, p. 248.

21. Ibid., p. 247.

22. Ibid., Figure 1, p. 241.

23. Ibid., p. 239.

24. Ibid., Figure 13, p. 274.

25. Ibid., Figure 14, p. 275.

26. Ibid., Figure 15, p. 277.

27. Ibid., pp. 272–273, 276.

28. Chris Lee, "Using Customers' Ratings to Reward Employees," *Training*, May 1989, p. 42.

29. "Zero Defections: Perfecting Customer Retention and Recovery," Gold Book Series for Senior Management (Advisory Board Company, 1990), p. 43.

CHAPTER 8. Keeping in Touch: Customer Retention through Customer Contact

1. David C. Jones, "Existing Clients Can Offer A Valuable Market," *National Underwriter Life & Health/Financial Services*, October 24, 1988, p. 46.

2. John A. Goodman and Arlene R. Malech, "The Role of Service in Effective Marketing," *Handbook of Modern Marketing*, Victor P. Buell, ed. (New York: McGraw-Hill, 1986), pp. 88-6.

3. For more information on Marriott's HGA program, see Chapter 4.

CHAPTER 9. Customer Encounters of the 4th Kind: Keeping Customers through Multiple Relationships, Cross-Selling, and Customer Partnerships

1. Rosabeth Moss Kanter, *When Giants Learn to Dance: Mastering the Challenge of Strategy, Management and Careers in the 1990s* (New York: Simon and Schuster, 1989), p. 89.
2. For more information on the DLA training anecdote, see Chapter 3.
3. Dave Zielinski, "Focus on customer retention is a proven profit strategy," *The Service Edge*, June 1990, p. 3.
4. Tom Eisenhart, "Cross-Marketing Spells Sales Success," *Business Marketing*, November 1988, p. 63.
5. Carla Furlong *Marketing Money* (Toronto: Gage Educational Publishing Company, 1989), pp. 164–165.
6. Donald Shoultz, "Bankers Balk at Learning How to Get Foot in the Door," *American Banker Consumer Survey*, 1989, p. 42.
7. Ibid., p. 40.
8. Tom Eisenhart, "Cross-Marketing Spells Sales Success," *Business Marketing*, November 1988, p. 60.
9. Ibid, pp. 60, 62.
10. Ibid, p. 64.
11. Ibid, p. 58.
12. Ibid, p. 60.
13. Ibid, p. 65.
14. Ibid, p. 62.
15. Carla Furlong, *Marketing Money* (Toronto: Gage Educational Publishing Company, 1989), pp. 164–165.
16. Tom Eisenhart, "Cross-Marketing Spells Sales Success," *Business Marketing*, November 1988, p. 63.
17. Rosabeth Moss Kanter, *When Giants Learn to Dance: Mastering the Challenge of Strategy, Management and Careers in the 1990s* (New York: Simon and Schuster, 1989), p. 89.
18. Leonard Lee, "The case of Lee Valley Tools," *Optimum*, 1990/91, Volume 21-4, p. 70.

CHAPTER 10. Lead, Follow, Or Get Out of the Way: Translating the Customer Retention Model into Management Action

1. Tom Peters, *Thriving on Chaos: A Handbook for a Management Revolution* (New York: Knopf, 1987), p. 411.
2. Erica Wade, Tommy Jones, Paul Eakin, Lucretia Aloi, Vincent Ortiz, Jr., and Ron McGlynn, "The Human Side of Quality," *Fortune*, September 24, 1990, pp. 137–208.

3. Leonard A. Schlesinger and James L. Heskett, "Breaking the Cycle of Failure in Services," *Sloan Management Review*, Spring 1991, p. 22.
4. "Your Decisions Stink" *B.C. Business*, November 1991, p. 14.

CHAPTER 11.   The Buck Stops on Everyone's Desk: Staff Accountability for Customer Retention

1. Peter M. Senge, *The Fifth Discipline: The Art and Practice of The Learning Organization* (New York: Doubleday/Currency, 1990), p. 67.
2. Patti Schom-Moffatt, "Service with a snarl," *BC Business*, November 1990, p. 52.
3. Ibid.
4. Ibid.
5. Ibid.
6. Nancy Shepherdson, "Sales Management Training," *Bank Administration*, September 1989, p. 33.
7. Allan Taylor, *Interest: For and About People at the Royal Bank*, September 1992, p. 30.
8. David McInnes, "Sharpening the Service Edge," *Canadian Banker*, March/April 1991, p. 42.
9. Kathleen Hawk, "Sales Efforts May be Eroding Service Quality," *Bank Marketing*, September 1989, p. 6.
10. Frederick F. Reichheld and W. Earl Sasser, Jr., "Zero Defections," *Harvard Business Review*, September/October 1990, p. 111.
11. Anne Petite, *The Manager's Guide to Service Excellence: The Fine Art of Customer Service* (Toronto: Summerhill Press, 1989), p. 46.

CHAPTER 12.   Recognizing Good Work: Using Employee Incentives for Customer Retention

1. R.H. Woods and J.F. Macaulay, "Rx for Turnover: Retention Programs that Work," *Cornell HRA Quarterly*, May 1989, pp. 78–90.
2. John A. Byrne, "The Flap Over Executive Pay," *Business Week*, May 6, 1991, p. 90.
3. John A. Byrne, "How CEO Paychecks Got So Unreal," *Business Week*, November 18, 1991, p. 20.
4. John A. Byrne and Kathleen Kerwin, "Salaries At The Top Finally Stop Defying Gravity," *Business Week*, April 15, 1991, p. 30.
5. John Naisbitt, "New Programs, Incentives Boost Employee Morale," *Inside Guide*, June/July/August 1992, pp. 16, 22.
6. Kate Bertrand, "Sales and Service: One Big Happy Family?" *Business Marketing*, December 1988, p. 38.

7. John Naisbitt, "New Programs, Incentives Boost Employee Morale," *Inside Guide*, June/July/August 1992, pp. 16, 22.
8. Peter Larson, "All Work and No Play?" *Vancouver Sun*, February 19, 1992, p. 136.
9. "Your Decisions Stink," *B.C. Business*, November 1991, p. 14.
10. Rosabeth Moss Kanter, *When Giants Learn to Dance: Mastering the Challenge of Strategy, Management and Careers in the 1990s* (New York: Simon and Schuster, 1989), p. 234.
11. Tom Ehrenfeld, "Merit Evaluation and the Family of Measures," in the article by Thomas Teal, "Service Comes First: An Interview with USAA's Robert F. McDermott, *Harvard Business Review*, September/October 1991, p. 122.
12. Dean P. Wilson, "Seeking Service Quality," School of Bank Marketing (Washington, D.C.: Bank Marketing Association, 1988), p. 28.
13. Chris Lee, "Using Customers' Ratings to Reward Employees," *Training*, May 1989, p. 43.
14. Dean C. Minderman, "Why Incentive Plans Fail (And How to Avoid It)," *Credit Union Management*, February 1991, p. 13.
15. Ibid.
16. Ibid, pp. 13, 16.
17. Rona Maynard, "The Next Labor Crisis," *Report on Business Magazine*, June 1990, p. 48.
18. Ibid, p. 45.
19. Benson P. Shapiro and Stephen X. Doyle, "Make the Sales Task Clear," *Harvard Business Review*, November/December 1983, pp. 72.
20. Aaron Bernstein with Richard Brandt, Barbara Carlson, and Karen Padley, "Teaching Business How to Train," *Business Week/Reinventing America*, Special issue 1992, p. 86.
21. Joel Jacobson, "Canadian Business Told to Stop Complaining," *Mail-Star*, November 19, 1991, p. B12.
22. Carla Furlong, *Marketing Money* (Toronto: Gage Educational Publishing Company, 1989), p. 147.
23. Ibid., p. 153.
24. Quoted in Herbert V. Prochnow and Herbert V. Prochnow, Jr., compilers, *The Toastmaster's Treasure Chest*, 2nd ed. (New York: Harper & Row, 1988), no. 612, p. 39.

CHAPTER 13. What Works Today May Not Work Tomorrow: Adapting Your Customer Retention Strategy

1. Tom Peters, *Thriving on Chaos: A Handbook for a Management Revolution* (New York: Knopf, 1987), p. 259.
2. Dean C. Minderman, "Why Incentive Plans Fail (And How to Avoid It)," *Credit Union Management*, February 1991, pp. 13, 15.

3. Bruce Rawson, "The PS 2000 task force on service to the public: the chairman's comments," *Optimum*, 1990/91, Volume 21-4, p. 19.
4. Michael Jackman (editor), *The Macmillan Book of Business and Economic Quotations* (New York: Macmillan Publishing Co., 1984), p. 46.

Epilogue Notes

1. "Contrails", *Inside Guide*, October 1990, p. 70.

Index